BLACK PERIL
WHITE VIRTUE

BLACK PERIL
WHITE VIRTUE

SEXUAL CRIME IN SOUTHERN RHODESIA, 1902–1935

JOCK MCCULLOCH

INDIANA UNIVERSITY PRESS
BLOOMINGTON AND INDIANAPOLIS

This book is a publication of
Indiana University Press
601 North Morton Street
Bloomington, Indiana 47404-3797 USA
www.indiana.edu/~iupress
Telephone orders   800-842-6796
Fax orders   812-855-7931
Orders by e-mail   iuporder@indiana.edu

The paper used in this publication meets the minimum
requirements of American National Standard for Information
Sciences—Permanence of Paper for Printed Library
Materials, ANSI Z39.48-1984.

Manufactured in the United States of America

Library of Congress Cataloging-in-Publication Data

McCulloch, Jock, date
    Black peril, white virtue : sexual crime in Southern Rhodesia,
    1902–1935 / Jock McCulloch.
        p.   cm.
    Includes bibliographical references and index.
    ISBN 0-253-33728-3 (cloth : alk. paper)
     1. Sex crimes—Zimbabwe—History—20th century. 2. Zimbabwe—Race relations—
    History—20th century.   I. Title.

HV6593.Z55 M33 2000
364.15'3'09689109041—dc21   99-055755

    1 2   3   4   5   05   04   03   02   01   00

TO JANE CONNELL

Contents

Acknowledgments

Like so many books, this one was written by accident. While working in the Zimbabwe National Archives in 1994 I was struck by the amount of official correspondence dealing with sexual conduct. It seemed that white males, for they were the ones writing the reports, keeping the records, and complaining about the threat of rape, had an intense interest in other people's sexuality. The reasons were mysterious. Hence this book.

The research on which this work is based was carried out in the National Archives of Zimbabwe, South Africa, and Kenya. I would like to thank the staff and directors of the archives in Harare, Nairobi, Cape Town, and Pretoria. Special thanks are due to Maria Olivier and her wonderful staff in Pretoria. I must also thank the National Research Council of Zimbabwe for granting me the right to do research and the Department of Economic History at the University of Zimbabwe for providing me with an official base.

I must also thank Sally Trautman for giving me a place to hang my bicycle, Anthony Chennells for his pioneering work on colonial fiction and for coffees too numerous to mention at the Italian Bakery, the late David Beach for his example, and Carl and Katerina Hallencreutz for their friendship. I must also thank theologian Isabel Mukonyora for helping me to better understand the bewildering history of Zimbabwe.

One of the pleasures of working on this book was a conversation carried out between Melbourne and Ulm with Rob Turrell. Rob was working simultaneously on a history of capital punishment and mercy in South Africa that covered much of the same period. Rob read the entire manuscript and commented at length on its flaws and strengths. His advice was invaluable. Pavla Miller and Bruce also read parts of the draft with varying degrees of acuity. All books begin life with innumerable flaws. Thanks to the editorial skills and care of Kate Babbitt, this book now contains far fewer than before.

Funds for travel were provided by the Australian Research Council.

North Fitzroy, September 1999

BLACK PERIL
WHITE VIRTUE

INTRODUCTION

THE UMTALI OUTRAGE

At a little after 8 P.M. on Saturday, October 17, 1908, Miss Janette Falconer, who worked as a shop assistant in Umtali, a small town near the Mozambique border, left the Cecil Hotel for her lodgings. It was her habit to take her evening meal at the hotel in the main street and then walk the short distance to her boarding house. She was carrying a lantern and leading her small dog on a chain. It was dark. She had walked only a short distance when she became aware of footsteps behind her and then of an African man standing next to her shoulder. As she held the lantern to his face he struck her twice in the chest, knocking her to the ground. She tried to struggle to her feet but he was too strong. While she was on the ground he attempted to rape her. In recounting the assault Miss Falconer later said: "My dress was a good deal torn. I was bruised considerably. While I was screaming and struggling a gentleman came up. My assailant ran away."[1] Miss Falconer's rescuer was Robert Sterling, Umtali's veterinary surgeon. He had been walking up the main street from the railway station. As he passed the Royal Hotel he heard screams. He ran toward a flashing lantern where he found Miss Falconer. She was hysterical and her clothing was torn.[2]

On Sunday morning Miss Falconer went to the police station and gave a description of the man who had attacked her. As she was leaving the station she identified her assailant as the man being led into the police compound. Singana, a native of Nyasaland who worked as a housepainter in Umtali, was immediately charged with attempted rape.

Miss Falconer lived alone in a boarding house. She was single, white, and certainly respectable. In Southern Rhodesia at that time women like Miss Falconer were unusual: The imbalance between the sexes was such that few women escaped marriage. The judge and members of the jury viewed the attack upon her as particularly grave because of her perceived asexuality.

Singana was tried twice for the crime. At the first trial held at Salisbury in the first week of November the jury failed to reach a verdict because of doubt over Miss Falconer's identification of Singana. At the second trial

Singana was found guilty of attempted rape. In his report, the presiding judge, Justice Watermeyer, commented on the seriousness of the attack, suggesting that Singana had probably lain in wait for Miss Falconer with the intention of raping her. The assault was so serious he could find no grounds for clemency. At the first trial the jury had been divided over the question of Singana's identity, but having heard the evidence twice Watermeyer was satisfied on that score. Acting under the terms of the Criminal Law Amendment Ordinance of 1903 he sentenced Singana to death. At the time it was necessary for death sentences passed in the territory to be ratified by the British High Commissioner, who was resident in South Africa.

The case was controversial. To settlers it was another example of the threat posed by the black majority that outnumbered them by almost thirty to one. Whites resented the lack of protection offered by the British South Africa Company (BSAC) that administered the territory. They also resented the lack of support from the British government and the British public, neither of whom, they believed, understood the circumstances under which they lived. Both Resident Commissioner James Fair and High Commissioner Lord Selbourne were aware of those political realities. They were also aware of the need to maintain the perceived fairness of the legal system. While the majority of the white community favored Singana's execution there were others, including the Rev. John White of the Methodist Church, who were disturbed by doubts regarding his guilt.[3]

Having read the trial transcript, Selbourne noted a number of inconsistencies. There was no evidence that the assault was aggravated; neither was there serious injury to the victim. There was an absence of proof of intent because according to Miss Falconer the assailant did not even expose himself. Even more serious were doubts about the identity of the assailant. Selbourne observed that it was difficult at any time for Europeans to identify Africans and that the assault took place at night. Selbourne wrote to Fair: "Under these circumstances I feel the gravest doubts as to whether the prisoner was sufficiently identified and therefore whether he was rightfully convicted at all."[4] He commuted Singana's sentence to ten years' hard labor and requested that an inquiry be held.

Selbourne's decision caused an uproar in Salisbury. He had questioned the competence of the presiding judge and the administration of justice in the territory. He had also failed to calm settlers' fears about Black Peril. Attorney General Robert Tredgold, who prosecuted the case, was hurt by the suggestion that the trial had been conducted improperly. He was adamant that the assault upon Miss Falconer had been severe and that it was most certainly of a sexual nature. He commented: "I would explain that when in court she (Miss Falconer) was wearing a somewhat unusual amount of jewellery including a fairly substantial hanging chain or necklace. As I was nearing the important question to be put (about the motive of the assault) she almost interrupted me saying: "His purpose could not have been robbery. I had all these (pointing to her jewellery) and he made no attempt to touch them."[5] Miss Falconer was positive in her identification of Singana. She told the court: "I shall never forget his face."[6] Justice Watermeyer likewise justified his handling of the case and defended the jury's verdict. For him a key factor in the trial was the evidence and demeanor of Miss Falconer, which left no person who was present in any doubt as to the seriousness of the crime.[7] Despite such protests, Mr. Hulley, of the Native Commissioner's Office in Umtali, was appointed to conduct an inquiry.[8]

Hulley carried out a thorough investigation, speaking to all of the witnesses and a number of residents whose testimony had not been sought at the time of the trial. He interviewed Mr. Beck, Singana's employer, who spoke highly of him. He found no evidence that Singana was familiar with Miss Falconer's movements.[9] Evidence from an African named Saulus established that at the time of the assault he was with Singana some twenty minutes' walk from the Cecil Hotel. This evidence, and the testimony of other witnesses, convinced Hulley that Singana could not have been at the scene of the crime and that the assault was in any case not sexual. In uncovering the identity of Miss Falconer's assailant Hulley visited the native location where he spoke with a man named Shikube.[10] Shikube was employed at the Bank of Africa which was situated near the Cecil. Shikube's duties included looking after the baboon kept at the back of the bank. The baboon, a half-grown male, was in the habit of escaping from the compound; in the days leading up to the attack on October 17 it had escaped twice, on one occasion attacking the children of an Umtali resident. When asked where he had been on the night of the assault Shikube became frightened but finally confessed to what had happened. On that evening the baboon had escaped and Shikube had finally caught the animal in a tree. He had chained the baboon and was leading it back to the bank when he came across Miss Falconer: "I wanted to pass a lady who was carrying a light. This was on the path near the newspaper office. A dog belonging to the lady made a rush at the baboon. The baboon jumped on the lady. She fell down. I pulled the baboon off and ran away with the baboon. I tied the baboon up and waited."[11] He was afraid the baboon had bitten the woman.

Hulley was certain that Miss Falconer had seen the baboon but in her fear and excitement the fact made no impression on her brain.[12] Judge

Watermeyer was less charitable and suggested Miss Falconer had invented much of her evidence. Upon receiving Hulley's report Selbourne granted Singana a pardon. The circumstances surrounding the reprieve were never made public and Miss Falconer subsequently wrote to the high commissioner asking him to re-open the case.[13] Selbourne refused.

In the context of Southern Rhodesian courts the Falconer case was unexceptional. At the trial no testimony was offered in Singana's defense and there was no forensic evidence establishing the intent to commit rape. Questions about the identity of the accused were ignored and the jury, like the bench, accepted without reservation the victim's account of the assault.[14] Yet the case was important for a number of reasons. Without Selbourne's intervention an innocent man would have hanged. The reprieve also soured relations between Salisbury and imperial authorities. Selbourne's successor Gladstone spent his first years in office trying to heal the wounds. What was most remarkable about the trial was the willingness of a jury to convict a man on flimsy evidence. At that time courts in other parts of the British Empire habitually found men innocent of rape in the face of overwhelming proof of guilt. Judges and juries assumed that it was a woman's duty to restrain male desire; if a man transgressed the victim was culpable. The need for eyewitness testimony or forensic evidence worked to the disadvantage of women. In contemporary New South Wales in Australia, for example, there were glaring discrepancies between the incidence of rape and the number of prosecutions.[15] But under the sway of fears of Black Peril in Southern Rhodesia those conventions were often abandoned.

THE MORAL PANICS

In the period from 1902 to 1916 colonial Zimbabwe was swept by a series of moral panics, of which the attack upon Miss Falconer was part. The perceived threat posed by black men to white women was such that in 1903 the Legislative Council passed what was perhaps at that time the only law in the British Empire prescribing capital punishment for attempted rape.[16] As many as twenty men were executed for sexual crime and another two hundred were jailed.[17] Such assaults were perceived not just as an attack upon the body of a woman but as an attack upon the white community itself.[18] It is significant that no such threat was felt on those rare occasions on which an African killed a settler. Such murders, no matter how brutal or senseless, never provoked the same degree of anxiety.[19] The panics, which were known colloquially as Black Peril, were elaborate events. There were trials, public rallies, petitions to members of the Legislative Council, letters to the press, and deputations to the resident commissioner. The most dramatic cases strained relations between settlers, the BSAC, and imperial authorities in Cape Town and London. Black Peril hysteria was also important in South Africa and forms a significant element in the region's history. It was eventually exported to the far-flung colonial society of Papua New Guinea, where the same term was used and a law based upon the Rhodesian ordinance of 1903 was enacted.[20]

There were two striking features about the panics. The first was the gap between the fear of assault and the incidence of rape. That gulf was so extreme that historians have tended to treat Black Peril as a form of psychopathology.[21] The second was the means used to combat the threat. Over a period of thirteen years the state introduced a swathe of legislation but the death penalty of 1903 was the only ordinance directed specifically against offenders. Most Black Peril legislation was designed to restrain the sexual impulses of white women. The Immorality Suppression Ordinance No. 9 of 1903, for example, prohibited women from having illicit sexual relations with black men.[22] The terms of that ordinance were extended under the Immorality and Indecency Suppression Ordinance No. 1 of 1916 which prescribed two years in jail for any girl or woman who by words, writing, signs, or suggestion enticed a native to have illicit sex. The legislation suggests that Black Peril was as much about gender conflict within white society as about racial conflict between settlers and Africans. It is significant that in the history of Southern Rhodesia no white man was executed for rape.[23]

Black Peril was original in its intensity but in constructing the panics settlers borrowed freely from existing conventions. The misogyny of the legislators who wrote the morality ordinances was imported. So too were the prevailing codes of sexual conduct, which were far stricter for women than for men.[24] During the decades from 1880 to 1930 women achieved some of the rights of citizenship. It was also a time when women were blamed for a perceived moral decline of British society evident in rising divorce rates and falling fertility. Those changes were reflected in the contrary notions of female chastity and carnality prominent in medical and legal discourse. Ironically, the doctrine of sexual anesthesia was exploited to effect by feminists to justify their involvement in social movements and in the exercise of familial authority.[25] Similarly, in Southern Rhodesia the ideals which shaped the morality legislation were used by women to gain access to a hitherto forbidden public domain.

There were ample precedents for the racial stereotypes upon which the panics were based.[26] Victorian scientists produced as many narratives about the sexuality of primitives as they did about metropolitan proletariats. In the same year as the Umtali outrage, Sigmund Freud, who had no firsthand experience of the colonial world, published an important essay on the sexual instincts.[27] Freud believed that Africans, Aborigines, and Pacific Islanders lacked a period of sexual latency which in Europeans acted as a counter to the sexual drives. That absence explained both the hyper-sexuality of indigenous peoples and their lack of civilization. It is interesting to speculate about how Freud would have explained Black Peril. He would probably have referred to the absence in African men of internalized controls over the sexual impulses. Although couched in a very different language, such views were cited frequently by the BSAC police.

European psychiatrists who worked in Africa in the period between the wars produced a rich if idiosyncratic literature on the "African mind." One of them, the South African psychiatrist B. J. F. Laubscher, wrote a monograph on Black Peril. There is also a small literature about sexuality and empire from the 1940s and 1950s of which Octave Mannoni's *Prospero and Caliban* and Frantz Fanon's *Black Skin, White Masks* are the most notable examples. However, sexuality was not a part of nationalist discourse and Fanon's contemporaries showed no interest in such questions. Kenyatta, Nkrumah, Lumumba, and Cabral, for example, wrote at length about identity and culture, but not about sexual conduct. That problem lay on the other side of the colonial divide.

There have been various seasons in the literature on the sexual politics of empire. Those seasons run in conceptual rather than chronological sequence and there is little evidence of a steady progress in the understanding of events as complex as Black Peril. Some authors writing in the 1970s were better informed than their successors about current debates within social theory. In 1990, for example, the British historian Ronald Hyman published *Empire and Sexuality: The British Experience.*[28] The book, which touches on the moral panics, is innocent of any concept of gender and was written in apparent ignorance of the gains made by feminist scholars over the preceding twenty years. Writing in 1950, Octave Mannoni was more willing than Hyam to view sexual behavior in terms of colonial dominance.[29]

Historians who wrote about Black Peril during the colonial period did so against the grain.[30] Without a concept of gender or a theory of power/knowledge sexual crime had little meaning as a field for historical inquiry. One of the few exceptions was Philip Mason's *The Birth of a Dilemma: The Conquest and Settlement of Rhodesia* (1958).[31] In his critique of settler rule Mason was preoccupied with two questions: How did British justice work in Southern Rhodesia? In what ways were settlers morally superior to the people they ruled? The contradiction between imperial intention and practice was obvious in the judicial response to Black Peril. For that reason Mason was drawn, almost against his will, into discussion of the moral panics. He was critical of white rule in regard to land, labor, and segregationist policies. But when writing about Black Peril Mason found excuses for the behavior of white male courts and white male legislators. There is in fact a sharp contrast between Mason's liberal political economy and his sexual politics.

Mason makes no mention of Miss Falconer or Singana but it is possible to construct his likely response to that case. Like his contemporaries he assumed that rape was caused by an excess of male desire. He also felt it significant that white pioneers came from a society which was sexually repressed.[32] Black men were uncivilized, he argued; they were cruel to animals and unrestrained in their sexual conduct.[33] That barbarity was linked to Black Peril in the contrast between what he saw as a civilized community of settlers and a black majority which had few constraints on its behavior. Black Peril arose from a lack of sexual discipline among black men. Mason would have conceded that the jury made a mistake, but Singana was not lynched nor was he executed. In that sense the legislation was a success.

Mason had no means to unravel the conflicts which underlay Singana's trial. How, for example, could he explain the determination of males to control female bodies? For that reason Mason's material remains fragmented. More than two decades were to pass before an historian again wrote at length about Black Peril.

By the late 1960s second-wave feminism, the work of Michel Foucault, and the gay liberation movement saw sexuality gradually established as a legitimate area for research. But at the very moment when that history came into focus historians were moving away from the study of European settlement to explore the workings of African agency. To write about Black Peril during the nationalist period was to hark back to an historiography which conceded primacy to white ruling minorities. The best history written in the 1960s and 1970s was looking in the opposite direction. For that reason the silence surrounding the moral panics returned.

The history of settler societies was an unfashionable subject in the 1980s when Dane Kennedy wrote *Islands of White: Settler Society and Culture in Kenya and Southern Rhodesia, 1890–1939*.[34] Kennedy was interested in the ways in which ruling minorities created their own culture. Although he showed no interest in post-structuralist theory he treated Black Peril seriously.

Kennedy argues that the high points of Black Peril panic in Southern Rhodesia, 1908 and 1910–1911, corresponded to peaks in the rates of white immigration. The other outbreaks occurred at times of economic decline. Kennedy admits that although the fear of Black Peril touched all settlers there was little correspondence between the incidence of sexual crime and the level of white concern.[35] Those fears were manipulated for political ends and the outbreaks of Black Peril accusations were contrived by settlers for political advantage. Black Peril was in effect a conspiracy. According to Kennedy the scares served the purpose of enforcing solidarity among new arrivals.[36]

How would Kennedy have explained the case of Miss Falconer? He would probably have argued that the trials were designed by the white male elite to embarrass the high commissioner and the British government. Possibly they also reflected settlers' fears of being swamped by a black majority. As we shall see, Kennedy was right about the political advantages wrought from the panics. But he was wrong in supposing that Black Peril was invented for political ends. Having read the trial transcripts, I have no doubt that Miss Falconer believed she had been the victim of sexual assault. The juries at Singana's trials and the press which reported them were also sincere in their fears for the safety of white women. There was no conspiracy to convict Singana. It is also true, as we shall see, that the Falconer case, like the other major Black Peril assaults, was used to political advantage by white men and women.

The past two decades have seen many changes in academic fashion. One of the most notable has been the emergence of post-colonial studies. Post-coloniality draws on many sources but perhaps none has been more important than the work of Edward Said. Said's *Orientalism* raised new questions which were quickly taken up by literary theorists with an interest in the colonial world. The result has been a rich and diverse literature on race and colonial representation. Those working in the field, such as Spivak, Nandy, Pratt, Sharpe, Strobel, McClintock, and Tovgornik, have generally relied upon published sources such as novels, travel writing, and memoirs. Historians were slower to respond to a challenge which came from outside their discipline. Although writing after *Orientalism*, Kennedy, for example, made no use of Said's work in *Islands of White*. It took until the mid-1980s for scholars, who were mostly feminists, to begin to produce innovative research on marriage, female labor, religious beliefs, disease, urbanization, and mental illness.[37] Writers such as Vaughan, Barnes, Kelly, Jeater, Schmidt, and Mukonyora have shown that resistance to colonial rule was infinitely complex. They have also shown that it was gendered.

Unfortunately feminist historians working on southern Africa have yet to produce sustained research on Black Peril.

In the contemporary historiography on the region there are two explanations for the moral panics. The first assumes that some specific event within the political, social, or economic sphere caused anxiety among settlers. The fear was of a kind which could not be acknowledged and so it was displaced or projected onto an imagined threat. Sometimes historians identify the original fear, sometimes they do not. In his study of the Witswatersrand Charles Van Onselen refers to Black Peril as a "collective sexual hysteria" which in the period 1890 to 1914 embittered race relations in the Transvaal.[38] Van Onselen argues that the scares occurred at times when the incomes of middle-class and working-class white families were falling. He is careful to link the panics to specific events and he never suggests that the same factors necessarily explain Black Peril panics elsewhere. According to Norman Hetherington the moral panics which swept Natal in the 1870s were connected to the desire of the dominant classes to maintain control.[39] Sexual assaults upon women became symbolic of perceived threats to the property and authority of white males. Whenever there was a disturbance in the economy or the body politic, that fear rose to the surface. To varying degrees Van Onselen and Hetherington rely upon Freud's concept of projection. Among historians projection has been the favorite tool used to explain Black Peril.

The most creative work on Black Peril has come from Ann Stoler. In her review of the literature Stoler concludes that Black Peril was provoked by real or perceived threats to the internal cohesion or boundaries of white communities.[40] Where boundaries were fragile panics erupted. But in practice the difference between actual and perceived threats is problematic and to distinguish between the two requires careful historical research of a kind which is only now beginning. There is also the problem of timing. In Southern Rhodesia crises of the kind identified by Stoler occurred before Black Peril and continued long after the panics had disappeared. As elsewhere in southern Africa, relations of race, gender, and class were meshed in complex and unstable configurations which could vary dramatically from one period to the next or from one site to another. For that reason a general theory of Black Peril is fraught with dangers.

Michael Banton has shown that the stereotypes of African inferiority which emerged in the period from 1880 to 1914 were to a large degree the creation of settler societies.[41] There may have been economic and social elements common to white minority regimes, but there were also important differences. White settlement in Southern Rhodesia was distinguished by its setting, experience, and recruitment. The political and physical environment was often threatening. African resistance, drought, labor shortages, and cattle disease meant ruin for many families. Those particular circumstances, like Black Peril itself, were not repeated elsewhere.

Ann Stoler has also written an overview of sex, race, and gender in colonial settings, focusing upon the Dutch East Indies and Indochina.[42] In passing she makes reference to the British and Belgian Empires. Stoler shows that every boundary of race or gender was also a boundary of colonial authority. She argues that settler rule was based on two assumptions: that Europeans made up a natural community and that boundaries separating the colonizers from the subaltern races could be easily drawn. To control those boundaries required careful regulation of sexual and domestic life.

In exploring how white minorities resolved the complex asymmetries of race, gender, and class Stoler arrives at a more abstract question: the construction of whiteness and bourgeois subjectivity. Stoler suggests that the subjectivity of the Western European bourgeoisie was in part shaped by the trade in conventions, social habits, and personnel between the empires and their metropoles. In suggesting that the colonies may have been laboratories of modernity Stoler has reversed the shibboleths about a passive colonial world acted upon by imperial forces. The panopticon was possibly invented in Russia, monitorial schools in India, and nationalism in Latin America. Even factory production, according to Sidney Mintz, may have been imported into western Europe from the sugar plantations of the West Indies. The historiography of whiteness is just beginning.[43]

Nowadays there is little argument about the relevance of bodily disciplines to the exercise of public and private forms of authority. In *Discipline and Punish* and the first volume of his *History of Sexuality* Foucault shows how in western Europe criminal justice, medical practice, child-rearing regimes, marriage forms, and sexual pathologies have been tied to diverse centers of power. Foucault also shows that such phenomena must be understood in terms of their context. By identifying the various sites in which power is exercised post-structuralist theory has helped to open the way for a better understanding of Black Peril. The moral panics drew the settler state into conflict with imperial authorities and so it is necessary to examine state formations. The panics also provoked conflict between white men and women, which brings us back to families and more intimate expressions of male power. In using such insights it is important to acknowledge that, like theory, history itself is local and ephemeral.

Contemporary social theory carries within it assumptions about state formations and civil society derived exclusively from Western European experience. As Marx, Weber, and, more recently, Elias and Foucault have shown, modern European states have exercised unprecedented levels of authority over their economies and citizens. By comparison, colonial states were rudimentary in scope and function. Their means of administration were typically ineffective. They were also violent. In Southern Rhodesia, for example, state-directed labor policies were frustrated by African resistance, while medicine and education were largely in the hands of missions. Pass laws were more successful in clogging up magistrates' courts than in regulating the movement of workers. There were no "great confinements" of the mad or social outcasts because colonial states were incapable of such an achievement.[44] The moral panics of Salisbury, Umtali, and Bulawayo were contingent on particular alignments of imperial power and demography. To understand why the moral panics occurred and what they meant to settlers requires careful historical research.

In this book I argue that in Southern Rhodesia Black Peril was protean in its causes and effects. It tended to spill over borders, incorporating other controversies, borrowing rhetoric, undermining reform, and creating political opportunities. The panics helped to precipitate the jury crises of 1908 and 1912.[45] They also led to state intervention in the sexual conduct of white women, influenced controls over the movement of black women, and shaped the state's response to venereal disease. The panics encouraged the drawing of a *cordon sanitaire* between the white and black communities and suggested rules for the regulation of social distance and intimacy.[46] Although Black Peril followed rather than preceded the establishment of urban locations, it gave impetus to that system, thereby bolstering the very conditions under which the panics could be sustained. Black Peril also provoked a number of unexpected consequences. White women used the panics to castigate men for concubinage. The experience thus gained by organizations such as the Rhodesian Women's League was used to effect in the struggle for suffrage. It is only when linkages are made between those contests for authority that the impact of Black Peril becomes visible.

Black Peril accusations were driven by fear and the desire for retribution and cleansing. They also involved very real demonstrations of state power. The panics served the interests of the white community by dramatizing the dangers it faced, thereby giving it some leverage against its enemies. But as the history shows, those gains came at a price. The panics soured Salisbury's relations with imperial authorities and made whites more fearful. Black Peril outbreaks identify a number of key moments when the boundaries of race, class, and gender were being established. The panics were both an expression of the problems of constructing a white identity and a means by which it was achieved. That identity needed to be constantly repaired and re-asserted and so the panics were repeated.[47] By the time they had passed, Black Peril had gained an emblematic status.

The sexual controversies of Rhodesian society revolved around Black Peril, miscegenation, concubinage, prostitution, and venereal disease. In the period from 1902 until the mid-1930s those issues preoccupied legislators, newspaper editors, and community interest groups such as the Rhodesian Women's League. Discourses on sexuality served many purposes. Among other things they facilitated the classification of colonial populations into distinct human types. In Southern Rhodesia many whites were barely middle class and so white identity was problematic. Whiteness was not a singular category: it included poor whites, continentals, Jews, and Portuguese. It also included those who could pass as white such as Coloureds from St. Helens. The absence of clear racial boundaries created all kinds of problems for the state, which in turn were played out in Black Peril.

The stories that follow of Singana, Kutchi, Mrs. Cromer, and Alukulita were important in the unfolding of Southern Rhodesia's history. They are also relevant to wider imperial processes. The ways in which settlers in Southern Rhodesia reacted to the threat of sexual crime helped to shape the forms of political dominance. The peculiar place of white and black women in regard to patriarchal authority has something to tell us in general about the politics of race and gender.

In Southern Rhodesia discourses about sexual pathology helped to decide the most fundamental of bourgeois rights: the legitimate claims of men to property, which included control of the bodies of women, headship of a family, and citizenship. It was here that the essential features of a bourgeois sensibility and whiteness were developed. It was also the site of Black Peril.

TWO

BLACK PERIL: THE CRIMES

THE CONTEXT

Kenya and Southern Rhodesia were, with the exception of South Africa, Britain's principal settler colonies on the continent. As such they stood in type between temperate colonies such as Australia and Canada and tropical colonies such as Sierra Leone and the Gold Coast. The temperate colonies were sparsely populated and their native inhabitants quickly succumbed to introduced disease and systematic violence. The situation in Africa was very different. In Southern Rhodesia, for example, in 1900 blacks outnumbered whites by more than thirty to one and white farmers and mine managers depended heavily upon black workers. In much of sub-Saharan Africa white communities were minuscule and the maintenance of cultural norms and racial boundaries came to have particular importance.

During the first thirty years of colonization settlers in Southern Rhodesia lived under the rule of the British South Africa Company (BSAC), a commercial company founded in 1889 by Cecil Rhodes. The BSAC speculated in gold mines and alienated millions of acres of land in the hope of making quick profits. From the moment of settlement in 1890 until independence ninety years later the major issues for settlers were access to land, mining leases, and the availability of cheap labor. As elsewhere in the colonial world it was land and labor that created wealth.

In the first decades of the twentieth century miners and farmers struggled with little success to produce goods for a world market. Most settlers lived in cramped small houses with poor food and little sanitation. There were few schools or hospitals. Despite high wages many families found the cost of living prohibitive. The Legislative Council which was supposed to represent their interests was divided between mining interests, large maize growers, and small producers. The colony drew its legal system, civil service, and native policies from South Africa.

The BSAC was ruthless in its pursuit of wealth. The dispossession of land and cattle and the imposition of hut taxes and forced labor meant that within less than three years there was armed resistance. In 1893 the Matabele fought a determined war and a second war, or *chimurenga,* erupted at the beginning of 1896. By the end of the last week of March of that year one hundred and twenty-two white men, five women, and three children had been killed. Nearly all the dead lived in isolated homesteads or camps. By early April the survivors were huddled in fortified settlements in Bulawayo and Gwelo. The eventual total was around ten percent of the European population.[1] According to Terence Ranger: "The sudden unexpected risings in which the house-servants, the customers in the stores, the respectful old men, suddenly turned into killers, burnt themselves deep into white Rhodesian consciousness."[2] The rebellion was arguably the most serious single blow to colonization in southern Africa. It became a permanent feature of settler culture, feeding the racism which whites brought with them from Britain and South Africa.

The revolt weakened the position of the BSAC. The company was forced to meet the costs of imperial intervention and to compensate settlers for their losses. Whites were bitter at the BSAC's failure to protect them and with some justification: At the outbreak of war there were only forty-eight white police in the whole of Matabeleland.[3] Even so, the rebellion strengthened the position of settlers, who gained constitutional and financial concessions that included the establishment of a Legislative Council. In 1903 they won parity in the council and in 1908 a full majority. Despite those gains they remained vulnerable. In 1911 there were twenty-nine blacks for every white. Ten years later that ratio had fallen only slightly.[4] Following the *chimurenga* fears of further resistance persisted and the BSAC police were placed on permanent alert.[5] In the context of southern Africa such fears were justified; there was an uprising in northeastern Mashonaland in 1900 followed by the Bambatha rebellion of 1906 in Zululand. During World War One there were further revolts in Portuguese East Africa and Nyasaland.

Settlers had reason to perceive the physical environment as dangerous. Periodic droughts and human and cattle diseases were a constant threat to family life and economic success. To those real hazards settlers added a number of imaginary fears. Intense tropical sunshine, for example, was supposed to cause congestion of the blood and neurasthenia in blondes.[6] Because of the supposed danger of sexual precocity brought on by a tropical climate, parents preferred to send their children to school in England when possible.[7] Such ideas were conflated with the fear of living in proximity to colored races. According to one contemporary authority: "The nervous troubles of white men in the tropics are often due to the privations of pioneer life. . . . Nervous strain is more likely due to interracial friction than to climate."[8]

The victory of 1897 over the Shona and Matabele did not end the troubles which plagued white settlement. Primary resistance may have ended but Africans still refused to do waged labor and they continued to compete too successfully against white farmers. In 1904, for example, blacks produced over ninety percent of marketed food.[9] White farmers needed state intervention to limit peasant competition and to gain the best labor for themselves. They also wanted government support in the form of rail concessions. Settlers remained in conflict with the BSAC, which dominated economic activity until long after 1923 when the company's charter ended. There were also at odds with imperial authorities and with various philanthropic groups within Britain such as the Aborigines Protection Society. In addition colonization was dogged by economic recession, drought, cattle disease, and the influenza epidemic of 1918.[10] Those crises did not foster a natural community of interests, and white society was deeply divided. The most flagrant divisions were between miners and farmers, both of whom competed for the company's favor. The white community was also split by ethnicity. In the wake of the Anglo-Boer War relations between British and Afrikaners were strained while so-called continentals, including Greek, French, and Portuguese minorities, were greatly disliked. There were also cleavages between poor whites and those who had been successful. In terms of Black Peril perhaps the most important divisions were between white men and women. It was in that setting of conflict and perceived vulnerability that the attack upon Miss Falconer occurred.

The administrative framework in Southern Rhodesia was unique. The permanent executive was formed not by the British government but by the BSAC, which appointed the administrator, the executive council, and the civil service. Until 1907 the elected members of the Legislative Council were in the minority and even after that date the company still exercised financial control. A resident commissioner was appointed by Whitehall and he reported directly to the high commissioner in South Africa, who in turn held an imperial veto over racially discriminatory legislation. Gladstone, the high commissioner from 1910 to 1914, soon found that whites resented any interference and he spent his first two years in office assuaging settler discontent over supposed Black Peril incidents. The role of the resident commissioner was to preserve imperial interests and in particular to ensure that the company did not provoke a further rebellion.

The perspectives of the BSAC and the British government were distinct. The company wanted to make money by alienating land and driving Africans onto the labor market. The British wanted somehow to protect African interests while devolving power into the hands of settlers. That strategy was made more difficult by the company, which was hostile to both settler power and imperial influence. Britain hoped that eventually the absorption of Rhodesia into the Union of South Africa would strengthen pro-imperial forces and solve the problem of native policy in southern Africa.[11] That strategy was opposed by Afrikaners who did not want more imperialist voters in their midst. In their turn Rhodesians feared being swamped by Afrikaners and in 1922 they upset Whitehall by rejecting union or incorporation with South Africa.

During the first decade of colonization Salisbury consisted of a scattering of public buildings and residential areas.[12] It was smaller than Bulawayo and in 1904 had 2,000 white residents and over four hundred houses and shops. Many plots of land for housing were kept off the market by the Company in the hope of forcing a rise in price. Salisbury's sparse appearance was also magnified by the large commonage which cut through its center. The town was divided between the *kopje* in the west, the home of storekeepers and artisans, and the causeway in the east, where BSAC officials lived. With the development of a business center came the first residential suburb, known today as the Avenues, which was home to company managers, bankers, and mine engineers. The failure of the gold industry to produce a second Rand only added to the economic gloom which plagued the first years of colonization and in 1904 not a single new building was erected. Six years later there was still no street lighting, and water and sanitation had scarcely improved since Salisbury's foundation two decades earlier. It was not until the end of World War One that Salisbury became a commercial and administrative center serving mining and agricultural industries.

Even before the influx of a large African population urban space was structured according to color. In 1892 a town pass system was introduced and a residential area for Africans opened one kilometer south of the *kopje*. Both were modeled on Transvaal practice and those who failed to register were subject to prosecution. The system was designed to control the movement of labor and on first entering a town a worker was obliged to report to a registry office. The same strategy was used in Bulawayo and other urban centers, but it never ran smoothly. Passes were often ineffective and there was no proper control over the location.[13] Complaints about the behavior of African servants led to a police crackdown on pass offenders. In response, in October 1907 the Salisbury council set up a new location.[14]

The location was under police control and occupancy was granted on a monthly basis, supposedly to keep out undesirables. Although many workers preferred to live on plots outside the city limits, over time evictions, police raids, resettlements, and removals forced many into the location.

Urban black communities were predominantly male and according to official estimates in 1911 the African population of Salisbury was 6,400, of whom 6,065 were men. Many urban dwellers were aliens; in that year almost half of the town's blacks were from Nyasaland, Northern Rhodesia, or Portuguese East Africa.[15] The European community was heavily urbanized and by 1911 half of the territory's 23,000 whites lived in towns.[16] Black Peril was always an urban problem and almost all "outrages" occurred in Bulawayo, Salisbury, or Umtali.

Recent histories of South Africa have emphasized how segregation served various and often contradictory interests. It offered white farmers cheap labor and gave mine managers access to migrant workers. To missions and native affairs department officials it promised to shield rural communities from the ruthless environment of the cities; to a white proletariat it offered protection from competition in labor markets.[17] Such ambiguities did nothing to temper the philosophy and in Southern Rhodesia the number of constituencies the policy was intended to serve increased the vigor with which racial separation was pursued.

Yoshikuni has claimed that in the period before 1910 there was no specific policy of segregation in Southern Rhodesia and that the system of African locations came about in an ad hoc way.[18] Whatever its origins, urban segregation was never successful in imposing the kinds of disciplines of which legislators dreamt. Location life was sustained by tea parties, dances, football matches, religious meetings, and night schools. Locations were the site for protests against excessive rents and prohibitions on the brewing of beer. The independence of location life increased rather than soothed the fears of the white community.

Settlers were in the main drawn from the lower middle or working classes of Britain and South Africa. Most were in trade rather than the professions and they were aggressive in their desire for social and economic betterment. They made a considerable effort to isolate themselves within physical, linguistic, social, economic, and political boundaries. The society they created was far smaller in scale than white communities to the south. It was also idiosyncratic. As two sympathetic historians would later write of them: "White Rhodesian society in some ways retained a curious archaic quality; the values of Edwardian England survived as in a kind of sociological museum."[19]

BLACK PERIL

According to a confidential report written by the local Criminal Investigation Department (CID) during World War One, Black Peril was any rape or assault with intent to commit rape by an African on a white female. It included indecent assault, acts, or overtures, and the molesting of women for the purpose of exciting or satisfying "bestial desires."[20] In theory it embraced indiscreet gestures, familiarity, or even friendship. In practice Black Peril covered crimes ranging from the brutal to the absurd. Serious sexual assaults upon white women were rare, but police, like the public, believed that many assaults were not reported and that the incidence of Black Peril was far higher than records suggested.[21] They were also certain that most assaults were committed by men employed as servants, an opinion supported by court records. In terms of the size of the white population Black Peril cases were common but accusations of actual rape were rare. In the period from 1899 to 1906 there were fifty-three assaults reported in Bulawayo but only two rapes. In Salisbury in the period from 1907 to 1914 there were sixty-three assaults.[22] But those figures have to be seen in light of the extravagant definition of sexual crime used by victims, the police, and the courts. In other contexts many of those incidents would not have come to the attention of police let alone have resulted in a prosecution.

The first notable assaults occurred in Bulawayo in 1901. Those crimes were debated by the town council and in the local press and were followed in the first half of 1902 by a number of minor incidents in Salisbury. September 1902 saw the first major Black Peril crime when a young African named Charlie was charged with having raped Ada Flower at Bulawayo.[23] The case caused bitter feeling in the town, and before a trial could be held an attempt was made to lynch the accused. A distressed acting attorney general wrote to head office: "I myself was present assisting the magistrate to quell the riot in which the police were very nearly overpowered receiving a severe wound in the course of the melee. The whole affair seems to have been very cleverly engineered and I am unable to tell you anything definite until I have reports from the proper quarters."[24] The attorney general demanded that the BSAC apprehend the men involved. He also moved the trial from Bulawayo to ensure a fair hearing.[25] Charlie was eventually tried at Salisbury, found guilty of rape, and sentenced to thirty-six lashes and twelve years' jail. The *Bulawayo Chronicle* criticized the sentence and demanded the death penalty.[26] No charges were laid over the lynching but within twelve months the Criminal Law Amendment Ordinance introduced the death sentence for rape and attempted rape. There was no lack of determination in Salisbury to push through sentences and yet it took seven years from the passing of the ordinance in 1903 for a man to be hanged for attempted rape. As we shall see, the reason for that delay rested with the Office of the High Commissioner.[27]

Following the ordinance of 1903 there was a hardening in the jail sentences imposed. In 1904 a case involving a man named Ziku, which was probably a simple housebreaking, resulted in a conviction of assault with intent to commit rape and a sentence of five years' hard labor.[28] In January 1905 a laborer named Mudzingawe was charged with the rape of Johanna Katrina Oliver at Grootfontein, where she lived with her stepfather.[29] The district surgeon J. Ritchie Brown found Johanna to be *virgo intacto* but he was unwilling to say that rape had not occurred. Mudzingawe was found guilty and Justice Watermeyer sentenced him to fifteen years' hard labor. As sentences increased the definition of sexual assault was widened. In April 1913 Mananga, an African laborer from Umtali, was charged with having broken into the house of Mrs. Emma Palmer and assaulted her with intent to commit rape.[30] Mrs. Palmer was in bed with her baby and another child was asleep in a cot beside her. Her teenage son was in an adjacent room and two servants were close by. Mrs. Palmer awoke to feel a hand on her arm. Her screams woke the household and the accused was captured at the scene of the crime. There was no evidence of intent and even the victim admitted in court that she could not be sure as to Mananga's purpose. In the eyes of the jury the crime was made worse by two facts: At the time of the assault the victim's husband was in England, and Mrs. Palmer was deaf. Mananga was found guilty and sentenced to twelve years' hard labor and twenty-four lashes. As was usual the trial was well publicized.

On occasion it was sufficient for an African to break into a house where a white woman lived for him to be charged with sexual assault. In July 1924, for example, a man named Musima was tried for the attempted rape of Sussanah Couldrey, a married woman of Salisbury.[31] On the night of the crime the victim awoke in her bed to find the accused with his hands on her leg. Mrs. Couldrey's husband was at the time asleep four feet away. Musima was found guilty and sentenced to ten years' hard labor. Four years later, in May 1928, a servant named Munemu was charged with attempted rape. He was also arraigned on a separate charge of housebreaking.[32] Both charges referred to an incident which took place at the home of Phyllis Atkinson, who lived with her husband in Selous Avenue, Salisbury. On that evening the victim went to bed at around 10 P.M., sleeping as usual with her husband on one side and her four-year-old daughter on the other. She awoke at 4 A.M. to feel a cold hand on her "private parts." "My husband woke" she told the court, "and he switched on the light. The door was open. I found my daughter in bed. I noticed a smell of native in the room. I got out of bed and looked under the bed and there I saw a native."[33] Munemu, a servant employed by the Atkinsons, was found guilty and sentenced to two years' hard labor and fifteen cuts with the cane.

In cases brought under the Immorality and Indecency Suppression Ordinance of 1916, which proscribed sexual relations between white women
and black men, the slightest indiscretion could have serious consequences. In one case a man named Akutizwi was sentenced to two years' hard
labor and ten cuts with the cane. While resting his bicycle against the bur-
lap door of a privy, Akutizwi had lifted the flap, exposing a young woman
who was inside.[34] Although such cases were uncommon, the heavy penalties handed down to offenders were not. Almost a decade later a servant
named Joseph was charged with *criminal injuria*.[35] He had written a letter
to a young Salisbury woman, Johanna du Plessis, declaring his love and
asking her to meet him at a certain place. The court found that Joseph had
lewd and lascivious intent and was therefore guilty as charged. He was
sentenced to two years' jail.

The major Black Peril panics occurred between 1902 to 1905 and 1908
to 1911. The cases which took place after those dates drew upon conventions which the earlier panics established. Each case had particular features
in terms of the time and place of the assault and the degree of violence involved. There was also much variation in the reaction by the press. Many of
the cases had an abstruse quality which makes the public response to assaults difficult to understand. Rarely was there a simple relationship between
the nature of the crime and the reaction. At one time a trivial incident could
lead to panic; at another a serious rape would attract little comment.

THREE SEXUAL ASSAULTS

The major Black Peril cases aroused intense debate and had repercussions far beyond the courtrooms of Rhodesia. Towns were small and gos-
sip-ridden and so in addition to the comprehensive and often hysterical
newspaper reporting there was room for endless speculation. The trials
were often characterized by an ambiguity between the symbolic status of
the woman and the intrusions of privacy which came from the press. Even
though the papers usually suppressed the victim's identity, in such small
communities her name would have been common knowledge. The press
often wrote of Black Peril as a threat to family life; the worst assaults were
presumed to threaten white settlement itself. The following cases, three of
which resulted in the death penalty, illustrate some of the complexities of
Black Peril and its importance as a site for political struggle.

MRS. CROMER'S DILEMMA

One of the most important Black Peril trials was held before Justice Watermeyer at Salisbury in October 1910. The accused was a servant
named Alukuleta, the prosecutor Attorney General Tredgold. Recovering

the story of the trial is difficult. The transcript, the judge's report, and other essential papers are missing. The resident commissioner's files are incomplete, as are the list files from the Salisbury Criminal Court. Of the 3,500 files in that series it is the only one which has vanished.

Bessie Cromer, the victim, was the wife of James Cromer of Umtali.[36] The accused, Alukuleta, was employed in the Cromer household. On the evening of the assault Cromer was away from town and the victim was alone in the house with her four children. According to Mrs. Cromer, late that night she heard a sound and moments later she was seized by the throat. A black man forced her back onto the bed saying "Keep quiet or I will kill you."[37] He smelt strongly of liquor and, according to Mrs. Cromer, there was partial penetration. Alukuleta was found guilty of rape and sentenced to death. In forwarding the case notes to Cape Town for endorsement the resident commissioner commented: "The evidence of this case seems very clear and I can see no grounds for recommending any remission."[38]

The case was in many ways typical. The press wrote about the safety of women, the defense of civilized values, and the sanctity of white social space, namely the towns. It wrote of the responsibilities of government toward citizens, which always meant the past negligence of the BSAC and the British administration. There was some special pleading about the hardships of pioneer life in which women were unsafe. It also dramatized the failure of the state to protect white families, a criticism which harked back to the *chimurenga* of 1896.

The new high commissioner Gladstone had good reason to confirm the sentence. The attorney general and the resident commissioner had both endorsed the death penalty, as had the press. His predecessor Selbourne had already alienated settlers with his reprieve of Singana. But Gladstone believed firmly in the need for a fair judicial system and he prided himself on his knowledge of the law. He was unconvinced that attacks upon women were increasing and that Alukuleta's death was necessary to prevent further assaults. On December 20, 1910, he commuted the sentence to life imprisonment.

The reprieve aroused deep resentment in Rhodesia and it featured prominently in the South African and British press. During December and January a series of protest meetings were held in Salisbury and Umtali. At the height of the controversy a rumor circulated that Gladstone had suggested Black Peril would cease if women locked their doors and windows at night. The rumor, which Gladstone subsequently denied, inflamed public opinion because it implied that women had invited such attacks. The South African press claimed Black Peril was so common that white men were afraid to leave their wives alone and that the only the death penalty would prevent further assaults. One editorial observed: "White women must be protected at all hazards, and any weakness in this respect would only open the flood-gates for a seething tide of horrors."[39] The Women's Unionist Association of Johannesburg petitioned Gladstone to introduce the death penalty for attempted rape; one meeting at The Wanders Club was attended by over 2,000 citizens.[40]

The British press was preoccupied with the legal distinctions between Gladstone's duties as governor of South Africa and as high commissioner of Rhodesia. There was concern that as the Crown's representative he had acted on his own volition rather than on the advice of his ministers.[41] The *Daily Mail* and the *Pall Mall Gazette* viewed his actions as dangerous and called for greater protection of women. On February 8, 1911, the issue was raised in the House of Lords.[42] In reporting the debate the press suggested that Gladstone's action was unconstitutional and against the interests of settlers.[43] Prime Minister Asquith was questioned in the House about Glad-stone's competence.[44] Debate moved quickly from discussion of the re-prieve to the scope of the high commissioner's powers, the very issues which rankled settlers.

During January and February the resident commissioner's office in Sal-isbury was inundated with letters of protest including complaints from the Salisbury Chambers of Mines and the Kimberley Reef's Miners Associa-tion. Typical of that correspondence was a resolution passed by the Sal-isbury Council which in part read: "It is much to be deplored that the High Commissioner has thought fit to interfere with the course of justice and it is felt that his action is bound to have a most injurious effect upon the native mind, and to endanger the safety of many women in this sparsely popu-lated country."[45] Petitions were collected by citizens at Hartley, Gatooma, Umtali, and Bulawayo. Most telling was a petition signed by over 1,200 Rhodesian women.[46] In 1911 there were less than 6,000 white women in the territory.[47]

With Gladstone's approval, in the first week of February a letter he had written to the administrator explaining the reasons for his decision was published in the Rhodesian and South African press. The letter showed that Gladstone had doubts about the question of intent. He was also reluc-tant to endorse the death sentence for a crime for which there was no death penalty in South Africa.[48] The charge of rape and the jury's verdict de-pended upon statements made by the complainant and the accused. Be-cause of her distress, the evidence of Mrs. Cromer could not be taken liter-ally, in Gladstone's view. The prisoner's admission before a magistrate that he had raped Mrs. Cromer was compromised by the use of an interpreter. Furthermore the admission was not substantiated either by a doctor or by the complainant. Gladstone believed that Alukuleta entered the house to find food and drink: He had first gone to the meat safe, the keys to which were found in his pocket. He also noted that the trial judge had preferred a verdict of "assault with intent."

The public response was generally unfavorable. In a letter to the press, Charles Coghlan, a prominent member of the Legislative Council and future prime minister, claimed that the number of Black Peril assaults had only fallen since the death penalty was introduced in 1903.[49] In order to improve his standing with settlers Gladstone decided to visit Rhodesia in May, but Resident Commissioner Burns Begg warned that feeling had been fanned by further Black Peril cases.[50] He told Gladstone: "A number of Rhodesians who have visited Cape Town, Johannesburg and Pretoria have conceived the idea that you do not take an interest in Rhodesia because you have not, so it is alleged, made opportunities of discussing Rhodesia with them when they have met you or have not sent for them for that purpose when they have called at Government House."[51] Concern for Gladstone's safety was such that the visit was delayed.

In October 1911, almost exactly a year after Alukuleta's trial, a colleague of Mr. Cromer's named Coe came forward with new evidence.[52] He told Gladstone's staff that Mrs. Cromer had been having an affair. When discovered in bed with her lover Alukuleta she had accused him of rape in order to protect herself. That was why Mr. Cromer had been absent during the trial and why he had subsequently left his wife. The conventions of settler society make Mrs. Cromer's behavior understandable. Her husband, like any white man, could at little cost have had a sexual relationship with a black woman: The number of half-caste births in the territory proves that many did. The penalty Mrs. Cromer faced was a prison sentence and ostracism.

Gladstone knew that if the details of the case became public there would be a scandal and for that reason he put the matter aside. He justified his action to himself in the following way: "Assuming the story of the prisoner to be practically true he committed a serious crime in entering the house by night, making free in the kitchen, taking the keys and demanding intercourse—even though his story to his council that he had in June been asked to have connection is true. Two or three years imprisonment would not be an unreasonable punishment."[53]

Over the next three years Gladstone worked hard to establish good relations with Salisbury. In 1914 he was due to leave his post and he decided to resolve the matter. He wrote to Burns Begg: "About two years ago I consulted the Chief Justice formally and he favoured releasing the prisoner after five years—the sentence to which he would have been liable under Section 3 of the Immorality Suppression Ord, S.Rhodesia, 1903."[54] (That ordinance proscribed voluntary sexual relations between white women and black men.) Despite the objections of the resident commissioner and the attorney general, Alukuleta was released.[55] Gladstone knew that his actions would alienate public opinion and under the circumstances his decision was brave. The BSAC charter was due to end in 1914, opening the way for an amalgamation with South Africa.

The missing documents make it difficult to recover what exactly was known about Mrs. Cromer. The CID was unable to locate her husband, who it was rumored was living in South West Africa. It was Coe's testimony alone that convinced the police and Gladstone of Alukuleta's innocence. As with Miss Falconer the case involved a secret known only to a few within the administration. That secret was kept not to protect Mrs. Cromer's reputation but to protect the integrity of the Salisbury judiciary. It was also kept to protect the high commissioner's office. Gladstone remained silent. The stakes in the case were high. To speak out would have alienated public opinion in South Africa and Southern Rhodesia, which no doubt would have seen such a story as a fabrication. Coe's revelations were potentially more damaging than Gladstone's supposed comments about closed windows and doors. In Britain such an admission would have galvanized opinion against an incompetent and racist judiciary, thereby compromising the prospect of union with South Africa.

Gladstone's first years as high commissioner were marred by an infidelity in one of the territory's smallest towns. Conflict between his office and settlers was kept alive by the attempts of a woman to protect herself, the determination of a male judiciary to enforce the death penalty, and Gladstone's own commitment to the impartial application of the law. Mrs. Cromer's dilemma was caused as much by the politics of white marriage as by the play of imperial interests. Within that web of circumstances settlers used the case as an opportunity to embarrass the high commissioner and secure the first executions for the crime of attempted rape. I will now turn to those cases.

THE HILLSIDE AND CAPE AVENUE OUTRAGES: 1911

Within the space of ten weeks two Black Peril assaults shocked the white community of Salisbury. The first occurred at Hillside, an outer suburb, in January 1911, the other in Cape Avenue. At that time Cape Avenue was the most prominent street in the residential area and was used during late afternoons by nannies and children.[56]

The first attack involved Mrs. Annie Watson, who lived with her husband at Hillside, a detached suburb lying to the east of the town. Mr. Watson was a constable who was often absent at night. On the day of the assault he left home at around 8 P.M. and his wife went to bed.[57] Some time later Mrs. Watson was awakened by knocking and saw an African on the other side of a French window. He indicated that he wanted sex and when she refused he broke the glass with his fist and caught hold of the sleeve of her nightgown. She struggled for some minutes and finally he ran away. The next morning she identified her assailant as a laborer named Bonali, who worked for a neighbor. Clothing taken from Bonali showed bloodstains while Mrs. Watson's nightdress was stained and the arm was torn. Dr. Orpen, the government pathologist who examined the victim, found numerous scratches and cuts on her shoulder and there was skin missing from her right hand. At the preliminary hearing Bonali made a confession of sorts when through an interpreter he told the magistrate: "I don't know why I should have gone to the house—Satan told me to go there."[58] He did not admit that his intention had been to rape Mrs. Watson and the Crown presented no evidence to support such a claim.

With memory of the Cromer case still fresh there was a public outcry. Even before the trial Mrs. Watson's sisters wrote to their local member asking him to ensure the death sentence was carried out.[59] In his summation the judge commented that unless there was some extenuating circumstance, namely reprehensible conduct on the part of the victim, he was obliged by law to pass the death penalty. In so doing he misinterpreted the ordinance of 1903, which left the matter of sentencing to the judge's discretion. As a result the attorney general, Tredgold, feared the verdict was compromised.[60]

Tredgold believed the assault was premeditated, for although she suffered no serious injury only Mrs. Watson's resolve had saved her. Yet for reasons which are not clear he recommended the sentence be commuted. Resident Commissioner Burns Begg was concerned about the need to protect white women from blacks; "whose aboriginal savagery is covered, even in the case of boys constantly employed in towns, by a remarkably thin veneer."[61] He asked for a statuary punishment as a deterrent and on June 27 Gladstone confirmed the sentence of death.[62]

While Bonali was awaiting trail another Black Peril assault took place in Cape Avenue. In the second week of March, Mary Duthie, a woman in her late twenties, was walking down the avenue in the early evening when she became aware of footsteps.[63] Before she could turn around she was seized from behind and thrown to the ground. Her assailant apparently made no attempt to steal her bag but put his hands inside her clothes as far as her waist. When she screamed he ran away, leaving her holding his coat. Miss Duthie was carrying nothing of value except for a brooch which was fastened with a pin to her jacket. In a thinly disguised attack upon Gladstone the *Herald* commented: "This occurrence only serves to illustrate the daily menace that exists for white women here, despite assurances from high authorities that the danger is exaggerated."[64]

The accused, a laborer named Nyamadzi, pleaded guilty to assault with intent to rob but not guilty to the charge of attempted rape. As at most Black Peril trials no witnesses were called for the defense and counsel made so little attempt to forward his client's interests that the judge urged him to make more effort. Although there was no forensic evidence to support the charge, as required under law, Judge Watermeyer rejected the plea of robbery and agreed with the jury that Nyamadzi's object was rape: "I consider this a very bad case. A lady—Miss Duthie is the sister of the Super General of Education—was attacked whilst taking an evening stroll through the best residential part of Salisbury. She only escaped by being able to scream loudly enough to be heard some 200 yards away."[65] He sentenced Nyamadzi to death. In his report Tredgold acknowledged that the accused was short and of slight build while Miss Duthie was unusually tall and muscular. That fact combined with the locality meant the crime could not have been completed.[66] Even so, for the first time in his career Tredgold called for the death penalty. The resident commissioner agreed. He too believed the case pointed to a slackening in the "natives'" respect for the inviolability of white women and for that reason he endorsed the sentence.[67]

No appeals were lodged and on August 4, 1911, Bonali and Nyamadzi became the first men in Southern Rhodesia to be hanged for attempted rape.[68] Settlers claimed the deaths would prevent further assaults and they celebrated the executions, at least in the letters to the press and Legislative Council debate, as a victory over Gladstone. Bonali and Nyamadzi were certainly unlucky. They died in the shadow of Mrs. Cromer's infidelity, which created a set of complexities against which the high commissioner was powerless.

Despite the deaths of Bonali and Nyamadzi, within fifteen months there was another attack in Cape Avenue. In November 1912, Kuchi, an African worker, was charged with having assaulted and attempted to rape Eleanor Judd.[69] Mrs. Judd, a nurse, was attacked as she was on her way to night duty. She and her assailant were riding bicycles in the same direction along

Cape Avenue at around 8 P.M. Kuchi, who was riding behind Mrs. Judd, deliberately ran into her back wheel, so she claimed, throwing her to the ground. He then hit her in the face with a clenched fist. Although he did not attempt to undo her clothes, Mrs. Judd was certain as to his purpose. Kuchi then stole her bicycle, leaving his own in its place. Mrs. Judd's bicycle was later found in Kuchi's possession.

It seems likely that Kuchi, who was riding a borrowed bicycle, accidentally ran into Mrs. Judd. While struggling to his feet he pushed her in the face or upper body. In fear he ran off with the wrong bike. When questioned through an interpreter, Kuchi told police: "I did not sleep with her; I merely ran into her with my bicycle. It was an accident."[70] During the trial Kuchi was not called to give evidence and only a feeble defense was offered on his behalf. The jury retired at 10:58 A.M. and at 11:10 returned a unanimous verdict of guilty of attempted rape. The death sentence was imposed. The case was as absurd as that of Singana and the evidence against Kuchi was just as insubstantial. Gladstone had the courage to commute the sentence but not sufficient courage to overturn the verdict. Kutchi was to endure fifteen years in prison and twenty-four lashes.

One panic fed the next and public reaction often depended upon a sequence of trials. None of the cases cited so far involved rape and with the exception of Mrs. Watson none involved any degree of violence. No defense was offered for the accused, the judge was sometimes incompetent, and juries rushed to judgment. The question of intent was usually the weakest part of the prosecution's brief. That weakness was ignored because police, juries, and judges assumed that the accused must have wanted to rape the victim.

SOME THEMES, SOME EXCEPTIONS

It is difficult to be certain how many men were executed for Black Peril, and Lawrence Vambe's figure of thirty hangings between 1903 and 1933 is probably exaggerated.[71] Certainly in that period at least twenty men were executed and over two hundred were imprisoned and flogged. Few charged with such crimes gave evidence in their defense. They were tried in a foreign language under a belittling nickname and most spent their trials silent and probably uncomprehending at the ritual being played out. They were accorded no distinguishing features, for there was nothing in their lives in which courts took an interest. After 1912 there was a gradual lessening in the numbers charged but until the early 1930s men were still being sentenced to death.

The crimes differed greatly from sexual assaults in other parts of the British Empire. In England, for example, assailants were usually in positions of authority over their victims. The reverse was true in Southern Rhodesia, where assailants were often in the employ of the women they attacked. However, the elevated status of women as subordinate members of a ruling minority did little to empower plaintiffs. The panoply of the law was to protect women; it was also designed to ensure their dependence upon men.

Rhodesian courts assumed that there could not have been a pre-existing sexual relationship between the woman and her assailant. Consequently the kinds of strategies used elsewhere by defense counsels were absent. Counsel did not attack the character of the victim or question her sexual history or status. With notable exceptions courts were sympathetic and vigorous cross-examination was seldom used; sometimes it was waived. In the majority of cases penetration had not occurred and so the degree of stigma attached to sexual assault was also diminished. On occasion, as with Miss Falconer and Miss Duthie, victims were treated by courts and the press as heroines who had fought off vicious assailants. Even so, a rape trial can hardly have been a pleasant experience for them. Some women were not believed and when guilty verdicts were achieved the attorney general and high commissioner sometimes refused to ratify the sentence.

At most Black Peril trials the same cast acted out the same drama: a silent accused, a stoic victim, a sympathetic court, homilies from the bench, and harsh verdicts. The oddness of Miss Falconer's assault was typical of an oddness in many of the cases. The trials were theatrical and involved studied displays of power, but for whom? No attempt was made to publicize the verdicts outside the white community and suggestions of a return to the old English practice of public executions were rejected as barbaric. The trials and the outrage which surrounded them were not designed to instill fear into potential assailants. African workers had far more reason to fear the casual violence of employers than they did the morality legislation.

Black Peril fears were fueled by the press, by Legislative Council debate, and by women's organizations such as the Rhodesian Women's League (RWL). There was tacit agreement among those groups about what made a crime significant. But from the distance of almost a century it is difficult to identify what those elements were. We do know that the panics justified attacks upon the office of the high commissioner and the BSAC administration. The major Black Peril crimes occurred in two waves; the first from 1902 to 1905 and the second from 1908 to 1911. There were other crimes outside those dates but they added little to the design of the panics. Most Black Peril incidents involved trivial assaults upon victims of unimpeachable character. Crimes became *causes cèlébres* not only because of the degree of violence, the place of the attack, or the identity of victim. The external factors which made a crime important were not always obvious.

Most Black Peril crimes involved little physical injury, and during the early colonial period there was only one fatal attack upon a white women.[72] On March 9, 1916, the mutilated body of a fifteen-year-old girl was found beside the Salisbury railway track. Newspaper reports suggested the motive was rape.[73] The victim was Sussanah Thomas, who lived with her father three miles down the line. Thomas was employed as a shop assistant and on some evenings she was in the habit of returning home alone. The inquest concluded that three or more assailants had been involved and the victim had died from any of a number of injuries: her liver was ruptured, a steel hatpin had been driven into her brain, and she had been suffocated.[74] Three weeks after the inquest two African men named Thausern and Mzulu were arrested although there was little evidence linking them with the murder. Those charges were eventually dropped and in June two other men were charged. They too were released because of lack of evidence and the case disappeared quietly from public view.[75] There was no proof that the murderer was black but the CID and the press never considered the possibility that the assailant could have been white.

The murder of Sussanah Thomas was of a kind common in Britain at the time but rare in Southern Rhodesia. The lack of publicity surrounding the case was also notable. The crime was far more serious than the Cape Avenue outrages yet there was little coverage in the press, there were no rallies, and there was no debate in the Legislative Council. The murder took place at a time of crisis, which could have lent it importance. The BSAC's charter had expired in 1914 and there was uncertainty about the colony's future: In 1916 many men were absent fighting an imperial war in Europe. Almost 2,000 whites fought in the war, which was a massive contribution for the small population. More than seven hundred men died.[76] But it was an isolated crime that did not fit the pattern of Black Peril, and it illustrates the very special nature of the panics. World War One brought settlers together in support of imperial authority, whereas Black Peril had united them against it. Sussanah's murder fulfilled the worst fears of whites. But the circumstances meant that the case could not be invested with the right kind of imaginative purpose and so it was useless as an emblem.

Few men who were tried for Black Peril escaped without a prison sentence and those who did owed their good fortune to the court's perception of the plaintiff. Juries were willing to convict men on flimsy evidence but they did demand a high degree of respectability from victims. An unusual independence or even eccentricity could be sufficient for a woman to lose the law's favor. Three cases heard at Salisbury between 1909 and 1913 in which the accused was found not guilty illustrate the problems faced by victims.

In November 1909 a domestic servant named Kwiendainda was charged with the attempted rape of Miss Andrie Darvel at Salisbury.[77] The press coverage of the case betrayed a levity unprecedented at a Black Peril trial, and in contrast to the usual practice the name of the victim was published. Miss Darvel, a French national, ran a coffeehouse on Pioneer Street. On the day of the assault she was by her own admission drunk when the accused, who was in her employ, attacked her. Miss Darvel managed to fend him off with a chair and then with her clothing badly torn she ran into the street screaming. A passing policeman, Constable Watson (who may well have been the husband of Mrs. Annie Watson), arrested Kwiendainda, whom he found sitting at the back of the house. There were no signs of a struggle.

Kwiendainda's evidence was disjointed. He had been helping his mistress to find a lost bracelet, so he told the court, when she asked him to fetch the police. An argument between Miss Darvel and another woman then followed. Justice Watermeyer instructed the jury that there was a lack of evidence to support the charge and the case was dismissed. The *Herald* reported with some mirth that when the verdict was announced the accused "danced a jig."

Kwiendainda may well have been innocent and the evidence produced against him was weak. But that was not why he was acquitted. The verdict arose more from a desire to malign Miss Darvel than a wish to see the defendant's rights protected. Miss Darvel was cross-examined at length, which in itself was unusual. The police took the trouble to gather evidence against the plaintiff, and witnesses were called whose testimony undermined her case. Justice Watermeyer was unsatisfied with the evidence presented by the Crown, yet in other Black Peril trials he used very different standards. The fact that the victim was foreign (that is, French), that she lived on Pioneer Street (which was the center of white prostitution), and was supposedly drunk were the telling factors. Miss Darvel was in the court's view a prostitute and therefore she did not warrant protection.

The second case took place in April 1910, when a laborer named Kolale was charged with the robbery and rape of Miss Mary Simms. Kolale, who was undefended, pleaded not guilty. On the morning of the assault Miss Simms had been walking in the Collie Gardens when she was attacked. She was thrown to the ground and held by the throat. Her assailant raped her, then stole her purse. The assault had all the elements of a *cause célébre;* the crime was completed and it took place in daylight in a recreational area used by white families, an area as sacrosanct as Cape Avenue. The victim was young and considerable force was used. Miss Simms's experience in court, however, was very unlike that of Miss Falconer eighteen months earlier. Dr. Orpen, who examined Miss Simms, found no bruising and no trace of semen.[78] He made much of the fact that because she was not a virgin he was unable to tell whether penetration had occurred. In other cases involving married women who had borne children Orpen never mentioned such a problem. Orpen's evidence, like the jury's acquittal of Kolale, resulted from the victim's status; Miss Simms was unmarried and had a small child.

The third case involved a domestic servant named Zuzi, who in December 1913 was charged with attempting to rape Mrs. Appelbee, who lived in the Hartley district.[79] Elizabeth Appelbee's husband had died four years earlier and despite appeals from the Women's Guild, a voluntary association of white women, who believed it unsafe, she continued to live alone at her isolated farm. According to the indictment, Zuzi, who was employed by Mrs. Appelbee, caught her by the wrist and tried to pull her into a hut with the intent to commit rape. Zuzi made no attempt to leave the district and was arrested the following day in the main street of Hartley. According to Zuzi, on that morning he had argued with Mrs. Appelbee over his pay. "She took 12/- out of a box and put it on the table and said she wanted me," he told the court. "She then gave me the Ginger Beer and caught me by the braces. I ran out of the hut and took my blankets, she said she would have me arrested."[80] Another witness verified that Mrs. Appelbee was a bad employer who never paid proper wages but he retracted a statement made earlier to police that she had asked "boys" to sleep with her. After a brief deliberation the jury returned a verdict of not guilty.

The case was unusual because it occurred in the countryside rather than in a town. Most significant of all, the jury chose to believe the accused. From this distance in time we have no way of judging Zuzi's evidence. He may have been telling the truth or he may have been using the standard defense adopted by men charged with sexual crime. We do know that his allegations reinforced the unsympathetic attitude of the police and judiciary toward Mrs. Applebee. The key to the verdict was the victim's decision to live alone. That decision, taken against the advice of the Women's Guild, suggested to the jury that the claims made against Mrs. Applebee were true. Her independence was proof of an unreliable character and sufficient to disqualify her from the law's protection.

Miss Falconer's demeanor greatly impressed Justice Watermeyer, as did that of Miss Duthie, whose brother held an important public office. The opposite was true of Andrie Darvel, Mary Simms, and Elizabeth Applebee. Each was viewed by the court as unchaste. Yet the claim of seduction a-gainst Mrs. Applebee was not substantiated, and no proof was offered that Miss Darvel was a prostitute or that Miss Simms's indiscretions extend-ed across racial boundaries. The three women were distinguished not by their relations with black males but by their independence from white men. None of them was under the protection or authority of a man and it is that which explains their experience at court. The cases expose a number of powerful assumptions about female virtue which underlay the judicial re-sponse to rape. A court's refusal to believe a woman who had been raped was hardly novel; what was notable was the resilience of such beliefs in the context of Black Peril. There were clear rules governing the loss of sta-tus through sexual failing which were obvious in the treatment of Mary Simms. The rules about autonomy were more ambiguous, but as the trial of Miss Applebee's assailant suggests, the issue of male authority was as important to the judiciary as the victim's probity.

There were other sexual crimes involving white victims which fell out-side of the boundaries of Black Peril. White households were filled with male servants and it was common for mothers to leave small children in the care of African youths or "picannins." During the period 1900 to 1916 several cases of the indecent assault of white children by "picannins," or young black servants, came before Rhodesian courts.[81] They were never viewed as Black Peril crimes and the sentences imposed were consistently lower than in trials where the victim was an adult. The age of the accused precluded capital punishment. In contrast, contemporary British courts viewed the assault of a child with abhorrence and offenders were punished severely.[82] It is likely that in Southern Rhodesia a belief in the sexual anes-thesia of children worked to the advantage of the accused. If the child was not physically injured courts tended to believe no permanent harm had been done and the sentence was adjusted accordingly.[83] That such attacks had no weight as Black Peril crimes suggests that in Southern Rhodesia, as in Britain, male anxiety about female desire was crucial to the politics of rape.

The conventions in cases where the victim was African were very dif-ferent. The story of how such assaults were viewed from the African side has yet to be written. We do know that in the eyes of magistrates the immorality of black women diminished the seriousness of sexual crime.[84] White offenders were not charged unless there was some unusual circumstance compelling authorities to bring a case to court. Those circumstances relating to the status of the victim or her assailant made it less likely for a prosecution to succeed. The formalities of the law were carefully followed but rarely was there a serious effort to achieve a conviction. Men who were obviously guilty were acquitted because courts disregarded the evidence of African witnesses.[85]

There were a number of notable differences between Black Peril assaults and sexual attacks by white men upon black women. When the victim was white the act was rarely completed and the charge was usually attempted rape; in white-on-black cases the crime was rape. With Black Peril the most flimsy evidence was sufficient to bring about a conviction, while in cases involving white assailants convictions were rare. When the victim was white it was common for the judge to comment upon the strong physique of her assailant. In trials of white-on-black assaults judges and prosecuting attorneys rarely mentioned the physiques of assailants or their victims. The most notable difference, however, was the court's view of the seriousness of the assaults. To the judiciary and the BSAC administration, crimes against black women were of little importance and neither the attorney general nor the resident commissioner saw fit to bring the unjust verdicts which were common in such cases to the attention of imperial authorities.

THE POLITICS OF SEXUAL ASSAULT

It is difficult to assess the CID's claim that many Black Peril assaults went unreported. Women in Southern Rhodesia had more incentive to report an attack than did women in other parts of the British Empire. Courts were sympathetic and plaintiffs were not subjected to the crushing ritual of cross-examination. The experience of a trial may have been harrowing, but it is notable that women like Miss Falconer, Miss Duthie, and Mrs. Judd came forward.

Black Peril trials always fell into a wide political arena yet the actual cases were fashioned from insignificant details. There were the identity, age, and background of the victim and the time, place, and type of assault. There was also a context for each crime in terms of adjacent cases or other events which often influenced the judicial outcome. The high commissioner's intervention in Mrs. Cromer's case, for example, ensured the executions of Bonali and Nyamadzi. None of those elements was interpreted in a stable manner so that at one time an assault in a public place in daylight would be viewed as particularly serious while at another such a site would lessen a crime's gravity. Many convictions were achieved without proof of intent and there was often doubt about the identity of the assailant. By law it was necessary to have forensic evidence such as torn clothing or proof of penetration. In practice, medical testimony, especially that offered by Dr. Orpen, who appeared at several trials, was capricious.

The transcripts of Black Peril trials have a dreamlike quality. That quality was enhanced by the lack of identity given to the accused, who in transcripts invariably appeared as an anonymous man driven by desire. The same was true of the victim, who in the press became an iconic figure without name or circumstances. That ethereal quality allowed Black Peril crimes to be more easily transformed into symbolic attacks upon the white community itself. The panics were largely irrelevant to Africans, who faced more important hazards in their dealings with employers and the colonial state. It is unlikely that Black Peril made servants more fearful of the law or more aware of racial boundaries. Black Peril certainly made whites more insecure by amplifying their existing fears. The panics did create an issue about which white males could agree.

During the first decades of colonization settlers worried about African resistance, disease, access to land and labor, and the cost of transport. They worried about rinderpest, droughts, the BSAC administration, and the threat of being swamped politically by South Africa. Black Peril fell somewhere among those anxieties, in turn reflecting and influencing other fears. Rhodesians were also people with a grievance. They held grievances against the BSAC, the British government, the high commissioner, missionaries, philanthropists, the Portuguese, Coloureds, Jews, continentals in general, Afrikaners, and especially Africans. They also felt put upon by the physical environment in which they lived. Rhodesians viewed their situation as far more difficult than that faced by settlers in South Africa or Australia and they were aggrieved that people in England did not understand their plight. In contrast to settlers in Kenya who were better connected, they often complained they had no one in Britain to champion their cause. Many of their grievances converged in Black Peril. It was the issue which had the widest ambit and for which, like so many of their woes, there was no solution.

The play of imperial interests meant that events in Southern Rhodesia were very much influenced by circumstances to the south. It was also true that some of the moral legislation was borrowed from the Cape and the Transvaal. That does not explain why sexual fear struck such a chord with

Rhodesians. Nor does it explain why they chose to invent Black Peril, albeit it from the most flimsy of materials. It was not a simple pathology to which the white community was victim as it claimed white women were victim to the sexual predations of black men. The fear was chosen and valorized and much effort was spent in maintaining it. Although after 1912 the scares subsided, the shadow of Black Peril stretched well into the 1930s when the press still carried stories of "a seething tide of horrors." Rhodesian society was deeply marked by the panics. They shaped both public administration and settler culture.

THREE

VIOLENCE AND JUSTICE

Minority rule in Southern Rhodesia was often brutal. Fears of further resistance and the frustrations of an unsuccessful economy were conducive
to assaults upon workers. As Ian Phimister has shown, eleven-hour days,
beatings, poor food, and the withholding of wages were used routinely by
mine managers to extract compliance.[1] Two types of violence characterized
social and labor relations: state violence and the violence of civil society.
The two were intimately connected: Mine managers and farmers frequently
cited the weakness of the state to justify their attacks upon employees.
They also used those assaults to demand a more powerful state to bring
African labor into line.

The BSAC administration acknowledged that during the first decade
of settlement assaults by Native Police did occur but such acts were supposedly aberrant and flogging was always officially condemned.[2] However,
there is evidence that in the period before 1914 flogging "was the unofficial
policy of the Native Affairs Department."[3] We do know that in the space of
a decade as many as seven officers were dismissed for that reason. Those
dismissals, like the surrounding circumstances, suggest the practice was
common.[4] The *cause cèlébre* was the de Laessoe case of 1907, in which the
native commissioner for Belingwe was found guilty of forced labor and
assault. Like other offenders, he claimed that he was forced to resort to
violence because his office held no authority.[5]

Prior to World War One the mining industry was hampered by a lack
of manpower, machinery, and even fuel. Between 1903 and 1911 the number of white employees doubled while the black workforce increased five-
fold. Even so, labor shortages were acute and a state-run system of *chibaro,* or forced labor, was introduced.[6] Southern Rhodesia drew workers
from various countries in the region; many miners were migrant workers
from Nyasaland. Mine compounds were harsh places. There was no family
life and interethnic conflict was rife. Petty crime and sexual offenses were
common and alcohol was a problem. Managers were responsible for small
and isolated communities and they were prone to the same fears that

plagued most whites. They also needed to assert their authority over a labor force which often engaged in theft or in damaging plants in retaliation for low wages and poor rations. Compounds inspectors, native commissioners, and the police were willing to leave the matter of discipline to managers. That decision and the isolation of the mines encouraged violence. According to van Onselen, miners were reluctant to complain about assaults, which was why so few cases came to the attention of authorities.[7]

Labor relations were regulated by a system of master and servant, location, and pass ordinances. The ordinances were designed to curtail the mobility and rights of labor. Masters and servants ordinances set out the most draconian terms of employment for black workers. Location ordinances were intended to control the movement of labor in and out of urban areas. Pass ordinances required male workers to carry a pass which also served as a record of employment. The loss or incorrect signing of a pass could result in jail. Although the ordinances were based upon South African precedent, Southern Rhodesian law was often more severe.[8] In theory the ordinances gave employers and local authorities sweeping powers; in practice the laws were largely ineffective. Employers had the right to see a refractory worker fined or jailed but that did not solve the problems of labor shortage or indiscipline. Legislation was incapable of preventing workers from making economic choices which best suited their interests rather than those of capital. Disciplinary beatings were common and the instrument often used was a *sjambok*. In his memoirs of mission life in West Africa Albert Schweitzer described how such a weapon was made: "When a hippopotamus is killed, its hide, which is from 1/2 inch to 1 inch thick, is cut into strips about 1/2 inches wide and nearly 5 feet long. One end is nailed to a board, the strip is twisted into a spiral, and the other end is nailed down. When it is dry that supple, sharp-cornered, and justly dreaded instrument of torture is ready."[9] Such a whip could kill.

In most cases in which a white man was accused of having killed a worker the only witnesses were blacks and juries were loath to accept their testimony, no matter how compelling. The quality of jurors was often poor and judges were sometimes incompetent in their interpretation of the law, thereby increasing the likelihood of unsound verdicts. Physicians colluded in undermining the judicial process. At trial after trial courts were told by expert witnesses that death had resulted not from a savage beating but because the deceased had a fragile spleen which ruptured at the slightest blow.[10]

In 1909 and again in 1912 the jury system was thrown into crisis. The system had been under question for some years because of verdicts in Black

Peril cases. Ironically, it was the failure of juries to convict whites for homicide that eventually brought Rhodesian courts into disrepute. The ways in which courts dealt with Black Peril and culpable homicide established an indifference to the proper workings of the criminal justice system.[11] Settlers had a remarkable ability to subscribe to the ideal of British justice yet be untroubled by discrepancies in its application.

THE FIRST JURY CRISIS, 1908–1909: LAIDLAW AND BATTLEFIELDS

During 1898 two cases came before the Salisbury High Court in which the accused asked for trial by jury. It was, they claimed, the inalienable right of an Englishman. In the following weeks there was much discussion in the press about the superiority of such a system because judges, who until that time had sole jurisdiction, were perceived as too far removed from the lot of the "common man."[12] In response to popular demands, in 1899 legislation for a jury system was introduced to the newly established Legislative Council. From its inception the system had symbolic importance. It was also to prove decisive in Black Peril trials or trials where a white employer was charged with having killed an African worker.

Under the Juries Ordinance of 1899 criminal trials in the High Court were heard by a judge and jury of nine men whose verdict had to be unanimous. The key criterion for jury service was a property qualification, which meant that the High Court and its juries, like the Legislative Council and its constituents, was composed exclusively of males. Whites took pride in their legal system. Writing in the 1950s, Philip Mason observed: "Rhodesia has on the whole been fortunate in her judges, of whom little more need be said than that they have maintained the standards of their profession."[13] Contrary to Mason's view, in the period from 1908 to 1912, a series of crises over the administration of justice exposed the often brutal nature of labor relations and the underlying antagonisms between settlers, imperial authority, and the British South Africa Company.

Court records suggest that before 1905 juries were willing to convict settlers on the testimony of black witnesses. A notable case from 1901 was that of George Binns, a storekeeper of Mazoe who was charged with the culpable homicide of Kafromingo, an employee.[14] According to two witnesses, Binns assaulted Kafromingo with a *sjambok* and then kicked him until he lost consciousness. Binns denied having kicked the deceased except to the shins and claimed that Kafromingo had been stealing; when confronted he ran away and fell down a hill. Although evidence from the BSAC police supported Binns, he was found guilty and sentenced to two years' hard labor. But by 1908 juries had become impervious to the testimony of black witnesses.

In the first week of May 1908, William Laidlaw, a farmer of Kinvarra, was charged with having murdered a "houseboy" named Neti.[15] At the first trial held at Salisbury the jury failed to reach a verdict and at the insistence of the attorney general the case was re-heard at Bulawayo. The evidence submitted at the two trials was the same and Justice Watermeyer presided over both.

The evidence for the Crown was given by five of Laidlaw's workers, including a man named Rusiri.[16] On the day of the crime Rusiri had been gathering hay when he saw a "boy" walking on the road to Salisbury. Laidlaw wanted to know who he was and sent Rusiri and two others to fetch him. Finding Neti's registration certificate defaced, Laidlaw had him stretched out between two poles and beat him with a stick. Laidlaw, who was wearing heavy boots, then kicked him three times to the back of the neck. Neti was finally tied to a tree so that his feet were off the ground and he was left in that position all night. In the morning he was dead. The evidence given by the other witnesses, Mbamagwa, Goosha, Ndabengwe, and Mpaseni, depicted a brutal assault which they were powerless to stop. Mbamagwa told the court that while Neti was being beaten he cried out "I am being killed."[17]

Defense counsel sought to prove that Neti was a thief and that Laidlaw had not contributed to his death. The key witness was the district surgeon, Dr. Thomas Stewart, who had performed the postmortem. Stewart, who knew the accused, began by altering his report as to the cause of death. In his original statement he had cited spinal meningitis but requested that the word contusion be substituted instead. He told the court that there was no evidence of meningitis and the cause of death was heart failure. Stewart was certain that the beating inflicted by Laidlaw had not contributed to Neti's death. Laidlaw's wife and young son also gave evidence and while they had nothing to contribute directly to the case their presence no doubt conjured up for the jury the image of another white family ruined by refractory labor.

The case for the defense was carefully thought out, albeit poorly presented. All members of the jury would have employed black workers. No doubt many held grievances which the defense exploited to advantage. Laidlaw's council told the jury Neti was a thief and that by inflicting a disciplinary beating Laidlaw was merely doing another employer a favor. Laidlaw was found guilty of assault and sentenced to six months' hard labor. At that time the average sentence for an African convicted of stealing a bicycle was between three and nine months.

The trial was notable for the injustice of the verdict. It was also notable for the inept performance of Dr. Stewart. In altering his statement Stewart adhered to the code observed by physicians in such cases; he emphasized an ambiguity between primary and secondary causes of death. According to Philip Mason, the jury may have been confused by the medical evidence and therefore gave Laidlaw the benefit of the doubt.[18] That was not the view of the high commissioner, Lord Selbourne, who was shocked by the verdict: "The evidence produced went to show that Laidlaw, after causing his unfortunate victim to be bound hand and foot, beat and kicked him unmercifully and finally had him tied up to tree, where he was left to pass a night of torture and was found dead in the morning."[19] However, Selbourne did not intervene and the sentence stood. The case was not the first to alert him to problems in the application of the law in Rhodesia and it was soon followed by others.

For a number of years there had been complaints about the burden of jury service; following the Laidlaw verdict, in June 1908, an ordinance increasing the size of the role was passed by the Legislative Council.[20] While the change was a technical one, Attorney General Tredgold took the opportunity to attack the jury system itself. He told his fellow counselors that in cases involving white and black men juries had been motivated by ideas they should never have entertained. According to Tredgold, "Apart from the question of colour he had found the greatest difficulty in Salisbury, even in the clearest case possible of getting a conviction against a white man at all."[21] He wanted the system abolished and a judge to sit with the assistance of assessors. He also warned of the threat of retaliation from Africans if such abuses continued.[22] Tredgold found little support. The majority of members did not want the matter of justice left in the hands of officials, by which they meant the BSAC.

Five months after the Laidlaw trial four white men, Murdo Macauley, John Fraser, George Murray, and James McBryde, were charged with culpable homicide. The case, which followed the deaths of two workers named Mangesi and Sixpence at the Battlefields Mine, was heard in November 1908 before Justice Watermeyer. The prosecution case rested upon the testimony of African witnesses and an admission by Macauley that the beatings had taken place. The defense relied upon forensic evidence from the district surgeon and an attending physician. Battlefields contained many of the themes of mine life: brutal managers, violent compound police, and theft. There was also an allusion to Black Peril.

On July 9th, Mangesi, Sixpence, and a fellow worker named Jack were arrested at the mine compound by Native Police for the theft of 2 pounds from the Rev. Davies. Over a period of three days the men were flogged with a *sjambok* to get them to confess to the crime. All the accused were present and, according to the Crown, all took part. During their ordeal both Mangesi and Sixpence fainted and Mangesi tried to kill himself before the final beating. After being flogged on the third day the men were released. Within twenty-four hours Mangesi was dead; Sixpence survived a week. According to a native policeman named Damasky the men screamed as they were hit. "The flogging was very severe. I could not count the strokes," he told the court.[23] None of the accused denied that the floggings had taken place; they did deny that they could have caused serious injury. Murdo Macauley, a wood contractor of Battlefields, told the court that a number of "boys" at the railway station were searched following the theft and numerous stolen articles were recovered. Mangesi was arrested and warned that unless he told the truth he would be flogged. Macauley admitted that he had given him five light cuts across the shoulders and buttocks. After two days of questioning on the Friday morning the "boys" were each given a *sjambok* and they then thrashed each other. Macauley watched but took no part. When released Mangesi and Sixpence were in good health, McCauley claimed. He told the court that there had been attempted sexual assaults on white women at the mine, implying that Mangesi and Sixpence were involved.

Dr. Mackenzie, the district surgeon who conducted the postmortem, attributed Mangesi's death to a combination of shock, a weakened constitution, and a chill which caused pneumonia. Mackenzie also examined Sixpence, whom he found had also died of pneumonia. He explained to the court: "The usual cause of pneumonia is chill. The fact that these boys stayed out all night might give them pneumonia."[24] Evidence from Dr. Stewart, who had attended Mangesi and Sixpence, confirmed the postmortem findings. The attorney general who prosecuted the case made no serious attempt to cross-examine either him or Mackenzie.[25] To the jury the floggings were born of frustration at chronic thieving and were a preventative measure against Black Peril. They sympathized with the accused and accepted without question, as did the Crown, the testimony of Dr. Mackenzie. After ten minutes' deliberation the jury returned a verdict of not guilty on all charges and the men were released.

Following the acquittal the press was flooded with correspondence. One anonymous writer complained that such a miscarriage of justice would discourage blacks from taking up work.[26] An editorial in the *Rhodesian*

Herald pointed out that the justice system in Rhodesia had been questioned in the House of Commons and that any further cases would only increase calls for its abolition.[27] A letter from the Rhodesian Missionary Conference suggested that the verdict showed the unfitness of colonists to manage their own affairs.[28] One of the most notable letters was from Sam Lewis of Bulawayo.[29] Juries were right, he claimed, to support men who otherwise went unprotected. Like many who wrote to the papers, he related the Battlefields case directly to Black Peril and the inadequacies of the BSAC administration.[30] Two years later Lewis would himself be in court defending a charge of murder.

The Battlefields verdict made Tredgold more determined to change the jury system. It also dismayed Lord Selbourne, who wrote to the administrator, Milton.[31] "I have just read the records of the Battlefield's case with profound sorrow. Coming so soon on top of the Laidlaw case it constitutes nothing less than a public danger, let alone the deep stain on the British name."[32] He suggested that trial by jury be abolished in cases where whites were charged with crimes against blacks. Milton explained that in the Battlefields case the counsel for the defense used his twelve challenges to exclude every citizen of repute or intelligence from service. The verdict, in Milton's view, was a reflection of the baser elements within the white community.[33] Although he was unconvinced by Milton's claim that race had little to do with miscarriages of justice, Selbourne retreated from his demand for new legislation.[34] The high commissioner was in a difficult position. He had recently commuted the death sentence imposed on Singana for the attempted rape of Miss Falconer and did not want to further alienate the white community.[35]

Judges Vintcent and Watermeyer believed that, in general, trial outcomes were fair and that Rhodesian juries were more intelligent and careful than were those in the Cape.[36] Having examined the figures, Attorney General Tredgold agreed.[37] The returns for Salisbury, however, suggested otherwise; of nineteen trials where the accused was a European there had been five convictions and thirteen acquittals. Although the returns from Bulawayo were more favorable, there were still serious discrepancies.[38]

After hesitating for several months Selbourne eventually made an official protest to the resident commissioner:

> These two miscarriages of justice are a stain on the British name and they constitute also a public danger. Not only is it a matter of national honour that justice should be administered truly and fairly between man and man of every colour throughout the British Dominions but I am profoundly convinced that it is only possible for a mere handful of my fellow coun-

trymen to fulfil their task of governing vast bodies of natives if they rule them with scrupulous justice as well as with absolute firmness.[39]

Selbourne wanted the law amended so that such cases would be tried by a judge and assessors.

At the end of May Selbourne's dispatch was presented in the Legislative Council, but it only antagonized the elected members. A select committee which had been established to consider the problem found that miscarriages of justice had occurred but not in sufficient number to suggest the jury system had failed. The attorney general warned the council that the issue was not simply the right to trial by jury but the fitness of Rhodesians to manage their own affairs, a fact of which no doubt they were well aware.[40] He found little support. One member, Mr. Brown, commented that Selbourne had never seen the seamy side of "native life" in Rhodesia and that the people advising him were driven by sentiment aroused by the slave trade. Selbourne was caught between his anger over Laidlaw and Battlefields and his fears about what the consequences would be if he intervened. The secretary of state shared Selbourne's concerns and warned that if necessary he was willing to legislate by proclamation.[41] A copy of the secretary's letter was sent to the resident commissioner and its contents were no doubt made known to the Legislative Council. That threat brought no change.

It is difficult to estimate how many African workers were killed by white employers. We can be sure that Laidlaw and Battlefields were unusual only in that they became *causes cèlébres.* In the six months before May 1910 nine cases involving the murder, culpable homicide, or serious assault of a black man were heard in the Umtali and Salisbury high courts. The assaults occurred on farms, in mines, and in domestic service. Many of the beatings had an almost sexual intensity and in every instance the relationship between the assailant and the victim was that of employer and employee.[42] In most cases the accused was found not guilty or at worst given a suspended sentence and a fine. In trials involving black-on-black violence, verdicts were very different. The average sentence for culpable homicide was two years' hard labor.[43]

Apart from those cases which went to court there were others which failed to pass a magistrate's hearing or were not pursued by police because of a lack of evidence. Witnesses were always Africans who had cause to fear both their employers and the police. Many workers were migrants who were constantly on the move and even if police dutifully gathered evidence they often had difficulty tracing witnesses. For those reasons the cases tried in the High Court probably represented only a fraction of such killings. Besides assaults which led to death there were others which did not result in serious injury. There would also have been the threat of assault to which, presumably, all labor was subject. In the months following the first jury crisis, cases in which a white man had killed an African continued to come before the High Court. The trials of Miller and Butcher are representative.

In November 1909, that is, almost exactly a year after the Battlefields killing, a BSAC policeman named Jordan Miller was charged with the culpable homicide of Kaporomandia.[44] Witnesses claimed that following an argument Miller had beaten and kicked Kaporomandia in the stomach so violently that he died. Surprisingly, the postmortem showed no signs of external violence or damage to the abdominal organs. According to the attending physician the heart was "very flabby" and he attributed death to shock following the effort Kaporomandia expended in running away (from Miller) or to a blow, not necessarily severe, to the stomach. Miller was acquitted. In May 1910 Frederick Butcher, a manager at the Eldorado mine, was charged with the culpable homicide of Kamzimbi, who had died following a beating.[45] Witnesses gave evidence of the savagery of the assault and the circumstances of Kamzimbi's death. Dr. Peall, who conducted the postmortem, found that there were numerous small cuts on the surface of the body and much dried blood, which he attributed to the use of traditional medicine. The deceased also had a ruptured spleen, which Peall concluded was probably caused by external violence. He attributed death to peritonitis and pneumonia. Butcher was found not guilty. The transcripts suggest the verdict was as iniquitous as the Battlefields verdict.

For a white man to be jailed for culpable homicide usually required some circumstance which alienated the jury. One such case was that of MacLaren Forbes, who in May 1910 appeared in the Salisbury High Court charged with the murder of an employee named M'tuna.[46] On the night of the shooting, Forbes, who managed a store at Lomagundi, had paid the staff their wages and then demanded that M'tuna and two other workers play cards with him. When they refused Forbes became angry, dragged M'tuna into the store and shot him. In his defense Forbes claimed the rifle had discharged accidentally and that he had no intention of harming the deceased. The jury found Forbes guilty of culpable homicide in the lesser degree and recommended clemency. The judge sentenced him to three months' imprisonment. Both the verdict and the sentence were unusual and require some explanation.

At the trial Forbes was unrepresented and it is probable that he was too poor to afford counsel. He was also young and apparently without family or friends, factors which in themselves were unlikely to have irritated the court. However, on the night of M'tuna's death Forbes had behaved in a way which members of the jury probably found unacceptable. It seems that his intention in asking the men to play cards within minutes of having paid their wages was to recover that money either by cheating or experienced play. M'tuna and his companions refused, they said out of fear. It was common for employers to cheat workers of their wages but the playing of cards was different; it involved intimacy.

After the Battlefields incident crimes against black workers continued and juries continued to acquit men who were guilty as charged. The rationales given by the accused were always the same. Labor was refractory and dangerous, there were few BSAC police, and so they were forced to take the law into their own hands. The verdicts, like the crimes themselves, were a form of revenge against a workforce seemingly impervious to legislative control. Juries used the verdicts to express their solidarity with the accused and to attack imperial authority in the person of the high commissioner. Throughout the Battlefields trial and the subsequent trials the resident commissioner made little effort to oppose the abuses of the legal system. He was already under pressure following the acquittals of Alukuleta and Singana and he did not want to further antagonize the white community.

The major culpable homicide cases occurred at the height of Black Peril panic and to juries, the administration, and the high commissioner the one set of injustices compounded the other. They raised the same problems of justice and imperial influence and they featured the same special pleading about the hardships of frontier life. The cases differed in the sense that culpable homicides were about the dangers faced by white men rather than those faced by white women. Behind the Laidlaw and Battlefields incidents lay a paradox. Employers wanted the state to provide the land, labor, and subsidies which were necessary for their economic success. But they did not want to be subject to regulation, especially with regard to their treatment of workers. The crimes and the verdicts were certainly a form of revenge against labor and the state; they were also a means used by farmers and miners to pressure both into compliance.

THE SECOND CRISIS: SAM LEWIS AND TITUS

In February 1911 Mrs. Duncan Thomson of Penhalonga, an isolated town to the north of Umtali, shot and killed a man who was attempting to break into her house. The next day a public meeting was held to express support for Mrs. Thomson and to raise funds as a form of compensation.

The police and the attorney general agreed that it was a Black Peril case and Mrs. Thomson was not charged with any offense.[47] It was one of several such cases at that time and there was high feeling in Salisbury and Bulawayo about the failure of the administration to protect women. Two months later the *Chronicle* reported the sentencing to death of Bonali and Nyamadzi for the Hillside and Cape Avenue "outrages." On that same day it announced that a prominent Bulawayo citizen named Sam Lewis had shot and killed an African newspaper seller named Titus. The report made reference to the Umtali outrage and the Penhalonga incident, suggesting that public opinion would probably be on Lewis's side.

Sam Lewis was born in London in 1860; as a young man he worked in various jobs, including a period as a mining engineer. He embarked for South Africa in 1888. After serving with the police he worked in general business, most notably as the contractor who planted the trees around the Wanders Cricket Ground. In 1895 Lewis left for Matabeleland, where he took part in the war. He also fought in the Anglo–Boer War as a captain in the Rhodesian Volunteers. After military service Lewis returned to Bulawayo, where he stood for election to the local council. He had some success as a contractor and he gained a reputation as a boxing referee. Lewis was a prominent member of the white community and in 1902 he organized an anti–Black Peril rally which led to the formation of a vigilance committee.[48] Following the Battlefields case Lewis had written to the *Rhodesian Herald* complaining of the lack of police protection for women.[49] Lewis had powerful friends and his arrest was in itself notable. Although there was no dispute about the events surrounding the shooting Lewis faced a second trial after the first jury failed to reach a verdict. The witnesses who gave evidence at both trials were the same and in most respects their evidence was identical.[50]

Lewis, his wife Katherine, and their two teenage daughters, Ivy and May, lived near the Bulawayo railway station. Titus, who was employed by the *Chronicle*, delivered newspapers (although not to the Lewis home). Soon after the family moved into the area Titus began making sexual overtures to the girls. According to May Lewis he repeatedly approached her and even followed her to school. He offered the girls money and on one occasion, according to May, "He [Titus] said that he wanted to go to the Veld and fuck me."[51] May and Ivy complained to their mother, who kept the matter to herself. Titus persisted in harassing the girls and eventually Katherine Lewis told her husband. A month later, on May 16, Lewis went with his daughters to the *Chronicle* office but they were unable to find Titus. The next morning they returned and were successful. Lewis then sent his daughters home in a cab and marched Titus from the building. A witness, Hayi Dumbira, saw Lewis take a revolver from his pocket and shoot Titus in the head. Lewis then walked down the main street toward the police station, where he met detective Harry Hammond. Lewis said: "It is alright Harry, I am just going to give myself up. He asked my daughter for a fuck and I have the revolver in my pocket."[52] According to Hammond; "He seemed to be well aware of what he was saying. He was quite calm. He was not excited."[53] The postmortem showed there was a hole in Titus's skull behind the right ear and a similar wound near the edge of the lips on the left side of the face. The bullet had passed through the throat and death was due to loss of blood.

Lewis was taken into custody and charged with murder. Before noon he was released on 1,000 pounds' bail. Immediate moves were made by the citizens of Bulawayo to raise a defense fund and on that first day 27 pounds was collected.[54] By the time he appeared at the preliminary hearing Lewis had received many telegrams of support and even one congratulating him on his action.

In opening the prosecution case Tredgold expressed regret that he had to bring such a charge against an old acquaintance. His regret must have been all the greater given the evidence against the accused. There was no reason in his work as a mining engineer for Lewis to carry a gun and the evidence showed that he had gone to the *Chronicle* office not once, but twice, with the express purpose of killing Titus. In both his opening and closing addresses Tredgold explained to the jury that the key issue was whether the act was deliberate or if Lewis had been unable to control his emotions.

The case for the defense was based on the testimony of Ivy and May Lewis and that of four other girls, Kathleen Swartz, Maud Wardell, Dora van Eden, and Florence Thorn, who claimed also to have been harassed. Maud Wardell said that an African man had approached her outside the *Chronicle* offices in early April and offered her money to go to his room. She had reported the matter to the police but nothing was done, a fact which clearly angered the *Chronicle*'s reporter and probably the jury as well.

Lewis's counsel, Mr. Russell, told the court that such an insult from a white man was bad enough: "But when beyond that, when this insult, this degradation, comes from a native, one of the race which, rightly or wrongly, for generations past, white people have considered absolutely below them in the human ladder—where such an insult comes from such a person, I submit absolutely that human nature has its limits, and one can quite understand a man being driven to do what Mr. Lewis did."[55] Police negligence had forced Lewis to act. The defense could not claim that in the territory's largest town the police were inaccessible and that therefore Lewis was forced to take the law into his own hands. Neither could it claim that his action saved his daughters from publicity. His only motive was to suppose that the law, meaning Lord Gladstone, would be too mild in its treatment of Titus if he were brought to trial. The murder was in effect an attack upon the office of the high commissioner.

Justice Watermeyer's summing up was very much in favor of Lewis and he gave the jury no useful guidance on important questions such as the issue of intent or the delay between Lewis being told of Titus's soliciting and the shooting. The jury retired at 3:15 P.M. and returned its verdict at 3:25 P.M. At the announcement of the acquittal many in the court cheered.

A number of factors contributed to the verdict. The first was the surrounding cases of Laidlaw, Miss Falconer, Battlefields, and most especially Alukuleta. The local press and the public tended to perceive those cases as analogous and were incensed by the high commissioner's failure to defend settler rights. The public knew nothing of the baboon which had attacked Miss Falconer nor of Mrs. Cromer's probable infidelity. The second factor was a photograph of a naked white woman found by detectives among Titus's belongings. The photo, which was entered into evidence, was cut from a newspaper and pasted onto cardboard. During the trial Titus's roommate was questioned at length about the picture, which was the most damning evidence against the deceased's character. Police went to some lengths to establish how it had come into his possession.[56] After weeks of investigation a store assistant named Louis Hendelman was charged with having imported obscene material. Ironically, his most serious offense, in the eyes of the white community, of having sold the photograph to Titus was in fact legal.

The case aroused strong feeling in Bulawayo and the jury had no hesitation in finding Hendelman guilty and calling for a severe penalty. Judge Vintcent agreed. He imposed a fine of 300 pounds and sentenced Hendelman to eighteen months' hard labor. The editorial in the *Rhodesian Herald* commented that the sale of obscene material to black men incited sexual crime and called for the introduction of legislation.[57] Four months later the Legislative Council passed, without amendment, the Obscene Publications Ordinance.[58]

Sam Lewis's defense was constructed from the testimony of his daughters, the photograph, and the supposed negligence of the high commissioner. Counsel succeeded in convincing the jury that the trial was about the maintenance of racial boundaries and established the shooting as a

Black Peril case. All the elements of Lewis's trial were familiar. The notable difference was the photograph. Symbolically the picture allowed access to the body of a white woman and could be passed through an infinite number of hands. The image was a particular kind of artifact which the press associated exclusively with urban life. The *Rhodesian Herald* reminded its readers: "The black criminal who molests white women and children is not the product of the kraal but of the towns where he comes into contact with depraved and careless white people."[59] The picture formed a remarkable contrast to the dominant images imported by settlers, the icons of Christ and Mary, which in Southern Rhodesia were also emblems of white authority. For a black man to have access to the picture of a naked white woman allowed him to achieve a degree of equality with white men. It was the idea of equality which the court, like the press, found intolerable. That resentment contributed to the acquittal of Lewis and the crushing sentence imposed on Hendelman.

The transcripts of both Lewis trials were reprinted in the *Rhodesian Herald* and the case received wide coverage in South African and British newspapers.[60] The Rhodesian press was sympathetic to Lewis and most papers related the verdict directly to the Umtali case. The *Bulawayo Chronicle* commented that it was difficult for the people of Rhodesia to accept a policy of weakness from their governors and in effect condoned both Lewis's action and the verdict.[61] The *Rhodesian Herald* noted that Lewis had stemmed a tide of lawlessness.[62] The attitude of those who supported Lewis was probably best expressed in a letter of protest which appeared in the *Herald*. Its author, who employed the pseudonym Sipan, was incensed at the suggestion that the jury had failed in its duty: "Lewis and others of us have lived many years in this country. We remember other cases where the authorities have neglected to act on complaints, notably the Rebellion, when the waiting for the danger to become imminent caused the deaths of between six and seven hundred people. We are therefore more apt to defend ourselves than are later comers."[63] The principal issues were the safety of women and the failure of the BSAC and imperial authorities to protect white families. To Sipan and others like him it was a Black Peril case.

Much of the South African press condemned both the verdict and the system of justice in Rhodesia. The *Pretoria News* referred to the decision as a travesty, while the *Rand Daily Mail* suggested that it eroded the foundations of the Empire.[64] The British press was equally hostile. The *Morning Herald* referred to the verdict as monstrous, while the *Times* called for the suspension of the jury system.[65] In the House of Commons the Secretary of State for the Colonies was asked if he proposed to take any action.[66]

While most of the Rhodesian public probably supported Lewis's acquittal, there was some opposition. The Rev. John White warned that Africans would lose respect for the law and spend as little time as possible in employment where they were exposed to murderous attacks.[67] He was also concerned about the threat of Black Peril and the need to convince the African that he must regard the person of the white woman as sacred. In a sermon given at Salisbury Cathedral the Rev. J. Simpson observed that a murder had been committed in a cold and deliberate manner and yet "in a territory over which the British flag flies, this man gets off scot free."[68] Simpson suggested that it would be a proper outcome if the imperial authorities abolished trial by jury. Simpson's sentiments were echoed by the Dean of Salisbury, the Rev. Harker.[69]

Attorney General Tredgold was embarrassed by the verdict, especially since he had moved the case to Salisbury in the hope of achieving a fair trial. Tredgold believed that part of the problem lay in the judge's failure to explain to the jury that an acquittal would have meant a dereliction of its duty. He rejected any suggestion that the jury was retaliating for the Umtali case.[70] Tredgold was particularly concerned about the repercussions: "The one real and apparent incidence of self-government which has been entrusted to the people of this country has been grossly abused. I have not refrained from giving public warning that the jury system was the one existing test of competency for self-government. That test has not been met."[71] In his opinion the Lewis case proved that the jury system had to be changed. To Resident Commissioner Burns Begg the acquittal was a miscarriage of justice.[72] He found it difficult to understand the jury's motives, "but possibly amongst them was a somewhat illogical feeling that by refusing to convict Lewis the jury marked their disapproval of Alukuleta's reprieve."[73] He doubted that a remedy lay in granting settlers further responsibility because that would only give them greater opportunity to behave badly.[74] In effect Burns Begg acknowledged that both the shooting of Titus and the jury's verdict were acts of revenge; the one against black males, the other against the high commissioner.

Despite the resident commissioner's misgivings, Gladstone made a state visit to Rhodesia in September. Such were the fears for his safety that he was given an armed escort. Gladstone spoke at a public luncheon at Salisbury during which he made reference to Black Peril and the Umtali case. He regretted the problems which had arisen over his reprieve of Alukuleta and told his audience that those differences were confined to a single case. "There can be only one principle namely the inviolable sanctity of our women, accompanied by strict justice and fair play for the subject races," he said.[75] The Rhodesian constitution, he explained, was particularly complex because of the division of powers between the Crown, the BSAC, the legislature, and the high commissioner. In that context an intolerable strain was placed upon juries which made change necessary. Gladstone's position was difficult and he had little choice but to be placatory.

The trial of Sam Lewis joined together for the first time Black Peril and culpable homicide. It was an explosive mix. A citizen had taken the law into his own hands because the state was too weak to defend white women against predatory black males. Lewis was politically ambitious. He had powerful friends and he had been involved in local council. There is no doubt that in shooting Titus he was sure that he would never be convicted of a serious crime. In fact he risked little. Lewis waited a month before confronting Titus and he chose the time and place of the murder. He shoot Titus in front of a witness and gave himself up immediately to police. His actions were utterly premeditated. Lewis's motivation may have been to make a public career for himself, to enhance his social status, or simply to humiliate the high commissioner. He succeeded in all but the first.

When the Legislative Council reconvened in December 1911, spokes-men for the Anglican Church and the native affairs committee demanded a change to the system. The Lewis case also changed Charles Coghlan's mind and as leader of the elected members he called for legislation in cases in-volving a European charged with a serious crime against an African. After prolonged debate the Special Juries Ordinance of 1912 was passed.[76] The ordinance covered all criminal cases involving a charge of murder, culpable homicide, rape, or robbery where the crime was committed by a European against a "native" or by a "native" against a European.[77] Such cases were to be heard before a judge of the High Court and a special jury consisting of five men of whom not less than four had to concur with a verdict. The jury was to be appointed from a list designated by the administrator and approved by the Legislative Council. No criteria were specified as to what qualified a man to sit on a special jury; that matter was left to the adminis-trator. According to Claire Palley, the ordinance was one of only two intro-duced at the request of imperial authorities; the other being the Immorality Suppression Ordinance of 1903.[78] Public response to the legislation was mixed and one anonymous citizen suggested the ordinance was a slur on Rhodesians' sense of justice.[79]

In fact it changed little. Innocent men continued to be convicted of Black Peril and guilty men continued to be acquitted of culpable homicide. As the result of chronic problems in achieving reasonable verdicts the jury system was again modified in 1927 with the passing of the Criminal Trials (High Court) Act.[80] According to Lewis Gann and Peter Duignan, the amendment, which introduced a system of trial by judge and assessors in cases involving black plaintiffs and whites, greatly improved outcomes.[81]

CONCLUSION

The Lewis case focused attention upon imperial authority, the failings of the BSAC, the administration of justice, and the safety of women. As such it shared much common ground with the Battlefields and Laidlaw incidents. The two cases also shared a preoccupation with gender roles and the defense of racial boundaries. In the Lewis and Battlefield incidents opposition to imperial authority was also important. Behind the trials lay the chronic violence of civil society.

On the surface the Lewis case was a patriarchal crime committed in defense of a daughter and the killings at Battlefields were simply disciplinary beatings which went wrong. In fact both were more complex. Sam Lewis behaved as if he were living in a frontier society when he was in fact resident in the colony's largest town. He was an ambitious man who had long been a Black Peril campaigner. The press and the resident commissioner were certain that the killing was politically motivated: Lewis shot Titus in order to attack the office of the high commissioner. Like the trial of Sam Lewis, the Battlefields and Laidlaw cases were evidence of a chain of violence which permeated colonial society.

The Lewis, Battlefields, and Laidlaw incidents occurred during the same period as the floggings committed by native commissioners, and to a degree they arose from the same circumstances. De Laessoe resorted to the *sjambok,* so he told the department, because his office carried no authority. In fact his superiors praised him for having imposed his will on the local community even as they censured him for using "unsound methods."[82] According to de Laessoe and Lewis, it was the weakness of the state which forced them to take matters into their own hands. The same justification was used again and again in cases of culpable homicide.

The pass, location, and masters and servants ordinances were designed to discipline labor. They made it an offense for a man to be without a work certificate or town pass or to be absent without permission from a master's premises between the hours of 9 P.M. and 5 A.M. The punishments provided for offenders were a reprimand, a fine, a suspended sentence, or jail. As the system grew so did the gulf between its purpose and what occurred in the labor market. Workers found endless ways of subverting the system; the ordinances proved a constant irritation for district commissioners and magistrates whose courts overflowed with offenders. Workers defaced passes, lost them, or shared them with friends. Prosecutions under the pass laws usually numbered more than 10,000 per year; in 1936 alone there were over 16,000 convictions.[83] The laws also proved a hindrance to employers, who were obliged to make a formal complaint and to present themselves and their offending workers at a magistrate's court. Employers were liable if they failed to sign a contract correctly and although such regulations were rarely enforced they were deeply resented.[84] Migratory labor further frustrated regulation; controls over the movement of workers from neighboring states were usually even more futile than those involving indigenous labor. The system did succeed in producing contrasting images of authority—the smooth, seamless world of the ordinances versus the endless messiness of their application. It is not surprising that the ineffectiveness of the state provided fertile ground for casual violence. Rather than providing evidence of the power of employers the beatings of workers were indicative of an absence of enforceable authority.

To offset their own inefficiencies and lack of capital employers set about exploiting labor. Mine compounds were hard places. As Charles van Onselen and Ian Phimister have shown, death rates from overwork, undernourishment, and inadequate housing were even higher in Rhodesia than they were in South Africa. In that context the killing of employees was an extension of economic imperatives.[85] The assaults were also suggestive of a lack of self-control common to a certain type of masculinity. In Southern Rhodesia male identity was centered on physical courage and independence. It was also crystallized around a dislike of BSAC officials and big capital, both of which in time became essential ingredients of Rhodesian nationalism. The elected members of the Legislative Council fought the threat of Black Peril; juries fought refractory labor. Together they formed a united front against their enemies—on the one hand the BSAC and imperial authority, on the other Africans.

The jury crises were important to Rhodesian claims for responsible government and hence were a focus for the struggle against the Company.[86] The BSAC charter was due for review in 1914, which gave particular urgency to the second crisis. As Attorney General Tredgold acknowledged, it was a test of the competence of Rhodesians to manage their own affairs. Imperial calculations about Rhodesia were always framed in terms of South Africa. In the period before 1923 jury service was by proxy a mark of citizenship. Policymakers could not afford to be seen to favor "native interests" because it would have alienated white South African opinion. Neither could they be identified too closely with the BSAC. It was that delicate balance which allowed the settler elite to flout imperial authority.

In 1910—that is, between the two crises—South Africa achieved union, which further inflated the importance of events in Rhodesia. The jury crises were in the end played out against a background of imperial intrigue which Sam Lewis for one sought to exploit.

Settlers viewed the crises in terms of their relations with the BASC. Many of those who supported Lewis agreed that the Company's failure to protect white families had forced him to kill Titus, a complaint which harked back to 1896. The crises were also a test of the treatment of African labor and therefore, within the terms of the charter, the Laidlaw, Battlefields, and Lewis verdicts were legitimately an imperial matter. Although both Selbourne and Gladstone were appalled by the operation of the legal system that commuted the sentences of Singana and Alukuleta, they were in effect trapped by Black Peril. The attorney general could not admit publicly the reasons why those cases involved a miscarriage of justice and so Rhodesians were able to blame the high commissioner. As a result the ordinance of 1912 was a weak compromise which diminished the status of Gladstone's office. Imperial intervention was out of the question because it would have embroiled the British government in an economically and politically expensive venture, the consequences of which could not be foreseen.

The beatings at Battlefields were intended to render labor compliant and to establish, at least symbolically, the power of employers. It is significant that Rhodesian courts treated such cases as analogous to domestic violence. In so doing they drew upon the models of patriarchal authority which underlay the masters and servants legislation. On occasion the violence against black men was sexualized and combined elements of fantasy and a desire for revenge which probably can only be understood in terms of psychopathology.[87] The worst of the assaults were committed at times of a labor shortage which daily reminded white employers of their dependence upon black workers. Black Peril fears suggested settlers were vulnerable to betrayal by the BSAC and Whitehall; the assaults were a futile attempt to re-establish their authority.

The moral economy of Southern Rhodesia was founded on two pillars—the threatened sexual violence of black men and the suppression of knowledge about the violence of white employers. The jury crises exposed the tensions generated by both. Black Peril and the killing of African workers were also to a degree expressive of the anxieties of white males; they suggest why the feminization of black labor in domestic service, the access white men enjoyed to the bodies of black women, and the rigid controls they imposed over the sexual conduct of white women were so important to them.

FOUR

LEGISLATING VIRTUE

A striking feature of rape is the discrepancy between the incidence of crime and the regularity with which offenders are acquitted. Those discrepancies have been obvious in British courts for more than two centuries as has the global impact of sexual assault upon the mobility of women. The judicial process is usually an ordeal for the plaintiff, who is required to describe the assault in detail. The question of consent is the standard defense and it is common for the accused to impugn the victim's character. Courts often take the view that rape is only a crime if the woman is chaste. Chastity is defined by a woman being under the tutelage of a husband or father. In her history of sexual crime in late-eighteenth- and early-nineteenth-century Britain, Anna Clark traces the process whereby the threat of rape became a means used by men to restrict women's access to public spaces.[1] That period also produced two of the most enduring fallacies about sexual assault: Women are safe so long as they remain under the protection of a male; rape is a punishment for those who stray. For many women such rhetoric offers little consolation because rape is commonly committed in the home or at work by men in positions of authority.

During the last decade of the nineteenth century less than one in five rape trials in Australian courts resulted in a prosecution. There was much debate in state parliaments about the best means to prevent rape and to punish offenders. In Britain, the death penalty for rape had been abolished in 1841. Some critics attributed the reluctance of juries to convict men to the death penalty and advocated lesser sentences as a means to ensure just verdicts. However, there were other factors which made acquittals likely. Medical examinations carried out by male physicians were often inconclusive and most cases were resolved on the basis of an assessment of the victim's character. Married woman who had been attacked in their own homes had the best chance of success at court while women who used public spaces at night, who drank alcohol, or were single, divorced, or separated were disadvantaged. In New South Wales amendments specifying "mitigating circumstances," thus allowing for a lesser penalty than death, were introduced but conviction rates remained unchanged. As a remedy, in the decade from 1898 to 1908, most Australian states replaced capital punishment with life imprisonment. Queensland abolished the death penalty for rape in 1899, and Western Australia followed in 1902.[2] In 1903 the death penalty for attempted rape was introduced in Southern Rhodesia.

There are a number of ways to understand rape; depending upon the discourse it can be seen as sex, violence, sin, or pathology. Rape can also be treated as a single isolated act or as part of a wider political process.[3] Where women derive their status as members of households and have no standing as individuals such crimes have particular significance for men. In the most patriarchal societies rape becomes a form of theft in which one man steals the property of another.[4] It was white men in southern Africa who spoke with greatest vehemence about Black Peril. For them the mere possibility of such crime involved the violation of their property rights over the bodies of white women and the breaching of racial boundaries.

MAKING LAWS

The BSAC Charter did not prescribe the legal code to be used in Southern Rhodesia and the company adopted the Cape system that was introduced in June 1891. The Cape model, based upon Roman-Dutch law, was flexible, and over time divergences between Cape law and Rhodesian law developed.[5] Customary law was reserved for civil cases involving Africans: It did not apply to criminal law, cases in which a plaintiff or defendant was a European, or cases in which it was thought "repugnant to natural justice or morality."[6] Apart from customary law the major difference between the Rhodesian and British codes were found in modifications to the jury system.

The Rhodesian judiciary was small, conservative, and closely allied with the BSAC.[7] During the period from 1898 to 1923 ordinances were vetted by the high commissioner, who could suggest amendments before legislation was introduced to the Legislative Council. The most common amendments were to secure equality for Africans; the initial version of the Criminal Law Amendment Ordinance of 1903 was rejected because it applied only to blacks.[8] To protect Africans from injustice any death sentence issued by the High Court was subject to review. The process, however, was of limited value. In the period from 1900 to 1912, for example, thirty-four Africans were convicted of murder in Matabeleland, of whom three were charged with the murder of a white. All three were executed. Of the thirty-one convicted of murdering an African, eighteen, or over 58 percent, were reprieved on the high commissioner's recommendation.[9]

Michel Foucault distinguished between a disciplinary society and one that is disciplined.[10] He acknowledged that laws achieve only a limited degree of mastery over a population.[11] The same social processes which prevent regulation also reshape and transform efforts at control. The creation of rules is often matched by their avoidance, remaking, and manipulation. Sally Moore has coined the term "regimentary processes" to describe those attempts to organize and regulate behavior through the use of explicit rules. In Rhodesia those rules included pass laws, masters and servants ordinances, and morality legislation. It is often impossible to predict the consequences of laws; we must distinguish between explicit rules, the circumstances under which they are invoked, and their effectiveness. Between each layer of law and intention there is room for incomprehension, mistakes, and transgression. In Southern Rhodesia the ever-spiraling number of offenders convicted under the pass laws was evidence of the inability of the state to enforce compliance rather than proof of its effectiveness. The same was true, in a rather different way, of Black Peril legislation.

White males had convinced themselves that Black Peril was an increasing threat and turned to the Legislative Council to create a mechanism by which they could control what in their minds was the source of the threat. The Legislative Council passed a number of laws to control the violence of black men and the vices of white women. Combating Black Peril was part of a wider project of creating a moral society and so they also passed laws regulating prostitution, white slavery, and the age of consent. The ordinances passed in Salisbury in the period from 1900 to 1916 show that while white men wanted to protect women from the threat of rape, they were more anxious about the disruptive power of female sexuality.

The first of the morality laws, The Criminal Law Amendment Ordinance of 1900, combined measures to protect young girls from sexual exploitation with the prosecution of brothel owners and procurers.[12] The ordinance, based upon British and South African precedent, made the running or leasing of such premises an offense punishable by a fine or prison sentence. A person found guilty of procuring a "girl" faced up to four years' jail. Legislators were careful to protect the men who used brothels (already a conspicuous part of Salisbury's landscape) and it was sufficient defense that a man should believe a girl to be a prostitute or above the age of fourteen for him to be innocent of any offense. The law was thus designed to protect girls, to suppress the activities of procurers and brothel owners, and to shield their clients from prosecution. Although no mention was made of race, the ordinance was applied exclusively to white females and it was intended to suppress the "white slavery" traffic which at that time so alarmed reformers in western Europe. Despite strenuous efforts by the CID in the period from 1900 to 1916, its officers were unable to uncover a single case of "white slavery." Thus, once passed the ordinance lay dormant. In terms of its ambiguous purpose and the absence of any need for its enactment the "white slavery" ordinance was characteristic of the Black Peril legislation that was to follow.

As the result of a number of assaults in Bulawayo in September 1902, Mr. Frames, an elected member of the Legislative Council, moved that the government impose the death penalty on blacks for rape or attempted rape. Public feeling was intense and Frames's motion, although defeated by the BSAC majority, found support within the chamber. In December the administrator Milton received a resolution from the ratepayers of Bulawayo demanding the death penalty. Milton was aware that such an ordinance would be unpalatable to Whitehall and for that reason he wished to soften the proposal. He told Selbourne, "I am in the circumstances prepared to advocate legislation on these lines on the grounds that it is almost impossible to obtain or even to seek evidence of the completion of the crime, which no European woman can be expected to admit, and which her friends, who are usually alone in the position to testify, are naturally anxious to conceal. It is indeed a position in which the person so deeply wronged has infinitely more at stake than the wrongdoer, and is virtually on her trial."[13] He argued, in effect, that the shame attached to rape was such that no woman would admit to being assaulted; once passed the ordinance would not be used. A year later the ratepayers of Bulawayo got what they wanted.

The Criminal Law Amendment Ordinance was introduced in the Legislative Council during November 1903. In its original form the ordinance referred to the suppression of black-on-white assault and the death penalty was limited to black males. Those clauses were removed at Selbourne's insistence.[14] In debate members spoke passionately about law and order and the right of men to protect their families without interference from imperial authority. Members were afraid that the Anglo-Boer War had undermined the respect of Africans for Europeans and that an increase in Black Peril assaults was an omen of further disorder. Frames told the council that the situation was so serious in Bulawayo that it was not safe for women to venture outdoors. "No nation would allow the weaker sex to be trampled upon by savages or by anyone else," he told his colleagues. "It might be said that such a crime was just as bad when perpetrated by a white person. He begged to dissent from that view. The native was no better or very little better than a brute in connection with crimes of this nature. It was very little better than bestiality and no woman who had been ravaged or raped by a native was likely to admit in any court of law that the crime had been accomplished upon her."[15] The ordinance had two purposes: to prevent Black Peril and, in the wake of the Anglo-Boer War, to ensure social discipline by making black men afraid of the law. Those purposes were indistinguishable. It was passed unanimously and there was no discussion of its most obvious flaw: It gave an assailant good reason to murder his victim.

Under the Criminal Law Amendment Ordinance a judge could impose the death penalty for rape or attempted rape. The death sentence was not mandatory and the question of penalty was left to the judge's discretion. Although no mention was made of race the law was only applied in cases of black-on-white assault.[16] In a matter of months an African man was hanged for rape but it was seven years before a man was executed for the crime of attempted rape.

Within weeks of the passing of an act in the Cape to prevent white prostitutes from accepting black customers a similar ordinance was proposed in Salisbury.[17] That motion met with little support and it took another six months before The Immorality Suppression Ordinance of 1903 was passed at the same sitting as The Criminal Law Amendment Ordinance. It made it a crime for a white woman to have sexual relations with a black man outside of marriage. Offenders faced a prison sentence of up to two years.[18] The surviving records are incomplete and all that remains is a brief account of the recommendations from a House committee and a summary of the final debate. In preference to adopting the Cape version in which illicit intercourse was confined to prostitutes, the council decided there was need in Rhodesia for more severe measures. The attorney general endorsed the amendment, claiming that it would help to achieve convictions. He made no comment on the fact that the ordinance was far wider in scope and therefore more severe than that used in South Africa. There was also some debate about penalties; it was argued successfully that a harsher penalty for black men would help to protect white women from the threat of blackmail. The connection between "White Peril" and blackmail was curious; no evidence was presented that such a threat existed or how a harsher sentence would work to the benefit of women. The most severe punishment was reserved for procurers, a policy in keeping with South African practice.

In submitting the ordinance to the high commissioner the administrator observed: "It is considered indispensable that the native should be liable for punishment for this offence otherwise there will be a great danger of blackmail, a form of crime, which I am advised, the native is fully acquainted, and it is also highly desirable to keep before the native the idea that illicit sexual intercourse between himself and a white woman is in no way to be tolerated."[19] According to Claire Palley, the legislation was one of only two ordinances introduced at the request of the imperial government.[20] That may have been so, but it was adopted with enthusiasm by the council and was not repealed until 1961, when it was rescinded as part of a general review of discriminatory legislation.

The exclusively male chamber fretted about the possibility of blackmail and the issue appeared with unerring regularity in Black Peril debate. There is not one case of such a crime in the CID files and so their fear needs some explanation. The raising of that issue, like the ordinance itself, suggested there was no safety within white households and that African servants, because that was the class of labor against which the law was directed, had a limitless repertoire for malice. The idea of blackmail was to an extent grounded in the specter of African literacy. The BSAC had no desire to educate the labor force and no wish to see black artisans replace whites. However, as the result of African initiatives in the decade to 1912 there was an explosion in the number of indigenous schools. By 1904 there were twenty schools with around 2,000 pupils; twelve years later the number of schools had grown to six hundred and fifty and the number of students had risen tenfold.[21] Blackmail served well as a metaphor for the economic dangers that faced white households and for the need to preserve their secrets. The establishment of the first schools coincided with the passing of the suppression ordinance. Paradoxically, through the means of the morality laws the Legislative Council managed to expose the domestic space to public scrutiny.

In Southern Rhodesia rape was allied with the fear of mass violence; the rape of a white woman was supposed to be the first step in a chain that would lead to an African rebellion. Administrator Milton acknowledged that the purpose of the ordinances was to prevent white society from being overrun by the black majority. What was at risk was not just civilized standards but community survival. The ordinances of 1903 were intended to control the sexual desires of black males through the fear of execution and to discourage the vices of white women through the threat of imprisonment. By distinguishing between chaste and unworthy women the legislation extended the authority of men. The two ordinances were passed in the one session and they preceded rather than followed the major Black Peril scares. Taken together, they contain the paradox at the heart of the moral panics: The first ordinance was designed to protect white women from assault, the second to protect the white male community from white women.

Over the next decade convictions of women under the Immorality Suppression Ordinance were rare, yet in 1916 a second ordinance increased the law's powers to restrain their behavior. In introducing the Immorality and Indecency Suppression Ordinance the attorney general explained that the legislation was not based on any moral considerations. It was "a law really to preserve the prestige of the white race in the country and to prevent anything being done which might endanger the existence of the honour of white women in this territory."[22] The bill, which supplemented existing legislation, distinguished between soliciting and the committing of sexual acts, thereby widening the scope of criminal behavior. A woman could be jailed for a year who by words, writing, signs, or other suggestion enticed, incited, solicited or importuned a "native" to have illicit sexual intercourse with her or to commit any act of indecency.[23] In the case of a black man an "act of indecency" included raising or opening any window, blind, or screen or the fly of a privy in order to observe any girl nude or semi-nude. There were severe penalties for black males and any alien found guilty of such an offense faced deportation. The only protection offered to the accused was the requirement for corroborating evidence. By expanding the domain of sexual transgression to include voyeurism, flirtation, and even friendship the legislation made domestic labor more hazardous for both white women employers and their black male servants.

During its passage through the council the legislation was debated at length.[24] Colonel Grey, who supported the ordinance, objected to the provisions relating to women, which he said were a slur on their character and exposed them to the threat of blackmail. White women, he argued, did not have sexual relations with black men and those Africans who made such claims were merely seeking some advantage. The legislation was a "Kaffir ordinance" and there was no need to refer to women at all. Mr. McChlery was critical of the proposal because it involved using the courts to arbitrate questions of morality. He wanted the terms "native" and "white woman" removed from the draft so that the ordinance would apply equally to all races. McChlery rejected the idea that Black Peril was increasing and suggested that the legislation would encourage white women of poor character to bring false charges against servants. In a rather curious argument Mr. Begbie claimed that the reason why Black Peril was unknown in Portuguese East Africa was because a certain class of Portuguese males cohabited with African women. That proved that the cohabitation of white women with black men could not possibly cause Black Peril. Mr. Cripps suggested that those women who were most chaste were most at risk from the threat of attack. He had heard it said that some white women did not regard black men as human and the legislation would make them more aware of the risks they faced. It would also encourage them to treat their servants better. He argued that sexual crime was caused by the separation of black men from their wives and that families should be allowed to stay together in locations. The attorney general suggested that the crime addressed by the ordinance was both common and the major cause of Black Peril. Most members of the council agreed and the bill was passed.[25]

Convictions under the morality ordinances of 1903 and 1916 were rare; in a review of the Salisbury High Court records from 1903 to 1940 I found no cases involving the prosecution of a woman. The few black men convicted were unfortunate. In May 1923, for example, a servant named Kaimulila who was employed at the Queen's Hotel, Salisbury, was charged with criminal injury.[26] His offense was that he tried to open a bathroom door at the hotel while a guest, Bessie Dawe, was in a nude state. Kaimulila, whose duties included cleaning the bathrooms, told the court that he did not know the room was occupied. He was found guilty and sentenced to three weeks' jail. In July of the following year a laborer named Chilumpa who was employed at Hildadale farm was charged with having forced open the grass wall of a privy to see Gladys Rose when she was semi-nude.[27] Although it was probable that Chilumpa had accidentally brushed against the privy he was found guilty and sentenced to a year in jail. Those cases which reached court mostly involved women who were washing, showering, or excreting, activities about which the British middle class was so sensitive.

The ordinances of 1903 and 1916 were enacted as a warning to black males. Yet no attempt was made to publicize the legislation and it is probable that few servants were aware of its existence. African men were at jeopardy from the pass laws, the imposition of taxes, forced labor, and the threat of violence from BSAC police and white employers.[28] In a dangerous world the risk of being charged under the immorality ordinances was trivial. The lack of publicity about the laws indicates that their purpose was to intimidate white women rather than black men. The legislation suggests there was no safety anywhere from the threat of sexual assault and it reinforced the dependence of women upon the protection of husbands and fathers. It was also a reminder of the need for women to retain social distance from their servants and to monitor their own behavior for any indiscretion. The legislation had wider fields of reference and through them white males addressed the BSAC and imperial authorities. To those audiences the ordinances were offered as evidence of the negligence of the Company and the high commissioner. In terms of that political project the African community was irrelevant.

PRECEDENTS

In Britain between 1885 and 1914 a massive increase in the number of prosecutions of brothel owners was accompanied by the suppression of homosexuality, obscenity, and eroticism in the arts. That austerity was part of the moral purity movements which swept the country in the late Victorian and Edwardian periods. The movements were supported by feminists, Christian reformers, and eugenicists who were concerned about white slavery, a falling birth rate, and the spread of venereal disease. The demographic transition and changes in the status of women were obvious factors that fueled the campaigns. A variety of organizations such as the White Cross Movement, the Church of England Purity Society, and the New National Scheme for the Deliverance of Unprotected Girls and the Rescue of the Fallen worked to strengthen the family and combat vice. Feminists used the opportunity to question male sexual conduct and thereby challenge patriarchal authority.[29] The movements had wide support—a demonstration held in Hyde Park in 1885 to demand the raising of the age of consent was attended by over a quarter of a million people.[30] In the Criminal Law Amendment Act of that same year the age of consent was raised from thirteen to sixteen years and increased penalties for brothelkeepers were introduced. The climate of fear about sexuality, the family, and the future of the white race was exported to the colonial world.

During the 1890s there was a flood of continental women into southern Africa, some of whom worked as prostitutes. Concern over the willingness of such women to accept black clients saw public authorities shift their interest away from contagious diseases toward the need to maintain racial purity. In December 1902 the Cape parliament passed the Suppression of Betting Houses, Gambling Houses and Brothels Act, aspects of which were soon adopted in three other provinces. The act was fourteen pages long and dealt with gambling, betting shops, brothels, and prostitution.[31] In the eyes of legislators the vices of gambling and prostitution were analogous and the act was conceived as a general attack upon immorality. It was not specifically about race and only three small subsections addressed miscegenation. Those parts of the law dealing with prostitution laid down heavy penalties, especially for brothelkeepers and those convicted of procuring young women. Sections 31 and 32 (clauses consistent with legislation used in Britain) were addressed to white slavery and allowed for jail terms for male offenders found guilty of using drugs or threats to procure women. The final parts of the act were novel in proscribing sexual relations between white prostitutes and black men.[32] A white woman convicted of having sexual intercourse for the purposes of gain with "any aboriginal native" was liable to two years' hard labor. The penalty for the woman's client was up to five years' imprisonment and twenty-five lashes. Heavy penalties applied to any person who ran a brothel where such intercourse took place. It was the first act passed after the Anglo-Boer War that proscribed miscegenation.[33] In no other Cape law was a man liable to penalty for buying sex and the session of parliament which passed the Suppression Act also passed the first urban location act. Both acts were designed to enforce the social and spatial boundaries separating the white and black communities.

During its passage through the House of Assembly the attorney general, Mr. Graham, spoke at length about the prevalence of brothels in Cape Town, suggesting that their number had swelled since the beginning of the war. He also condemned the willingness of some white women to accept black customers as a particular threat to public safety. "This is a matter of the gravest importance" he told his colleagues, "for once the barriers were broken down between the Europeans and native races in this county there is no limit to the terrible dangers to which women would be submitted, especially in isolated areas."[34] In the following year, 1903, it was suggested in the House that rather than protect women from a life of vice the act was encouraging harassment and blackmail.

As the legislation moved north it changed character and in 1903 an ordinance based on the Suppression Act was introduced in the Transvaal.[35] The legislation made no reference to gaming or gambling and the ordinance was designed specifically to suppress prostitution and miscegenation. Any white woman who had illicit sexual relations with a black man faced prison.[36] The penalties for a black man were set at six years' hard labor. Those clauses dealing with miscegenation made no mention of commercial sex, thereby widening considerably the terms of reference. Illicit relations were those occurring outside of marriage and a "native" was defined as any native of Africa, Asia, America, or St. Helena. What had begun in the Cape as an attempt to control prostitution was transposed into a law regulating the behavior of both virtuous and fallen women. The act was amended in 1908 and its provisions broadened to include inciting or soliciting for the purposes of indecent acts.[37] In the Orange Free State

and Natal similar legislation was passed in 1903. The phrase "for the purposes of gain" used in the Cape was omitted in Natal and the law simply
proscribed sexual contact outside of marriage. There was some debate in
the Legislative Assembly over jurisdiction but members decided that by
restricting the law to prostitutes the act would not "go far enough."[38] The
perceived threat of white-on-black sex was less prominent in the Free State
and the law was limited to prostitutes. No penalties were set for offending
blacks.[39]

The Salisbury ordinance prohibiting sexual relations between white
women and black men was passed in the same session which introduced
the death penalty for rape. Both were directed against Black Peril and each
formed one half of a broader piece of law-making. If black men were omitted from the Criminal Law Amendment Ordinance they were at the center of its companion, the Immorality Suppression Ordinance. White males
were absent from both. Within the fabric of those laws we can see a struggle for authority between white men and women. We can also see the linea-
ments of the British purity movements and their fears for the survival of the
white race. Those fears may have been imported, but in a frontier society
they were even more potent.

CONCLUSION

Black Peril was important in Rhodesia, the Transvaal, Natal, and the
Cape, but there is little evidence of moral panic in other parts of British
Africa. According to Helen Callaway, white women in Nigeria did not live
in fear of assault.[40] Similarly, in Northern Rhodesia sexual crime did not
give rise to hysteria.[41] Karen Hansen has suggested that north of the Zam-
bezi River the inferior status of male servants may have muted sexual fear,
thereby tempering relations between white women and black men.[42] Whatever the merits of such an argument, it does not apply to the south.

The Rhodesian laws were distinguished by their eclecticism and sever-
ity. Legislators in Salisbury were more anxious and arguably more vindic-
tive than their counterparts in the Cape and that was reflected in the penalties they imposed on black men and white women. The ordinances were
also part of a political struggle between elected members, the BSAC, and
imperial authorities. During debate of the Criminal Law Amendment Ordinance, elected members made pointed reference to the uprising of 1896,
thereby linking Black Peril to the Company's past failures to protect families. There were also important differences between Southern Rhodesian
and South African law in terms of focus. Legislators in the Cape sought to

suppress the activities of prostitutes but took no interest in the lives of chaste women; the Salisbury legislation drew within its ambit all women, thereby transforming the cumbersome Suppression Act into a Black Peril ordinance. Brothels were a target in South Africa but not in Salisbury, where Pioneer Street was flourishing at the time of the drafting of the laws. The centerpiece in the construction of a virtuous society was the death penalty for attempted rape. It was akin to a badge of honor which distinguished Rhodesians from settlers to the south. In 1903 the BSAC held a veto in the Legislative Council but was unwilling to oppose the death penalty for fear of alienating settler opinion.

The ordinances of 1903 were supposed to protect women from violence and ensure the safety of families. The legislation did not work in the sense that the major panics followed rather than preceded the ordinances. It seems likely they fueled Black Peril. That failure was rather different than the slippages between legal intent and social outcomes which Sally Falk and Michel Foucault have identified. In general Black Peril offenders like Singana and Bonali and those charged under the immorality ordinances of 1903 and 1916 were not guilty of any sexual crime. There were few assaults to remedy, far too few to justify in any instrumental sense the time spent on drafting new laws. There were also so few female offenders that it is difficult to explain the existence of the suppression ordinances. An explanation has to be sought outside the law in the expectations and demographics of the white community as a whole.

Settler society was conflict-ridden. White women were greatly outnumbered by men and they were much sought after as marriage partners. They were also subject to a swathe of discriminatory legislation which treated them as socially dangerous. Ethnic differences between British, Afrikaners, and continentals, like the presence of poor whites, were indicative of the lack of cohesion within white society. Racial borders were commonly broken by the transgression of white males. But instead of curtailing the behavior of men, legislators censured women. The morality legislation had three dominant features: It led to the execution of innocent men, it worsened gender relations within white society, and it offered to the public at large an explanation for Black Peril.

FIVE

EXPLAINING BLACK PERIL

The small literature on Black Peril has been heavily influenced by psycho-analysis. That science is not easy to characterize: It has been open to innovation and repeatedly split by factionalism. There are, however, I believe, three essential elements to Freud's theory. Practitioners generally agree on the primacy of the unconscious in individual and collective life; the anarchic power of sexual desire; and the causal relationship between sublimation and cultural achievement. Each of those assumptions has been influential in the understanding of Black Peril.

Octave Mannoni's study of the riots which swept the Malagasy in 1948, *Prospero and Caliban,* is probably the first full-length psychology of colonization. It is also the only study of its kind based exclusively on psychoanalytic methods. Mannoni lived in Madagascar from 1925 until 1947, working as an ethnologist and at one time serving as director general of the government information service. In November 1947 Mannoni entered analysis in Paris under Jacques Lacan.[1] Mannoni later claimed that during his years in Madagascar he cured himself of an obsessional neurosis. "I understood, moreover, why Rimbaud had cured himself in the desert. Dislocation can do the job of analysis. Being a white man among blacks is like being an analyst among the whites."[2]

During the riots there were rumors that European women had been raped by Malagasy men. The rumors were false and according to Mannoni were projections of the repressed desires of white males to themselves commit rape and incest.[3] Mannoni believed that just as Prospero projected his sexual guilt onto the figure of Caliban, so colonialists projected their own evil intentions onto the African. In a variation on this argument Philip Mason, who was familiar with Mannoni's work, suggested that the moral panics in Southern Rhodesia sprang from the sexual jealousies of white men.[4]

Frantz Fanon used a similar approach in his first book, *Black Skin, White Masks* (1952).[5] Written while he was a medical student, it is primarily a study of race relations in Fanon's home, Martinique. Social position in that island society was allocated according to skin color. Fanon believed that in Martinique, as in metropolitan France, racism arose from guilt over suppressed sexual desire. Among white men it was a response to repressed homosexuality, among women a defense against nymphomania. Fanon never wrote directly about Black Peril but it is easy to imagine how he would have explained the moral panics. Mannoni, Mason, and, to a lesser degree, Fanon believed that racism derived from flaws within individuals. When examined in the light of science or by reference to the "universal brotherhood of man" it becomes a disease which can be cured by appeals to reason. The argument that racism stems from individual faults may be reassuring in terms of potential solutions. However, racism in Southern Rhodesia had a more systemic cause; its roots lay in a powerful combination of ideology and material interest.

In the past two decades literary theorists have written extensively on colonial representation. The literature, which is rich and diverse, has also been much influenced by Freud's concept of projection. The myth of the Dark Continent, a place where strange and terrible things happen, was, according to Patrick Brantlinger, itself a means through which Europeans displaced their malevolent impulses onto Africans. To assuage their guilt for the slave trade and imperialism and to hide from themselves their own savage and shadowy impulses, Europeans created an imaginary continent inhabited by imaginary people.[6] Africa became more terrible as Europe became more civilized. Sander Gilman has amassed an impressive body of evidence from the arts and sciences about the construction of racial stereotypes.[7] Gilman presumes that phenomena such as Black Peril arose from the historical forces Freud wrote about in his metapsychology. In colonial settings the sexual repression characteristic of Western civilization bred fantasies about the desires of black males. The more white men repressed their own sexual impulses, the more intense the sentiment they displaced. Occasionally those fears erupted in racial violence.

There are a number of problems in the use of psychoanalytic methods to explain historical experience.[8] They are particularly weak in explaining the origins and effects of racism. Psychoanalysis offers no reason why sexuality should have been so important to settler elites or why sexual mythologies were so prominent in racial discourse. Freud and his school cannot explain why panics occurred at certain times and places and not at others. We know that Black Peril was important in Southern Rhodesia, the Transvaal, and Natal but absent from Northern Rhodesia, the Orange Free State, Nyasaland, and arguably Kenya.[9] Those variations are significant and require explanation. But that is not the only problem with such an approach. To treat Black Peril as a psychological phenomenon assumes that the panics were played out between sovereign individuals rather than between genders, classes, and ethnic communities. Such theory also ignores the very tangible consequences of Black Peril, consequences which in turn shaped future panics. Psychoanalysis is based on a radical individualism. Part of its appeal is that it is so effective in leaving the world unchanged.

Racism determines the life chances of both individuals and the political minorities to which individuals belong. It is not merely a set of ideas or beliefs. Racism is, among other things, an ensemble of material practices. Prejudices are institutionalized in state administrations, legal systems, and labor markets. Nowhere was that more evident than in settler societies such as Southern Rhodesia and South Africa. The term racial formation, currently popular among American sociologists, is a useful reminder that racial categories are created, inhabited, and transformed over time and place. They are primarily about power.[10]

There is no evidence that guilt played any part in Black Peril. The Battlefields and Laidlaw cases suggest that settlers in Southern Rhodesia felt no guilt about their treatment of the black labor force or about their expropriation of land. Some missionaries and philanthropists in Britain were remorseful about the effects of colonization but they had little in common with settlers in Australasia and the Pacific, where indigenous peoples were decimated, or with those in central and southern Africa, where they were not. Without justification the argument that racism is a projection of guilt attributes racism to the excessive decency of whites.

In colonial Africa relations of race, gender, and class were enmeshed in complex and unstable configurations. To explain the moral panics it is important to look first at how the white male elites who created Black Peril understood sexual threat.

CONTEMPORARY OPINION

The most important evidence we have about how male elites explained Black Peril is found in two reports. The first was the result of a public inquiry into sexual assault held in South Africa in 1912. The second is a confidential document produced by the Salisbury CID in 1915. The South African inquiry was given wide press coverage and excerpts from the final report were published by both the South African and Rhodesian press.

THE ASSAULTS ON WOMEN COMMISSION, 1912

The South African Commission to Enquire into Assaults on Women was appointed in June 1912. It had eight members, including three women, and was chaired by Mr. Melius de Villiers, the brother of the chief justice.

Almost three hundred witnesses were called, including magistrates, inspectors of locations, clergy, farmers, police, missionaries, vigilance committee members, and liquor retailers. Forty-six members were African men and fifteen were white women. A number of black women were interviewed but their evidence was not recorded and no mention was made of them in the final report. Although the terms of reference made clear that it was not to be a Black Peril inquiry and the commissioner corrected a number of witnesses who insinuated that it was, the transcripts suggest otherwise.[11] The inquiry dealt almost exclusively with assaults on white women by "colored" men and the final report was written around two themes; the threats to white prestige and the influence of alcohol, prostitution, urbanization, and domestic labor upon the passions of black males.

The transcripts and the report were very different from the materials produced in Southern Rhodesia. There was little of the strident tone characteristic of official correspondence from Salisbury and the racism and misogyny were less extreme. There was no reference to the hyper-sexuality of black men and no suggestion that sexual assault threatened the survival of white society. Surprisingly, even though much evidence was given about prostitution there was no mention of venereal disease. The usage of the term White Peril is another difference. As one witness, Mr. Graham Cross of Johannesburg, explained, Black Peril involved assault by a black man upon a white woman; "What is commonly known as the White Peril here (The Rand) is the cohabiting of white men with coloured women."[12] In the final report white women fared better than they did in the Salisbury review of 1915; white men fared worse.[13]

The commission reviewed the incidence of rape across all racial categories in each province of South Africa for the twelve years to 1912. It found that, according to court records, such crimes were unusual, with the rate of white-on-black rape being the lowest of all. In the Cape there were just thirteen cases in twelve years.[14] The incidence of Black Peril assaults was significantly higher; there were forty-one cases in that same period. The commission concluded that Black Peril crimes were comparatively common but that many cases went unreported because victims were reluctant to come forward.[15] In South Africa, as elsewhere, estimates of rape are always compromised by discrepancies between the incidence and reporting of crime. They are further compromised by the gap between the numbers of men charged with rape and those convicted. In that sense the views of the commission about the underreporting of Black Peril assaults may have been accurate.

Some missionaries and a majority of African witnesses referred to sexual liaisons between white men and black women as the cause of Black Peril. The commission agreed that it was a serious threat. De Villiers wrote: "We are distinctly losing in moral reputation and at the same time producing a harvest of legal, social and political problems by an ever increasing number of bastards."[16] Although the commission distinguished between the activities of poor and respectable whites, that did not solve the problem raised by evidence that white policemen were forcing themselves upon black women.[17] Even more disturbing was the testimony about sexual relations involving prominent white men.[18] For de Villiers, however, the most disturbing testimony of all was the allegations of voluntary sexual intercourse between white women and black men.

The commission was held in the shadow of the Anglo-Boer War, which had impoverished many Afrikaner families.[19] De Villiers was concerned about the influence of urban life upon blacks and in particular about their growing familiarity with the vices of poor whites.[20] In the eyes of the commission the most immoral whites were prostitutes who took black customers and those few women who took black lovers. It found that "in some of the cases in which undoubtedly such intercourse has taken place the facts seem to point to sexual perversion on the part of the female. In many other cases the medical testimony points to the view that the girls were of feeble mind."[21] The use of condoms by black men was seen as particularly offensive. It allowed perverse women to have sex with black men without becoming pregnant and thus being caught. Many witnesses believed the employment of men as domestic labor was the cause of Black Peril assaults. The commission found that while many offenders were servants, few servants offended.[22] There were also complaints from missionaries and black community leaders that white employers would withhold wages, claiming that a servant had committed an assault. Mr. Bertram Beets of the Pretoria police rejected that idea if only because of the stigma suffered by victims.[23]

Under de Villiers's direction the issues of punishment and deterrence were discussed at length. The former chief of police in Durban suggested that offending blacks be banished to an island such as Papua New Guinea. De Villiers was preoccupied with the possibilities of castration. During the initial hearings he asked all male witnesses their opinion of such a punishment. To his annoyance most suggested that it was too cruel. Eventually de Villiers's enthusiasm waned.[24]

In order to combat Black Peril the commission wanted the white community to curb what they called the "evil" of miscegenation. This could be accomplished, according to de Villiers, "not merely by administrative action, but mainly by upholding, and where necessary uplifting, the status and prestige of the white race, by maintaining the respect in which it should be held, and by doing away with aught and all that may tend to diminish that status, prestige and respect; and also by securing the moral elevation of the raw, uncivilized native whenever he comes into contact with a white population."[25] He also suggested that cohabitation, including marriage between the races, be prohibited; that prostitutes of foreign extraction who took black clients be deported; that a closed compound system at mines be established; and that conditions at locations be improved. In general, the commission treated Black Peril as part of a wider problem of white poverty. There was no suggestion that sexual crime posed a threat to white society and there was no reference to hyper-sexuality driving young black men to commit rape. Its major themes were the impact of urbanization and the social pressures leading to prostitution and miscegenation.

It is clear from Gladstone's correspondence that events in Salisbury were influential in his establishing the inquiry. Initially he wanted Southern Rhodesia to be included within its purview. That view was shared by de Villiers, who regretted that no hearings were held there.[26] Numerous witnesses made reference to Southern Rhodesia and in particular to the Sam Lewis case, which had taken place two years earlier.[27] White members of the commission implicitly endorsed Lewis's behavior and saw his trial as important because of the role played by pornography. The commission believed it significant that in South Africa such material had been found in the possession of offenders: "Since these pictures are freely circulated amongst the natives they can but serve to degrade the white woman in their eyes, and must have a pernicious effect in arousing their passions."[28] There was another sense in which events to the north were relevant. During the hearings de Villiers suggested that the Black Peril problem in South Africa had followed Lord Gladstone's commuting of the death sentence of Alukuleta. He believed that Black Peril had been imported from Rhodesia.[29]

THE CID REPORT OF 1915

Black Peril was of particular interest to the BSAC police, which in 1915 produced a report on the subject.[30] The CID's document was confidential and it was probably viewed by only a select few within the administration. There is no evidence that it was made available to members of the Legislative Council and there is no reference to it in the numerous council debates which touched upon Black Peril.

The report contained a brief summary of twenty-seven cases heard in the high courts of Salisbury and Bulawayo in the period from 1899 to 1914. Among that number were only two incidents of black-on-white rape.

In the majority of cases the assailant was employed by the victim as a domestic servant. Also, a majority of assailants were classified as "alien natives," that is, they were immigrant workers from adjacent colonies. Often the seriousness of a case was determined not by the nature of the assault but by its location. Attacks upon women living on isolated farms caused alarm, but there was greater concern about the few assaults that took place in daylight on the streets of Salisbury. While evidence of the intent to commit rape was often negligible, public reaction was intense, suggesting that the security of civic spaces was as important as the safety of women.

The CID offered two explanations for Black Peril. The first was that African males were so ruled by their sexual impulses that in the absence of normal outlets they committed rape. That was taken as self-evident and the CID made no effort to explain it. The second reason was White Peril. In contrast to South African usage, in Salisbury White Peril was defined as the degenerate or naive behavior of a white woman toward a black man. The CID had no colloquial term for the sexual abuse of black women by white men.[31] The evidence cited regarding White Peril was largely anecdotal; some of it was drawn from police files and some from hearsay. Little of the material was authenticated.[32] The CID regarded white prostitutes' offering of their services to black clients as a particular threat and a good part of the report was devoted to their activities. The account of prostitution then drifted inexorably into a general discussion on the relations of white women to black males and from there into an explanation of Black Peril itself.

The CID noted with alarm that in the period from 1899 to 1904 there were fifteen cases of prostitutes working with black men in Bulawayo. "On the question of prostitution by white women with natives" wrote the CID, "it is pertinent to state that the prevalance of Black Peril during the years 1902 and 1903 in Bulawayo was mainly attributed by the general public to the presence and operation of [white] women."[33] After prosecution the women were deported either to South Africa or to Europe.[34] It is unknown how many white women worked as prostitutes in Rhodesia during the first two decades of this century. We do know that prostitution was practiced on Pioneer Street in the center of Salisbury and that the industry was tolerated so long as the women did not accept black customers.

The CID's view of prostitution was selective. Relations between white men and black prostitutes did not, in the department's opinion, cause Black Peril. Neither did concubinage. The breaching of racial boundaries led to sexual crime only when the woman was white. The issue was not racial boundaries in general but the sexual transgressions of white women in particular.

Most of the instances of White Peril involved "decent" women. A representative case which appears to have been copied from a policeman's notebook reads as follows: "In this year [1915] an officer of the police whilst cycling past one of the residencies of the town noticed a female quite unclothed leaning out of a side door of a house calling her native servant to come indoors to the room. This would appear to be one of those indiscreet actions . . . as the lady is a well known, respectable married woman."[35] According to the CID the cause of such indiscretions was naiveté about the possible sexual interpretations of such actions and a lack of experience in handling servants. Even so, such episodes were considered both reprehensible and dangerous: "It must be admitted that the extraordinarily careless attitude permitted to themselves by white women in this colony in their domestic arrangements has had not a little to do with many attempts to criminal offence chargeable to persons who are human males not withstanding their colour."[36] But not all white women were innocent.

The report acknowledged that in a minority of cases "degeneracy," an "inherited" disposition which had been discussed by the de Villiers commission, encouraged sexual curiosity. One case from 1905 involved the wife of a well-known public official. Her husband made a request to police to find for his wife "an exceptionally clean Portuguese native—one used to house work and who always wore white limbo."[37] The woman then proceeded to force her sexual attentions upon the man, who, having complied, reported the matter to the police.[38] The CID concluded of such cases: "The white women implicated apparently [did not have] any other view than the illicit satisfaction of sexual desire due to unbalanced curiosity and an hysterical wish to experience comparative sexual relationships."[39] The department, like legislators and the white male public, borrowed freely from discourses about degeneration. As Daniel Pick has shown, by the turn of the century the concept of degeneration was transformed from a pathology affecting the individual to one affecting the body politic.[40]

The idea that a tropical climate could unbalance an otherwise stable temperament was common to many parts of the British Empire.[41] One Rhodesian intellectual, Dr. W. Hewetson, was so concerned about the impact of ultraviolet rays on blondes that he wrote a monograph on the subject.[42] That idea was shared by the CID, which feared that tropical conditions could have disastrous effects on white women: "In some instances when [nymphomania] is not inherent the climatic effect on the human produces the same form of temporary hysteria."[43] The condition was distinct from degeneracy and could be prevented by avoiding exposure to strong sunshine, the CID reported.

According to the CID white women were to blame for Black Peril, a view it supported with case histories. In so doing it followed the conventions used by the press and members of the Legislative Council, who highlighted the failure of women to discipline servants. To prevent further assaults the CID recommended that women develop a combination of self-contradictory traits. They were to be chaste yet remain alert to any sexual nuance, aware of sexual meaning yet innocent of desire. To ensure they did not transgress, the CID wanted women's behavior to be monitored by their husbands and the state, if only to protect the naive from themselves. In identifying servants as the major offenders the CID raised the question about the effects of migratory labor. However, it offered no comment on the management of locations, thus ignoring the gendered segregation of urban communities. The CID made no mention of concubinage, or ongoing sexual relationships between white men and black women, even though it had been cited frequently by the de Villiers commission, and also by women's organizations, as a cause of Black Peril.[44]

There were three distinctive features of the CID's report: a fear of the sexuality of African men, a distrust of the sexual impulses of white women, and a conviction that Black Peril threatened the survival of settler society. The South African commission of 1912 made little reference to any of those elements; the anxiety which dominated the CID document was absent from the South African material. The CID report was also marked by a contradiction between its conclusion that white women faced a threat of assault and the lack of evidence of sexual crime. It is that gap which has encouraged the use of psychoanalytic theory to explain Black Peril.[45]

A SCIENCE OF DESIRE

The idea that sexual behavior and even the sexual drives themselves are racially specific was common to Victorian ethnography. The most famous treatise on the subject, *The Inequality of the Human Races,* was first published in 1853. Its author, Arthur de Gobineau, observed that the white male's superior intelligence was matched by his inferiority in regard to physical sensation. By contrast, in the Negro "the strength of his sensations is the most striking proof of his inferiority" and his fate was marked in the shape of his pelvis.[46] Later researchers made similar claims, shifting the stigmata of race from the waist to the cortex.[47]

Although Sigmund Freud took little interest in racial theory, he believed that a facsimile of Europe's prehistory was to be found in the lives of the "uncivilized." For that reason his writings contain numerous references to primitives.[48] According to psychoanalysis, cultural achievement requires sublimation of the sexual impulses; on a number of occasions Freud referred to "the inverse relation holding between civilization and the free development of sexuality."[49] Freud believed that disgust, shame, and morality were the dams which suppressed desire and made the creation of an advanced culture possible.[50] Primitives were men and women in whom the libido was so strong that their mode of thinking was "still highly sexualized."[51] In his *Three Essays on Sexuality,* which is a centerpiece of the science, Freud commented on the absence of a latency period—that hiatus between infantile sexuality and adolescence—in what he called "primitives." He concluded that premature sexual activity explained the lack of cultural achievement among the peoples of Africa, Australasia, and the Pacific.[52] At the time he wrote *Three Essays,* no prominent psychiatrist, with the exception of Emile Kraeplin, had visited the colonial world and Freud's work was based on the second- and third-hand accounts characteristic of Victorian ethnography. Even so Freud's judgments about race and cultural achievement had a strong influence on the psychiatric literature produced in Africa during the colonial period.[53]

Southern Rhodesia's only asylum, at Bulawayo, was opened in 1908 but its successive superintendents published nothing on the subject of Black Peril. Therefore it is necessary to turn to the literature from other settings and in particular to the work of B. J. F. Laubscher, a South African physician, and J. F. Ritchie, a schoolteacher from Zambia, for an inchoate theory of African sexuality.[54]

Laubscher was physician in charge of the native wards at the Queenstown asylum. In 1937 he published a study titled *Sex, Custom and Psychopathology* which was inspired by a number of Black Peril attacks in the eastern Cape.[55] A self-professed Freudian, he was probably the first scientist to identify a cause for Black Peril. Because little was known about sexual crime in South Africa, Laubscher began his research by sending questionnaires to district magistrates in rural areas. He requested information on a range of offenses, including homosexuality, indecent exposure, rape, sodomy, and incest. With that data, which he limited to males and to those cases which reached a court, he set out to explain Black Peril.

Although magistrates reported that homosexuality was rare, from his experience at Queenstown Laubscher had formed the belief that it was almost universal in prisons and mental hospitals. In female patients it took the form of mutual masturbation, while he estimated that pederasty was practiced by at least 80 percent of men.[56] Laubscher found two reasons to explain such behavior; the immediate answer lay in the segregation of men from women, while the underlying cause was "the primitive organisation" of the sexual instinct. According to Laubscher, the African's sexuality had a compulsive quality and African men and women suffered from what can be termed hyper-sexuality. If normal outlets were unavailable, men would commit sodomy or rape and women would turn to lesbianism. That was why when deprived of female companions black men were a threat to white women. The solution to Black Peril implied in *Sex, Custom and Psychopathology* was either to extend segregationist policies on the basis of race, thereby excluding men from urban centers, or to end segregation in locations on the basis of gender. The demands of a capitalist economy for cheap labor and the desire of whites to keep urban populations of blacks to a minimum made either solution impossible.

Narratives about sexual conduct are often conflated with prescriptions about child care and it was in that guise that sexuality appeared in the work of J. F. Ritchie. For twenty-one years Ritchie served with the Northern Rhodesian Education Department and in 1943 he wrote an important monograph on temperament.[57] Ritchie had no medical training but he was so adept in the use of psychoanalytic theory that his work remained influential until the 1960s.[58]

Ritchie made little comment on sexual relations between adults. He did write in some detail about the mother's suckling of her infant, which in Freudian terms is the archetypal sexual relationship. Ritchie was appalled by African breast-feeding regimes, to which he referred as "one long debauch."[59] He found that the breast was given on demand and often the infant would drink with such gusto that it swallowed large amounts of air. Consequently the child's stomach wall expanded, acquiring an unusual elasticity.[60] He found that the child's need for milk would increase and so greed became ingrained into its physiology. A parallel with adult desire was implied and Ritchie moved effortlessly from discussion of breast-feeding to an analysis of adult sexual conduct. According to Ritchie, African children made a rapid transition from anal to genital eroticism and they would from an early age imitate adult behavior. Adults rarely experienced voluntary abstinence and beginning with the mother's feeding of her infant the sexuality of Africans was compulsive, he claimed. It was the African's need for instant gratification, noted also by the Salisbury CID and Laubscher, that threatened the safety of European women and justified the fears of white communities.

The notion of hyper-sexuality found vivid expression in the morality legislation and it underlay the CID's report of 1915. It is also visible in the transcripts of Black Peril trials and in anecdotes published by the Salisbury press. But in the hands of Laubscher and Ritchie it had disturbing implications. The segregation of urban locations by gender uncoupled the sexuality of migrant laborers from marriage, thereby raising the specter of predatory black males. Like his contemporaries Laubscher found some African mores such as *metsha,* or non-penetrative sex, unacceptable. To Laubscher *metsha* was evidence of excessive heterosexuality.[61] It was also proof that even in their perversions Africans lacked the sophistication cataloged by Krafft-Ebing and Havelock Ellis. In general libidinal energy was wasted and so Africans could not build the kinds of material cultures or the personal traits which, for Laubscher at least, were the hallmark of the civilized. African civilization was a cul-de-sac. Similar ideas can be found in Marx's asiatic mode of production, Weber's garden of magic, and in the concept of tradition so popular among modernization theorists of the 1960s.[62] When couched in terms of individual psychology they had particular force.

Psychoanalysis has provided popular interpretations of Black Peril because the panics have usually been viewed as neurotic. But even in that regard the science has been of limited value. To writers such as Mannoni and, to a lesser extent, Gilman and Gates, colonialism consisted of individuals and grand historical configurations with a void occupying the space between. They make little allowance for conflict between genders, classes, or the state. Their models of power are asocial in the sense that they see contests for authority occurring essentially between individuals. Psychological theories may explain a propensity toward the belief that Black Peril was a genuine threat. They may also be useful in explaining the climate of fear which accompanied the panics. They cannot explain why the Black Peril hysteria was so important in Southern Rhodesia.

A POLITICS OF NUMBERS

The panics had their beginning in Bulawayo in 1902 and a less definite end sometime after 1911. The judges who presided at the trials spoke of them as the most serious crimes to come before their courts and were willing, without corroborating evidence, to sentence men to death. The panics had distinctive features, suggesting they should have had an obvious cause. That cause has proven elusive.

Black Peril hysteria can be broken into two phases—the panics and the anxiety which followed. The panics that occurred between 1902 and 1912 began with a number of sexual assaults; they produced victims and assailants and widespread fear of further crime. White males responded to these panics with ordinances and executions. The second phase covers the period from 1912 until 1935, when the last of the Black Peril assailants was executed. By 1916 the panics had passed, as had the legislative response to sexual threat. The first phase began with an assault in Bulawayo; the second ended with the execution of a man named Ndachana.

The distinction between the first and second phases was not always clear. Perhaps the best way to distinguish between the two is in terms of fear and anxiety. Fear always has a specific object. For there to be fear there must be something to be frightened of. The fear itself may be unreasonable, such as a fear of the dark or open spaces. Even if a fear has no reasonable basis the removal of that object will offer a remedy. Panics are similar to fear and like fear they are ephemeral. Anxiety is a very different emotion. It is more nebulous and is characterized by the anticipation of a danger or threat. Fear is acute; anxiety tends to be chronic. The same anxiety can be evoked in different contexts and it may be shifted about. It is less likely to have a clearly defined beginning or end. Because it has no object there is often no simple remedy. After 1916 the anxiety generated by the panics lent itself readily to any number of concerns about health and racial hygiene.

The men who produced the morality legislation and who until 1919 had the sole right to vote were by choice absent from discussion of the causes of Black Peril cases. The CID report focused upon black men and white women, while members of the Legislative Council rarely mentioned concubinage as a factor which compromised racial boundaries and therefore provoked the sexual assault of white women. Most explanations of the Black Peril phenomenon produced by historians have also ignored the economic and social circumstances in which the panics occurred.

Behind the chimerical world of Black Peril lay the settler towns which were segregated by class, race, and gender. At the height of the panics there were twenty-nine blacks for every white in the colony, an imbalance which was obvious even in the white citadels of Salisbury and Bulawayo.[63] By 1909 Salisbury had a population of 2,000 Europeans and was comprised of a scattering of public buildings and residential areas.[64] During the period from 1901 to 1911 the white population doubled but white men outnumbered white women by more than two to one.[65] That imbalance was particularly obvious in the age range from twenty-four to forty-four years and competition among men for female partners was intense. With the growth in population Salisbury gained some pretensions to being a "white city." However, the ideal of ethnic purity of which settlers were so fond disguised the fact that the white community was divided between Britons, Portuguese, Jews, French, and Greeks. So-called continentals were disliked by the ruling elite even more than Afrikaners, who were themselves a conspicuous minority.[66] That ethnic diversity made the white community even more vulnerable to social and political factionalism. White society was fragile and was to remain so for more than a decade. Economic success eluded the BSAC and most settlers who had made the journey from South Africa or Britain. There was a huge gap between the expectations of instant wealth which settlers brought with them and the realities of a small and largely unsuccessful colonial society in which most men could not find a marriage partner or support a family.

The system of migratory labor created urban environments which whites could not effectively control. In 1911, when the official African population of Salisbury was more than 6,000, all but three hundred were males, of whom 85 percent were aged between ten and twenty-nine.[67] The structure of South African towns was very different and whites had less reason to fear being overwhelmed by blacks. In 1921 there were 153,000 whites in Johannesburg and 136,000 blacks. Fifteen years later the number of blacks in the city was only marginally greater than that of whites.[68]

Wages and salaries in Rhodesia were high but so were the prices of food and accommodation. The cost of basic goods and services was felt most acutely by middle- and lower-income earners, who were vocal in blaming excessive freight charges on the BSAC rail monopoly.[69] To placate those groups, in 1913 the administration commissioned an inquiry into the cost of living. The committee found that although salaries were as much as 50 percent higher than in Durban, prices of basic commodities were such that most men were worse off. Bread and milk were expensive and several witnesses estimated that to feed a family of four cost in excess of 30 pounds per month.[70] Clerks earned between 7 and 15 pounds, which made it difficult for an average working man to escape debt. Only those in senior positions could afford to support a family, and illness or the loss of employment could mean financial ruin.[71] Some witnesses referred to the inflated expectations which settlers brought with them from England and South Africa. The committee noted with some disquiet that all families and most single men employed servants. David McCullough, a soft goods merchant of Bulawayo, reminded the inquiry: "In a country where there is a black population the standard of living [for artisans] must be high. You cannot have whites living as natives."[72] Ironically, the committee found that the prejudice against skilled African labor was a major factor in the high cost of building, which in turn contributed to the inflated rents.

Single men had plenty of money; married men did not. Because of high rents civil servants tended to live outside of Salisbury, which meant that their wives were left isolated in outlying suburbs. Many men chose to have their wives and children remain in South Africa or Britain in the hope of being able to live more cheaply. The cost of medical care, especially for childbirth, also encouraged the practice of "sending away." By 1911 as many as a third of men in Salisbury were "grass widowers."[73] According to one witness: "I do not think this is a country for a married man; it is far cheaper for my wife to live at Home and for me to send her a certain sum each month."[74] Such complaints were suggestive of the difficulties white men had in establishing themselves as heads of families. They also provided a context in which the fears of Black Peril were played out.

In late-nineteenth-century Britain the dominant domestic form was the family in which the male was the breadwinner. That ideal was adopted by the bourgeoisie in the first half of the nineteenth century and was then taken up by the best-paid sections of the working class. By the first decade of the twentieth century the paid employment of married women had reached an all-time low, and although many proletarian women worked for wages the nuclear family in which the male was the primary earner was the dominant family form. Among the bourgeoisie and working classes it defined the responsibilities of men and the status of women and children. A man was expected to earn sufficient income to support a dependent wife who, because she was excluded from wage labor by marriage, lost much of her economic and social independence.[75] In Southern Rhodesia the contrast between African and settler families served as one of the boundaries distinguishing the ruling from the subaltern communities. Black women were supposedly drudges, white women were supported by servants. At the peak of the moral panics a third of the men living in Salisbury and Bulawayo were incapable of supporting a dependent wife; those who did struggled.[76]

But what evidence is there that family formations were relevant to Black Peril hysterias? We know that the panics cannot be explained by the incidence of sexual assault. We also know that the CID and the Legislative Council attributed Black Peril to the misdemeanors of women. That was why the morality legislation was directed as much against white women as it was against black men. Conflicts arising from low wages and high prices were fought out between men as breadwinners and women as homemakers. Many families lived in shabby gentility, a fact which caused great resentment. By "sending away" men lost status. They also lost control over their households, thereby undermining an essential ingredient of male identity. In that context the Criminal Law Amendment Ordinance was in part a response to female independence and to the failure of men to achieve the kind of economic success they expected. The conflicts between white men and women were elaborate: On one side lay concubinage, on the other the morality legislation.

CONCLUSION

It is not easy to judge the white community's response to the Black Peril assaults of 1902 and 1903. What was appropriate behavior at that time can only be answered in the context of perceived dangers. Many of the threats confronting settlers were physical. There was the possibility of armed resistance and of diseases in the form of malaria, black water fever, typhoid, and rabies. There was also the heat, which during the months of October and November many found intolerable. Political debate relied heavily upon bodily metaphors and those particular dangers lent weight to an imagery of society as a body. There was in fact a ready congruence between fears about the body and fears about the body politic. Legislative Council debate about Black Peril panic was always based on the assumption that assaults threatened settlement. Black Peril fears reinforced the logical link between corruptions of the body and political danger. Whites shared a conceptual language for crisis and it was corporeal. According to Mary Douglas, bodily margins need to be understood in relation to other margins. Like the human body a polity has boundaries and an internal structure.[77] She writes that "[s]ometimes bodily orifices seem to represent points of entry or exit to social units."[78] That was certainly the case with Black Peril.

The moral panics were fashioned from a variety of elements. There were a few assaults in Bulawayo, Umtali, and Salisbury, most of which in another context may have passed unnoticed; there were the racial and sexual stereotypes from Victorian Britain associating black skin with sexual excess; there was the fear of being overwhelmed left over from the wars of the 1890s, a fear magnified by the secondary resistance of African labor and kept alive by the racial imbalances in the colonial towns; there were the sexual anxieties borrowed from the British purity campaigns; there was the quest for respectability of an aspiring Rhodesian middle class unsure of its origins and even less certain of its economic future; there was the numerical dominance of white men which to a degree enhanced the bargaining position of women and reminded less successful men of their failure. Through each of those elements the chronic conflicts between settlers, the BSAC, and imperial authorities were played out. It is not easy to rank those factors but the wars of resistance, the gender imbalances, and the stresses of living in a frontier society were certainly important.

The reasons for racial segregation were complex, as were the factors which brought about the dramatic urban imbalance between black men and women. In 1900 a global outbreak of bubonic plague reached the South African cities of Cape Town and Port Elizabeth. Fearful of the spread of infection from black communities to white enclaves, public authorities quickly segregated Africans from Europeans. According to Maynard Swanson the fears of whites "focussed on the preservation of civilised society, which they believed was threatened with disorder and decay apparent to them in the festering 'hordes' of 'raw natives' at Cape Town and other urban centres."[79] Within weeks, the threat of plague reached Salisbury and was used to justify the establishment of an urban location which soon became a permanent feature of the city.[80] There is some dispute among historians about the importance of sanitation as a model for the management of urban environments and it is unlikely that it was ever the dominant cause.[81] But it did share with Black Peril fears the same powerful imagery of pollution, contagion, and social chaos. Black Peril encouraged the drawing of a *cordon sanataire* between the white and black communities and thereby reinforced the system of urban locations. The panics carried within them a design for the organization of urban space and suggested rules for the regulation of distance and intimacy. Although concerns about Black Peril followed rather than instigated the establishment of locations they gave impetus to that system, thereby encouraging the very conditions under which the moral panics could be sustained.

Black Peril was a rich metaphor. It symbolized the erosion of white male authority over women, it was an emblem for racial pollution, and it suggested that cities were unsafe. It was also a reminder of the threat of armed resistance. Each of those fears was predicated upon the weakness of the BSAC state. The state was perceived as weak because it had failed to ensure the subordination of the black majority. It also failed to provide the economic benefits which settlers wanted. White males wanted the state to supply and control labor. They also wanted the right to do as they liked with labor. Many of their demands were riven with paradoxes. The morality ordinances sanctioned concubinage for white males; they also shifted authority over wives and daughters from husbands and fathers to the state.

Black Peril hysteria served the interests of the white community by dramatizing the dangers it faced and giving it some leverage against the BSAC, the high commissioner, and the British government. It also gave settlers leverage against local missionaries, who were often critical of their treatment of labor and the expropriation of land. The scares enabled the state to identify Africans in terms of race while appearing to characterize them by their individuality, thereby satisfying at least one of the imperatives of liberal ideology. Black Peril reinforced the formal authority of white males in relation to white women. Women in turn used the panics as a means to challenge male dominance.

The panics were protean and they influenced public policy in complex ways. Black Peril fears were felt, for example, in the management of servants, the state's response to the mobility of black women, and in the campaigns to suppress venereal disease. Each of those contests for authority was influenced by Black Peril ideology and in turn heightened the importance of the panics to white men and women.

SIX

WHITE WOMEN

White women were subordinate members of a dominant race. For many of them the empire presented an opportunity for marriage and social advancement. Women went to Rhodesia as wives who drew their status from their husbands or to work in subservient roles in education, health, commerce, or missions. Colonial life was difficult and often dangerous, especially for young children. As Enid, the heroine of an early Rhodesian novel, reflected, "One hears so much of the brave Englishmen who go out into the lonely places of the world and pave the way to Empire—but what is ever said about the women? And after all the man always has his pipe, and gun and love of sport—but what is there for the average woman? Why should the woman always come off worst?"[1]

There were persistent problems with housing, diet, and climate, all of which were felt most acutely by women. There were also tropical sores, enteric fever, malaria, typhoid, and dysentery. Married women managed households and raised families, work which in a colonial setting had particular significance in preserving "standards."[2] As the wives of farmers or miners they worked hard, often in great isolation. Sometimes women ran small trading stores as did Mary Turner, the doomed heroine of Doris Lessing's *The Grass Is Singing*.[3]

Until recently, historians, like the colonial administrators before them, ignored the role women played in the creation of settler societies; it is only in the past fifteen years that a literature about white women has emerged. Besides famous individuals such as Mary Kingsley, Beryl Markham, Karen Blixen, and Sylvia Pankhurst, many ordinary women living unremembered lives were active in creating the wealth and sustaining the prestige of white minorities. In the writings of Karen Hansen, Margaret Strobel, Ann Stoler, Claudia Knapman, and Helen Callaway the ambiguities of their lives have begun to be understood.

While men made the rules of hierarchy and exclusion, women were anything but passive; voluntary bodies such as the Federation of Women's Institutes (FWI) and the Loyal Women's Guild entered vigorously into public debate. In 1919, for example, with the approaching end of the BSAC charter and the prospect of union with South Africa a number of women's groups, in particular the Women's Franchise Society, sought to exploit the opportunity by pressing for the vote. The passing of the Women's Enfranchisement Ordinance in that year, which was in part designed to strengthen the hand of Rhodesians in any amalgamation with South Africa, is an example of their successful use of political skills.[4] In South Africa white women had to wait until 1930 for suffrage legislation. Women's organizations such as the Rhodesian Women's League (RWL) were also active in seeking changes to the pass laws, changes in the training of female servants, and reductions in the cost of living. In Britain there were precedents for the involvement of respectable women in sexual controversies such as the repeal of the contagious diseases acts, the raising of the age of consent, and the suppression of prostitution. During those campaigns women were able to be vocal yet maintain their middle-class respectability. What was unusual about colonial women was the degree to which Black Peril panics gave them access to the political arena and their success in using that opportunity to advantage.

The state created by the BSAC was essentially masculine; in the period from 1908 to 1979 only three women served in the Rhodesian parliament.[5] Women were also excluded from high office in medicine and the law. In 1920, a year after women gained the vote, the Sex Disqualification Removal Ordinance extended to women the same rights men had to enter the professions or to be admitted to an incorporated society. However, in practice women were still denied access to positions of authority and were excluded from serving on juries.[6] Consequently the most obvious way for women to participate in public life was in carrying out good works. Organizations such as the Loyal Women's Guild and the FWI were active in providing aid for widows, orphans, and the insane.

Twelve months after white women gained the franchise, Ethel Tawse Jollie became the first woman elected to a Legislative Assembly in the British Dominions. Jollie was a leading figure in the Rhodesian Agricultural Union and the widow of Archibald Colquhoun, Rhodesia's first resident magistrate. Throughout her years in parliament Jollie was an energetic critic of both the BSAC and the British government and she was prominent in debate on Black Peril scares.[7] Her memoirs are filled with the creed of the average Rhodesian and the desire for self-government. In defending the actions of the early settlers Jollie argued that they had been given no support from Britain or the BSAC and she was critical of those, like Olive Schreiner, who pointed out that whites had been cruel. "[T]hey felt that their only chance of safety was to make themselves feared," wrote Jollie, "and as the arm of the law was practically non-existent, they dispensed a rough-and-ready justice of their own."[8] She acknowledged that errors had been made but suggested they were due to benevolence rather than malice: "Most of the mistakes made in dealing with the native comes from the conception that he is merely a white man in embryo—of a 'Child race'— which leaves altogether out of account the very unchildlike development of certain sides of his nature and desires."[9] Like her contemporaries, Jollie attributed the ruins of Great Zimbabwe to Asiatic builders because she was certain that Africans were incapable of such an achievement.[10] What was most distinctive about Jollie was her masculinist politics which frequently placed her at odds with the women's organizations.

Prior to 1939 writers such as Gertrude Page, Margaret Bachelor, Jane England, Blanche Longden, Sheila MacDonald, and Cynthia Stockley produced virtually all of Southern Rhodesia's fiction.[11] Women were also active in professional groups; from its inception the first association for those with an interest in science, the Rhodesian Scientific Association, had female associates.[12] Although white women were highly educated (the census of 1936 shows they formed almost half of the professional class), they were largely confined to a single profession, teaching.[13] The majority of middle-class males were clergyman, lawyers, and auditors; women accounted for 245 out of 295 teachers.[14] The census reflected the large number of missionary nuns, which makes the invisibility of women in the colonial histories of L. H. Gann, G. H. Tanser, Phillip Mason, and Colin Leys all the more significant.[15]

Settler women were self-consciously intellectual and the arguments they used in discussing respectability, the family, or racial hygiene were quite different from those favored by men. Women tended to place immediate controversies into larger historical frameworks to an extent which was unusual even in the Legislative Council, where debate was often pretentious. That intellectualism explains in part why women were able to play such a significant role in sexual politics, an arena from which they would otherwise have been excluded. Most of the issues about which women were vocal related to Black Peril ideology and associations such as the RWL exploited the panics as a means to create a political space within which they could maneuver. Just as British feminists had capitalized on the ideal of female sexual anesthesia to press for the raising of the age of consent and the abolition of the contagious diseases acts, Rhodesian women used their supposed vulnerability as a weapon against a male administration.[16]

During the early days of settlement men greatly outnumbered women and for most single men there was no female partner.[17] In 1904 there were 12,596 white males in Rhodesia and only 3,643 females with the imbalance being greatest between the ages of twenty-four and forty-four years.[18] That asymmetry was also more pronounced in certain towns; women were more scarce in Salisbury and Umtali, the centers of Black Peril hysteria, than in Bulawayo. By 1911 the settler population had almost doubled, but men continued to outnumber women until well into the 1930s.[19] To solve that problem some effort was made to attract females. Under the terms of the Empire Settlement Act of 1922 single women were encouraged to settle in the colony. The scheme, however, was a failure and in the period from 1922 to 1928 only thirteen women were recruited.[20]

Much of the fiction and some of the science written by men about the women of empire was damning. Often they were depicted as mean-spirited, socially ambitious, and racist. George Orwell's novel *Burmese Days*, set in the 1920s, contains a grotesque portrait of one of their number. Elizabeth, with whom the main character John Flory falls in love, is a philistine trying desperately to climb out of the lower rungs of the middle class and establish a comfortable life for herself. Loathing the Burmese and driven by banal ambition, she soon destroys Flory.[21] Like Orwell, many colonial historians have presumed that because of their sexual jealousy and opposition to concubinage white women ended a period of racial tolerance.[22] According to Octave Mannoni, the arrival of women in Malagasy ruined race relations because "European women are far more racialist than the men. Sometimes their racialism attains preposterous proportions."[23] He suggested that one cause of their behavior was overcompensation like that of the *nouveau riche* in their dealings with servants. White women were constantly trying to impress upon white males their superiority to Malagasy women, whom they secretly envied, while in their domineering behavior toward Malagasy men they sought revenge for their own misery.[24] Such prejudices against white settler women have been widespread. Writing of colonial Fiji, Claudia Knapman has commented, "There is no doubt that for Fiji there exists a commonly held picture (usually of the planter's wife) of the frivolous, idle, ill-tempered, narrow-minded, gin-drinking and servant harassing white woman."[25] According to Philip Mason, although white women in Rhodesia sometimes turned a blind eye to the presence of local women in the homes of bachelors they found it unthinkable that a white man could marry a black woman.[26]

The myth of the destructive memsahib contains two elements. First, by interfering with the access of white males to "native women" they supposedly widened the distance between indigenous society and colonists, thereby creating conflict. Second, their presence supposedly aroused the sexual appetites of black males, from whom they had to be protected. Such claims supposed that white women were simultaneously frigid yet sexually irresistible to black men, ideas found at the heart of Black Peril ideology. The evidence suggests, however, that the myth was hollow. Rather than being *responsible for* social tension, the arrival of women *coincided with* increased competition for land, the extension of wage labor, and urbanization, each of which strained race relations.[27] The stereotype of the frigid and vengeful memsahib reflected the equivocal status of women as subordinate members of a ruling class. It is only in the past fifteen years that such prejudices have been seriously challenged.[28]

PROSTITUTION

The disparity between the sexes in Southern Rhodesia favored both concubinage and prostitution. Even before the passing of the first morality legislation in 1903 the activities of some white prostitutes had aroused public censure. In the minds of men, colonial women were to be protected or controlled, and nowhere were such attitudes more obvious than in attempts to suppress prostitution and white slavery.

At the end of the nineteenth century there was a global diffusion of prostitutes from western and central Europe which reached as far as Buenos Aires and Sydney. At Europe's colonial periphery the lack of white women created a market for commercial sex and the development of the steamship and the telegraph allowed the establishment of an international trade. In southern Africa the surplus of males on the gold fields was such that in less than a decade almost 1,000 Jewish women entered South Africa to work in the burgeoning red light districts of Johannesburg and Cape Town.[29] The increased numbers of prostitutes aroused public concern. From the late 1890s the industry was suppressed through legislation to prevent white slavery that was passed in the Transvaal and the Cape.[30]

At the turn of the century Salisbury was a small town of 1,500 whites; the town had only the most basic amenities. One of the first issues addressed by the Salisbury council after its formation in 1897 was the presence of white prostitutes on Pioneer Street, where seven houses were used for "vice." There was much drunkenness and brawling and shopkeepers complained of a withdrawal of business from the adjacent *kopje* area. There were also claims that on the way to the cemetery mourners were embarrassed by having to pass by the brothels.[31] By 1908 there were nineteen prostitutes on the street but according to police the premises were conducted in an orderly fashion and there was no soliciting.[32] In November 1908 a group of ratepayers asked the government to suppress the trade. There followed a petition and a delegation which met with Attorney General Tredgold. The Salisbury council was unhappy with Tredgold's response and approached the high commissioner, again without success.[33]

During debate in the council on March 9, 1909, members agreed that since Pioneer Street was close to a recreational area used by families the situation was intolerable.[34] The presumed effect upon blacks was even more disturbing and the suggestion that brothels were a "necessary evil" contained in a letter sent by the administrator to the council only worsened matters. At the end of April it sent a petition to the high commissioner in protest.[35] According to the council there were nine brothels which lay directly between the town and the African location: "The native population is thus obliged to pass and re-pass, day by day, the whole stretch of the tainted area and the effect upon the native mind of visible and flagrant vice is too awful to contemplate."[36] The council believed that instead of suppressing brothels, which it was obliged to do, the government condoned their existence. The attorney general argued that the ordinance did not cover instances in which a woman ran a house by herself (which was the case in Salisbury) and that when no third person was involved he had no jurisdiction. Under Ordinance No. 13 of 1900, prostitution in itself was not unlawful or punishable; it was only punishable where it constituted a public nuisance. The government's position was therefore correct.[37] Both Tredgold and the administrator supported their case with evidence from the BSAC police which showed that there had been no offensive behavior from the women, that there were no adjoining houses, and that that part of the street was seldom used by Europeans or Africans.[38] The council was not assuaged and the issue was taken up by the Salisbury press.

According to the *Herald,* nowhere else in the British Empire was such a situation tolerated by police, who, since they were keeping the area under surveillance, were in effect supervising crime.[39] Although the *Herald* formally rejected the idea that the brothels were a necessary evil, it conceded that with the excess number of single white males in Salisbury the suppression of prostitution could encourage an even worse vice, sexual relations between white males and African women. The paper's solution was that such "unfortunates," the white prostitutes, should remain in that part of town least frequented by citizens.[40] In November 1909 a deputation from the council met with the high commissioner, Lord Selbourne.[41] Speaking for the council, Mr. von Hirschberg made clear how seriously it viewed the issue: "We feel that this is a question which affects the moral foundations upon which the strength of the British Empire has been and is being built."[42] The Rev. John White commented that no respectable citizen would venture down Pioneer Street and that only the previous week an African had been charged with criminal assault on a white woman who lived there.[43] The cemetery was situated close by and every funeral had to pass in full view of the premises, he added.

While Lord Selbourne wanted prostitution suppressed he did not understand why the delegation had come to him. He reminded them that his role in regard to the territory was to ensure that the constitution was honored and imperial interests safeguarded, nothing more. Rhodesians had the power to deal with their own affairs and yet he was being asked to coerce their elected representatives.[44] The mayor of Salisbury explained that Rhodesians were not fully self-governing and from experience the Legislative Council did not always act unanimously, which was why they had approached the high commissioner. The real reason, however, had to do with the precedent set by the Black Peril incidents. Like the moral panics, the issue was embedded in the chronic conflict between settlers, the BSAC, and imperial authorities and it was habit that such a delegation should seek to play one off against the other.

In February 1910, Mr. Brown, the mayor of Salisbury, wrote to Mr. Birchenough, a director of the Chartered Company. He explained that relations between the BSAC and the people of Salisbury were under threat because of the government's failure to remedy an obvious evil.[45] To Brown's delight, initially the BSAC supported the council: "The view of the Board is that, if proper evidence is forthcoming, the attorney general should not refuse to take action for reasons of policy, but that the law should take its normal course."[46] Attorney General Tredgold still refused to act and public debate about Pioneer Street raged until July 1911, when a petition signed by over two hundred residents was sent to the BSAC's head office. By that time the Company had withdrawn its support from the abolitionists.

What was ostensibly at stake on Pioneer Street was the creation of a family environment; beneath that idea lay the question of male authority over women. The issue involved a conflict between community standards, represented by the prestigious figure of the Rev. John White, and the local council; the wishes of white males to have access to commercial sex; the fear that suppression would increase miscegenation; and an intolerance of women not under the control of a man. At no stage was the issue of *White Peril* raised by those who favored the suppression of prostitution; it is certain that the women were not accepting black clients. If they had, the premises would have been closed.

The attorney general took no action because suppression would have been unpopular among his constituents, the white males of Salisbury. According to the census for 1907, the year in which Pioneer Street first became an issue, there were 14,018 Europeans in the territory, of whom 9,461 were men.[47] In Salisbury the imbalance was even more dramatic; outside of prostitution many males had no sexual access to a white woman. Out of deference to his constituents Tredgold made no effort to justify his action by raising the specter of concubinage.

The campaign for the suppression of prostitution involved the maintenance of racial boundaries, the assertion of masculine authority, and the protection of female virtue. In each of these goals fear of Black Peril was always an underlying factor. There were few white prostitutes but they were important because, since they were free of pimps or bullies, they were not subordinate to the authority of a man. They owned their own premises and their lives bore no resemblance to the suffering of those trapped by white slavers. Prostitutes probably earned more than many of the white males who were their customers. It is certain they earned more than women in "respectable" employment. They were arguably the only class of white women in the colony who enjoyed an authentic financial independence. It was their independence as much as the possibility that they would accept black customers which angered white male legislators.

The campaign against Pioneer Street also had a commercial significance to which none of the actors referred. It was about property values. Prestige was centered in the northeast of Salisbury and declined to the southwest. The *kopje* area offered cheap accommodation in tenements and boardinghouses in which black workers rented individual rooms. In early 1905 the issue of blacks moving into the area was raised by the town council and once a new location was established in 1907 the cries for their removal became stronger. By January 1908 the council began pressuring property owners to evict black tenants and within three months all free tenanted Africans had been removed.[48] That decision was part of the movement to have the *kopje* area and in particular Pioneer Street "sanitized." The campaign was led by Mr. Edward Coxwell, a town counselor and major property holder who skillfully exploited middle-class fears about social hygiene and segregation. Coxwell stood to gain financially if the area was gentrified and it was for that reason that he led the campaign.

Creating an environment fit for middle-class families was no easy matter in a frontier society. The struggle over Pioneer Street was part of wider tensions which were being played out within the white community. White males wanted access to commercial sex but they also wanted to appear respectable. In Salisbury, as elsewhere in southern Africa, male ambivalence toward women was obvious in the attempts to suppress prostitution. The campaigns always contained two contradictory themes; the desire to rescue fallen women and the desire to ostracize those women who were determined to maintain their independence from male authority.

WHITE SLAVERY AND BARMAIDS

The term "white slavery" was first used in the 1830s by London physician Michael Ryan to contrast the trade in the bodies of young white girls with black slavery, which in the British Empire had ended in 1833. Ryan associated prostitution with kidnapping and he helped promote an image of innocent girls forced by pimps and bullies into foreign brothels. The hysteria surrounding white slavery was intense and reached a peak in the period before World War One. In 1913, the young women employed at London's telephone exchanges were given official warnings to watch out for drugged chocolates.[49] Both the trade in women and its accompanying hysteria arose from a variety of social and economic changes which were reshaping European societies and their colonial dependencies. The term white slavery was misleading—the majority of women involved in the trade were Chinese and Japanese.[50]

The idea of female abduction appealed to feminists and puritans alike since both believed that no woman could rationally chose to be a prostitute. White slavery was useful to feminists in exposing the exploitation to which women were subject. In an age of changing gender relations it was comforting for men to believe that women were sexually passive and exploitable. The movement was encouraged by the work of purity campaigners, who were determined to ensure the health of the British nation through anti-obscenity statutes, the suppression of prostitution and venereal disease, and elevated ages of consent. By the beginning of World War One there were organizations fighting white slavery in a dozen countries. A series of international agreements were signed between 1902 and 1913, when a congress for its suppression was held in London by the International Abolitionist Federation.[51] There was also a vast amount of publicity in the form of films, novels, and plays. Although the moral concerns of legislators in Southern Rhodesia were often borrowed from Britain, that did not mean that white slavery had the same significance at the empire's edge. Nor did it prevent the Legislative Council in Salisbury from introducing ordinances designed to solve a problem which did not exist.

The Criminal Law Amendment Ordinance of 1900 combined the protection of young girls from sexual exploitation with the prosecution of brothel owners and procurers.[52] The ordinance made the running or leasing of a brothel an offense, allowing for fines and prison sentences. A person found guilty of procuring a girl aged between twelve and fourteen years or any so-called imbecile woman faced up to four years in prison. Legislators, however, were careful to protect the men who used brothels; if a man claimed that he believed that a girl was a prostitute or that she was older than fourteen that was considered sufficient grounds for acquittal. The law was thus conceived to answer quite contrary purposes: to protect young white girls from prostitution, to suppress the activities of procurers and brothel owners, and to protect their clients from indictment. Although no mention was made of race, the ordinance applied exclusively to white females. However, there is no evidence in the CID files of young girls being seduced by procurers. Once passed the ordinance lay dormant.

In May 1904 and again in 1910 international agreements were signed to suppress white slavery and in response the attorney general issued a number of memos on the subject.[53] While acknowledging that some men in the territory were living on immoral earnings he was certain there was no white slave traffic in Rhodesia. The issue remained important and debate about whether Rhodesia should become a signatory to those conventions continued for some years. There was also concern about white girls being forced into brothels in the neighboring Portuguese territory. In August 1912 the local press ran a series of articles "exposing" a traffic in barmaids between Salisbury, Bulawayo, and Portuguese East Africa (Mozambique).[54] The report proved groundless.[55]

The lack of evidence of white slavery did not prevent legislators from drafting laws to suppress it and in May 1916 the attorney general introduced The Criminal Law Further Amendment Ordinance.[56] The bill, which again contained no reference to race, was intended to protect young women and focused upon the activities of non-existent procurers and pimps. It was also designed to bring the laws in the territory into line with those of Britain and South Africa. The legislation, which excluded known prostitutes or those of poor character from its terms of reference, forbade the taking of any woman out of the territory for immoral purposes. In cases where intimidation, blackmail, drugs, or false pretenses were used, penalties of up to five years in jail and twenty-five lashes were allowed. The ordinance gained strong support in the council, although some members did point out its obvious deficiencies. The references to brothels, for example, had more relevance to the Cape (where contagious diseases acts had been used) than to Rhodesia, where, according to the attorney general, there were no brothels.[57] There was never any evidence that the legislation was justified and to understand why it was passed it is necessary to place it into context.[58] The ordinance was debated on the same day as the Immorality and Indecency Suppression Ordinance, and was based on the assumption that women were both given to moral lapses and helpless in the face of procurers. It was that fear which inspired one member, Mr. Cleveland, to move that the employment of barmaids in licensed premises be prohibited.[59]

In early 1915 the Women's Christian Temperance Union (WCTU) in Bulawayo collected a petition of more than six hundred signatures opposing the employment of women in bars and hotels. During October the Church of England Synod, which met at Salisbury, discussed the issue and Archdeacon Harker moved "[t]hat this Synod desires to express its strong disapproval of the employment of barmaids in this country, and calls upon the Government to introduce such legislation as will render such employment illegal."[60] According to the Synod young women were required to drink with customers, thereby exposing them to prostitution. The Synod was even more disturbed that African men employed to wash glasses saw white woman working in sordid circumstances. Harker's resolution to forbid the employment of barmaids, which was carried unanimously, was passed on to a sympathetic member of the Legislative Council, Mr. Cleveland.

Cleveland presented a petition signed by some 1,600 women, representing a large proportion of the adult female population, who demanded that the employment of women be prohibited. The petitioners were concerned about the demoralizing effect that working in such premises had, where white women were subject to innuendo and unseemly language. Cleveland told the council, "Natives have to perform work in the bar. They hear the conversation and see what goes on there. Your petitioners feel strongly that in the persons of the barmaids womanhood is shamed and humiliated before these natives."[61] Like his petitioners, Cleveland was sure that the presence of barmaids encouraged Black Peril incidents. In seconding the motion Mr. McChlery commented: "These natives in the bars heard coarse suggestions, obscene language and filthy jokes, and one boy told another boy what the white man said to the white woman in the bars. He had even known of natives trying to mimic the leer on the face of the white man when he had been talking to a barmaid."[62]

The major opponents of the legislation were bar owners. They believed that barmaids attracted customers and that the removal of women would have a bad effect upon business. Their case made sense in a society in which the only time many men encountered white female company was when being served in bars. While the Women's Christian Temperance Union collected petitions and the Synod held meetings, bar owners lobbied members of the legislative council. There is no evidence of the kind of pressure they brought to bear. What we do know is that they were successful and the motion was defeated.

The churches wanted an end to the vice in Pioneer Street, the government feared a reprisal from electors, and the *Herald* reminded its readers that the alternative was even worse. In the case of barmaids, the missionaries and a minority of members of the Legislative Council were directly opposed by commercial interests, which won the day. The controversies involved a perceived breech of racial and social boundaries. That breech was symbolized by the leer on the face of an anonymous black man, by the image of white families passing brothels on their way to picnic at the *kopje,* and by white girls being forced by pimps to have sex with black men in Portuguese East Africa. Each controversy had its own constituency defined by the very different interests of white men and women and also by the chronic divisions within white male society. The failed attempts to ban prostitution, suppress the chimera of white slavery, and proscribe the employment of barmaids were based on the idea of female sexual passivity or its alternative, female perversity. The apotheosis of each was found in Black Peril.

CONCUBINAGE

The socially accepted role for women in Southern Rhodesia was to protect the family and preserve standards. By pursuing the suppression of concubinage the women's organizations became involved in a bitter conflict with male legislators. In Southern Rhodesia there were two views of concubinage; men claimed it was rare and had nothing to do with Black Peril and women argued it was the major cause of Black Peril.

Within the British Empire concubinage between white males and indigenous women was common and involved a variety of domestic and sexual arrangements. In some instances the woman lived with her white male partner, in others the arrangement was more casual. In South Rhodesia the CID and members of the legislative council used the term to refer to any form of sexual contact between a white man and a black or Coloured woman. It covered both common-law marriages, which were rare and confined to isolated rural areas, and purely commercial sex.In the early colonial period, unless there was a scandal, local administrations, like the Colonial Office itself, tended to ignore such liaisons.[63] Until the first decades of the twentieth century local women in Africa, southeast Asia, and the

Indian subcontinent provided domestic services, including sex, to white males who could not otherwise afford to support a wife. Concubinage also eroded social distance and was therefore frowned upon by sections of the male community, including the missions. Others believed it had more sinister effects. According to Mannoni, the European males in Malagasy who found comfort in local women were soon demoralized: "When a European takes a Malagasy woman as wife or mistress, his subsequent transformation becomes so obvious. . . . [S]he gradually saps his will and intelligence."[64] Over time such ideas became dominant at the Colonial Office.[65]

The first serious attempt to proscribe concubinage occurred in January 1909 when the Secretary of State for the Colonies, Lord Crewe, issued a confidential memorandum.[66] According to Crewe, concubinage diminished an officer's authority and was likely to cause conflict with native populations. He threatened that any further breaches of discipline would lead to disgrace and official ruin. As intended, the memorandum had an influence in southern Africa and in June 1910 High Commissioner Gladstone wrote to Salisbury about cohabitation. He informed the resident commissioner: "I am gravely concerned about the growing evil which must result from whites cohabiting with blacks and the consequent dangers to sound and healthy administration."[67] He made it clear that any indiscretion would lead to dismissal and asked the resident commissioner to ensure all members of the administration were familiar with their responsibilities.

In Salisbury the subject was raised during the Native Affairs Committee of Inquiry of 1910–1911. A majority of commissioners favored the prohibition of marriages between black women and white men.[68] However, they saw little purpose in legislation unless concubinage was also banned.[69] The attorney general agreed and to prevent the growth of a half-caste population he wanted "ordinary illicit intercourse" to be made punishable. Although the committee made no mention of fears of Black Peril, Tredgold believed the issue was relevant. He told his colleagues: "It is clear, and recent representations from natives themselves have been most insistent on the point, that this intercourse is jeopardising the position of European women in the Territory. I therefore strongly urge that any legislation should include this point."[70] Such views were rarely expressed by public officials.

A number of women's organizations, including the Rhodesian Women's League, the Loyal Women's Guild, and the Women's Franchise Society, sought to improve the physical, intellectual, and cultural conditions in the home and to give women a forum for their social activities. In 1926 a Women's Institute was founded and a year later the Federation of Women's

Institutes of Southern Rhodesia (FWI) was created. The FWI embraced a number of political and philanthropic causes and it would be wrong to suppose that it was preoccupied with Black Peril or miscegenation. However, as was the case with other organizations, the issue of Black Peril was important because it shaped many of the issues taken up by the FWI. White women wanted protection from the threat of sexual assault. But they differed from their husbands, fathers, and brothers in their perception of the causes of Black Peril and therefore of the best means to combat it.

White women participated in public discussion of concubinage; most of their efforts were directed against the immorality ordinances of 1903 and 1916. While the latter was being debated in the Legislative Council both the WCTU and the Women's Franchise Society wrote to the administrator and to members of the council. They protested that the ordinance held women responsible for Black Peril incidents when in fact the source of the problem lay elsewhere: "We feel that the existing danger of this peril is very largely due to the bad example set by many white men in Rhodesia especially in the outside districts, in the use of native women and girls for immoral purposes. It appears to us that the native mind reasons that, if it is fit and proper for the white man to use his women immorally, it cannot be so great a crime for him to use the white women for the same purposes."[71] Once the ordinance was passed groups including the RWL kept up a stream of protest demanding that parallel legislation be passed for white males.

Women's groups pointed out that in the fourteen years from 1903 to 1916 only two women had been convicted under the Immorality Suppression Ordinance for having sex with a black man.[72] By contrast, transgressions by white men were common. In 1921 the RWL ran a campaign for legislation prohibiting concubinage. They gathered a petition, endorsed by the Synod of the Church of England, which was signed by more than half of the white female population.[73] In May the petition was presented in the Legislative Council by John McChlery, who moved that concubinage be made a criminal offense. According to McChlery the existing ordinances were unpopular because they demanded a higher standard of morality from African men than was demanded of whites.[74] He told fellow members that sexual relations between white men and black women had precipitated the rebellion of 1896 and that Black Peril attacks were a form of revenge. McChlery's amendment, like the petition itself, was an attack upon the Immorality Suppression Ordinance and for that reason it antagonized his colleagues.

The most vocal opponent of the motion was Tawse Jollie, the only female member of the chamber. Jollie frequently adopted stances at odds with the women's organizations and often her views revealed more about masculine orthodoxies than do the speeches of her male colleagues. She told the council that during her travels she had never heard the issue of miscegenation discussed and had been surprised when approached on the subject by the RWL. She had declined the League's request to present a petition on its behalf. While she supported the RWL's desire to preserve racial purity, Jollie did not believe in equality of the sexes because she felt there were many instances where women needed protection, not equality. She was also opposed to the idea that equality should be established by law between white and black women. "I consider it is really rather hypocriti-cal," she told the chamber, "to maintain that a native woman is as much degraded by intercourse with a white man as a white woman would be degraded by intercourse with a black man."[75] To protect that favored sta-tus discriminatory legislation was justified. Jollie was certain that every white woman other than a prostitute supported the immorality ordinance and rejected the idea that a white woman could be sexually attracted to a black man: "There was only one class of women to whom that applied, and those were the women who prostituted their sex and their race for money."[76] If, as the League maintained, those laws were harsh on women, that was the price to be paid for stability. From a woman's point of view no sacrifice was too great to prevent the growth of a "bastard" (mixed-race) population.

Jollie acknowledged that isolation encouraged some young men to en-ter into illicit sexual relations, but she believed a more important factor was training in early life. Boys needed discipline and self-control and so the solution lay in the hands of mothers, for it was they who set the moral standard. Jollie suggested that before making a judgment the council need-ed information from native commissioners, magistrates, the police, and certain doctors about the extent of the problem. She moved that a commis-sion be established to investigate the matter.[77]

Premier Charles Coghlan supported Jollie's amendment and justified the suppression ordinance in the following way: "It was not intended to put the white person in a different position from the native. It was because of the fact that a white woman living in a country of this sort was exposed to considerable danger, the converse of which her black sisters were not exposed to at all."[78] While he disapproved of concubinage, Coghlan did not believe that sexual intercourse between black women and white men was a crime against nature in the same way as sodomy or bestiality. Attor-ney General Tredgold defended the legislation because it protected white women; he was at a loss to understand why the League had opposed it. At the end of debate Jollie's proposal that a commission be established was defeated. So too was McChlery's original motion.

The reason for the council's decision is found in Coghlan's speech and in particular in the connection he made between the banning of concubinage and the specter of Black Peril, a connection which at first sight seems strange. The FWI and other women's groups had long argued that the Black Peril "outrages" were provoked by concubinage. They viewed the "outrages" as revenge by black men against the sexual privileges enjoyed by white males. In rejecting McChlery's motion, the council was rejecting that particular explanation of Black Peril while maintaining the right of white men to have sexual relations with black women.

In her speech Jollie managed to combine the idea of a dual mandate with a doctrine about moral purity of a kind then popular in Britain.[79] By characterizing those women who had signed the petition—that is, half of the white female population—as prostitutes, she offered the most candid rendition of the kind of patriarchal orthodoxies which dominated legislative council debate. She also quite explicitly mapped out the ideal of the passive woman who, unlike herself, was confined to the home under the protection of a man. The intensity of her opposition to the RWL's petition was indicative of the extent to which the document was perceived as an attack upon male authority; as she told her colleagues, women did not need equality, they needed protection. Jollie explained concubinage in terms of mothers who had failed to discipline their sons, thereby turning the problem away from white men and back onto white women. Her misogyny was more systematic than that of her male colleagues. That was why she understood so well what was at stake in the RWL's amendment.

Although the administrator opposed any change to the law or the holding of an inquiry, under pressure from the RWL he finally agreed to commission a survey.[80] The Native Affairs Department collected information from district officers. Most officers believed the arrival of more European families had brought pressure to bear on single men, who were less likely to offend as a result. At Salisbury, for example, it was claimed that only seven white men were known to associate habitually with black women and there was only one case of concubinage.[81] In the Bulawayo, Melsetter, Inyanga, and Ruspani districts there was little evidence of vice. By contrast the native commissioner at M'toko observed, "During the time I have been in this district it has never come to my knowledge that the natives are in any way disturbed or alarmed in their minds through interference with their women or girls by white men."[82] He believed that legislation was unnecessary because blacks would rather bring an action for damages than see such men imprisoned. At that time, 1921, native commissioners, like members of the Legislative Council, identified three problems regarding racial hygiene: The most important was concubinage, the next was black-on-white prostitution, and the last was the creation of a mixed-race population. They agreed that miscegenation was a thing of the past and that through marriage the few children produced by such unions would eventually disappear into the black community. After reviewing the evidence the administrator decided there was no need for further action.[83]

It is difficult to assess the accuracy of the Native Affairs Department's estimates. They were probably fanciful, as was indicated by the comment from the M'toko commissioner. White males were the last to admit that concubinage existed; the only sources of information used in the survey came from the Native Affairs Department and the police, both bastions of male authority. The survey was also compromised by the problem of definition with regard to sexual practice. For example, no allowance was made for contact between white males and black prostitutes. We do know that the Coloured population was growing in part because of the activities of white men.[84]

The RWL was not satisfied and in an open letter published in August 1924 it again attacked the existing legislation. It told the *Herald's* readers; "The 1916 ordinance penalises white women who are found guilty of the offence. Such cases are comparatively rare, yet the Ordinance says nothing about the very prevalent practice of white men cohabiting with native women, which, without a doubt, is contributing a large quota to the Black Peril problem."[85] The response from the CID was predictable. According to the department offenses were decreasing. Superintendent J. C. Blundell believed that since the existing law covered crimes such as rape, legislation of the kind used in Northern Australia which forbade sexual relations between white men and black women was unnecessary.[86]

In the following years the League continued to pursue the issue and in a circular distributed in 1925 by the Gwelo branch set out its objections to concubinage.[87] Such liaisons, it argued, damaged the prestige of Europeans and weakened the standing of white women. Black males resented such relations but were powerless to stop them. Miscegenation created a rebellious Coloured race and had a bad effect upon European children who saw white men living openly with "kaffir" women. The League made further representations to members of the Legislative Assembly, claiming that Black Peril was rife and that many cases of assault and criminal injury were not being reported.[88] In an article published in the *Rhodesian* in 1925, Mrs. Greta Bloomhill argued that the situation for white women was almost intolerable: "If she has a baby girl she cannot leave her for a moment. If she has elder daughters, her anxious thoughts follow her to school, to work, and about the home throughout the day. Even if she is childless, her nerves are constantly on edge—she is always in dread of terrible possibilities."[89] The remedy was to outlaw concubinage.[90] It is difficult to know how representative Bloomhill's views were of opinion within the League. We can be sure that they were almost delusional in terms of the actual threat of sexual assault faced by white women.

In its attempts to link Black Peril with concubinage and to have the legislation amended the Women's League faced strong opposition from a male-dominated parliament and bureaucracy. The missions were largely quiescent because they had little to gain by supporting the RWL and much to lose in the way of state patronage. Women also faced opposition from private citizens. Mr. A. Thompson, the manager of Wankie Colliery, wrote to the League setting out his objections to its campaign. He had lived in Rhodesia for many years and what evidence there was suggested that miscegenation was diminishing. "The opinion of the thinking native" he told the League, "is that the white men are the bosses in this country and have a perfect right to take their women, and if they (the natives) were the conquerors they would take the women of the people they conquered and when they pleased."[91] Thompson was adamant that on matters of sex the races should not be treated in the same way. A black woman who consorted with a white man did not lose any status and her marriage prospects were undiminished. In contrast, a white women who consorted with an African, like any "woman of high degree who consorts with a man of low degree[,] is usually a pervert and an outcast."[92] Despite its clumsiness Thompson's letter identified what was at stake in the RWL's campaign. Because it suggested an equivalence between women of both races, any amendment along the lines proposed by the League would have altered practically and symbolically the relations between white men and women.

TERRIBLE POSSIBILITIES

In 1927 the South African parliament passed an immorality act which was designed to discourage sexual contact across racial boundaries.[93] The act incorporated existing legislation forbidding sexual relations between white women and black males and extending it to cover white males and black women. For white men it set penalties of up to five years' jail, while a black woman faced the same penalty as her white sister, namely four years in prison. General Smuts, a one-time and future prime minister, opposed the act, believing public opinion was a better deterrent. He advised Rhodesian Prime Minister Huggins against introducing such legislation.[94] However, the South African law did give encouragement to those women's groups determined to see the existing law amended.

The RWL and the FWI held annual congresses at which a variety of issues were discussed and resolutions taken. At the FWI's 1930 congress, for example, it was resolved that a card indexing system be introduced for all male Africans that documented any criminal convictions; that Africans in villages and towns be subject to regular medical examination to combat the spread of venereal disease; that police protection be provided for white women living in isolated houses; and that bread in Southern Rhodesia be sold in wrappers.[95] The Institutes were more active than the League and under its secretary, Mrs C. Fripp, the FWI kept up a stream of letters and appeals to the premier, to the department of native affairs, and to members of the Legislative Council on a number of issues. Many of the resolutions endorsed in the period from 1927 to 1935 concerned the control of domestic servants, the prevention of venereal disease, and the suppression of concubinage. Each of those issues had its origin in fears of Black Peril.

Women's organizations were divided over the best means to prevent miscegenation, for although the FWI opposed criminalization, the RWL and the Loyal Women's Guild lobbied for a bill based on the South African act.[96] As a result, in 1930 Prime Minister Huggins sought information about the success of the South African law in order to gauge its applicability to Southern Rhodesia. The matter was discussed at length in the party caucus and the general feeling was that since miscegenation was on the wane legislation was unnecessary.[97] That did not end the matter and in May 1930 there was further debate in the Legislative Assembly. Huggins spoke of the fate of half-caste children rather than of the issue of Black Peril, claiming that the number of such births in the colony had risen alarmingly. At the request of the RWL he moved that the legislation be amended to cover relations between white men and black women. The attorney general, like the majority of members, favored the power of public opinion and the proposal was defeated.[98]

After three years of debate an act based on South African precedent was finally drafted. The bill, the Immorality Act of 1931, differed from South African law; it was directed against concubinage rather than against casual sexual relations. It imposed a regime of fines and prison sentences.[99] The bill had various critics, including the chief native commissioner. He believed that while the majority of the African population did not seek "equality of treatment in such matters" educated blacks would use the act

to push for further advantage.[100] Huggins favored legislation both to punish offending males and to ensure that white men be held responsible for
the maintenance of their offspring.[101] Male legislators and white women
viewed concubinage and miscegenation in terms of very different moral
economies and Acting Attorney General Speight was well aware of the
draft's narrow field of application. It was not the kind of bill sought by
Rhodesian women, for it was less a response to the threat of Black Peril
than a means to resolve the problem of who was to be responsible for the
care of Coloured children. Both were unpopular causes and the draft never
reached the house.

In opening the FWI congress at Bulawayo in November 1930 the chair
commented that with regard to the evils of miscegenation there were three
points on which all members agreed: "The horrible degradation of the
white father and through him to us all, as members of the British Empire;
the greatest fear as to the purity of our race in generations to come; and on
the bitter, bitter wrong done to the innocent offspring."[102] An emergency
resolution that the various branches study the question with a view to de-
bating the matter at a future congress was passed unanimously. The honorary secretary, Mrs. Fripp, who was also the Institute's leading intellectual,
prepared two reports on the problem; the first a confidential paper which
she presented in November 1930 to the FWI executive and the second titled
"Miscegenation or God's Step-Children" which was given to a private session at the FWI's conference in the following year.[103]

Fripp told the executive that while the Institute's priority (and that of
government) should be the maintenance of racial purity it should also seek
to redress the wrong done to mixed-race children. To imprison offenders
was uneconomic and un-Christian; a man in jail could not support his family and ex-prisoners could not find work. Instead of ostracizing offenders it
would be far better that they be reformed through accepting responsibility
for their actions. She rejected the idea that legislation of the kind introduced in South Africa in 1927 offered a solution; in the Union most offenders were Afrikaners, or what Fripp called "members of the Transvaal rural
peasant class."[104] Unlike the Afrikaner, "the British race alone had made a
firm stand in favour of racial purity and had very largely and very hon-
ourably kept to this."[105] Quoting from Tacitus on the rectitude of the early
Britons, Fripp suggested that those qualities had been maintained for 2,000
years through the influence of women on British society. All white women
in the colony were, out of instinct, opposed to racial mixing: "This instinct
would seem to be all the same perfectly sound from the scientific point of
view, since it is probably physiologically unwise to mate two race types so

widely different physically."[106] She found further comfort in the fact that
the later colonial period coincided with the ascendancy in Britain of the
"Great Middle Class" which encouraged good manners and emphasized
the purity of mind and body.

In "Miscegenation or God's Step-Children," Fripp identified two categories of transgressors. Casual offenders were not committed to vice and
formed such relations out of moral laxity. Hardened offenders had "gone
kaffir" and were beyond redemption.[107] World War One had let loose a
flood of sexual immorality which had encouraged casual offenders and it
was that problem which, according to Fripp, government should address.
She supported the ordinance of 1903 which protected white women from
the "demoralising effect on the native mind of white prostitutes selling
themselves to natives."[108] To combat the activities of black prostitutes (and
hence of miscegenation) it was necessary to stop the flood of woman who
were moving into the towns: "Merely to penalise the white male without
attempting to remove the growing menace of the immoral native woman in
our towns is to omit to extirpate the root of the evil. Remove the immoral
native woman, and you remove the temptation from the average man."[109]
Fripp wanted every African woman to carry a pass which could only be
issued at the request of her guardian.

While Fripp and Jollie differed over the means by which to suppress
concubinage, they both subscribed to a number of masculine orthodoxies.
Most notably, both believed that the threat of Black Peril was attributable
to the activities of white prostitutes. Fripp believed that any breach of racial boundaries could unleash a flood of sexual violence. In taking black
customers, white prostitutes lowered the prestige of their sisters, thereby
making all white women more vulnerable to the threat of sexual assault.
Like most members of the FWI, Fripp was also fearful of the growth of
urban black communities and she believed the best way to reduce their size
was to exclude women from locations. Like her colleagues, Fripp would
have had little if any contact with black women and she readily adopted
the misogynist views which were so often expressed about them in the
male-dominated legislative council. Fripp was less conventional than Jollie
in her views on racial hygiene, white destiny, and the threat of degeneration. Least orthodox of all was her conviction that in white women instinct
and science coincided.

Lobbying by the FWI continued and between 1930 and 1934 the question of legislation was considered by government on a number of occasions. In 1931 Prime Minister H. U. Moffat, who favored criminalization,
found that even within his own party there was considerable opposition to

the idea. Some members warned they would vote against legislation in the assembly.[110] The attorney general pointed out the practical difficulties of distinguishing between cohabitation and other forms of intercourse; evasion would be easy and such a law would bring the state into ridicule.[111] Despite such discouragement, three years later Huggins, who was sympathetic to the views of the FWI, again raised the matter at a caucus meeting. Once again he was defeated.[112]

CONCLUSION

In Southern Rhodesia women were excluded from positions of authority within the state, in medicine, and in the law. In response they focused their attentions upon racial hygiene and the maintenance of standards and were vocal about issues which were perceived as either antidotes to or causes of the threat of Black Peril. In the process they had some success in subverting male discourse. After 1910 tolerance of concubinage clashed with Colonial Office policy and women's organizations used the opportunity to press for revision of the morality legislation. However, gender did not guarantee solidarity and women's groups were divided over the best means to combat sexual threat. Like the Rhodesian Women's League and the Loyal Women's League the Federation of Women's Institutes wanted miscegenation discouraged, but unlike its rivals the FWI opposed legal penalties because they believed that community attitudes and the influence of middle-class culture were sufficient deterrence. Constance Fripp's "Great Middle Class" was a panacea to the conflict-ridden character of white society, a counterweight to the Afrikaners, poor whites, continentals, Coloureds, the morally flawed, and, in the remote distance, the blacks who stood eternally outside its gates.

The conflict over concubinage was particularly complex. It conflated the maintenance of racial boundaries with attempts to fortify the authority of men over women. It also provoked fears which were oblique. The subject of blackmail, for example, which was raised regularly in CID correspondence, at FWI meetings, and during council debate, was one of the justifications given by male legislators for their refusal to amend the morality ordinances. At an executive committee meeting of the Institutes held in July 1929 Mrs. W. Benjies warned that if miscegenation were made a criminal offense a conviction would drive many white men "to the dogs" and she asked delegates to consider the effect that a jail sentence would have upon the wife or mother of an offender. She was particularly disturbed that such a law would give native women the opportunity to blackmail their white partners.[113] That prospect suggested that the skills of literacy being spread by mission and African schools would be used for criminal purposes. Like so many of the fears which plagued whites, the threat of blackmail was groundless. There is no evidence in the returns from the Salisbury High Court of a single case of blackmail involving a black woman and a white man: The source of the anxiety has to be found elsewhere. It seems likely that behind the rhetoric lay a more realistic fear of a black middle class, which at that time was beginning to emerge. That class was distinguished by its literacy in English and its ability to challenge the social and economic privileges which whites wished to monopolize. It was the specter of such a class which found expression in settler fantasies about blackmail.[114]

Concubinage was also closely allied to notions of whiteness. But that notion was in itself gendered. Ann Stoler has argued that in southeast Asia concubinage was tolerated only so long as European identity and supremacy were stable; whenever it came into question white males shifted to the use of prostitutes or marriage with European women.[115] The opposite was true in Southern Rhodesia. Concubinage was proscribed at the moment when, for the first time, the spreading influence of homes and family life gave greater solidity to the white community. It was censured by women's organizations in order to enhance white supremacy rather than to shore up its decline. White males had a very different view of the dangers of miscegenation, at least where it involved themselves and black women. That was why the FWI's attempts to have concubinage criminalized produced such a complex politics. The campaign was seen by the legislative council as a direct attack upon male authority, which it was. The FWI wanted the codes of sexual conduct changed so that under the law white men would be treated the same way as white women. It was a kind of equality male elites did not want. Perhaps most important of all, the FWI's proposal attributed Black Peril to concubinage.

White women were blamed for Black Peril by the CID, by members of the Legislative Council, by the press, and by much of the administration. For that reason they were subject to discriminatory laws aimed at curtailing their sexual impulses. The moral panics focused attention on their failings as managers of servants, as homemakers, and as citizens and increased the authority of white men over them. Women lived in fear of sexual assault and even though that fear was unjustified it curtailed their access to social space. Their fear also sealed women off from contact with indigenous society; their views about Africans were even more fantasy-ridden than those held by white males.

Women were encouraged by men to blame the victims of Black Peril for their indiscretions and to monitor their own behavior for any sign of impropriety. While they had no wish to change the law regarding sexual relations between white women and black men they did want concubinage made illegal. That cause was doomed to failure by the power of male legislators. Women pressed for the introduction of black females into domestic service but the economic imperatives of a segregated labor system, the authority of husbands and fathers over the labor of young women, and their own fears of the sexuality of African females saw those demands frustrated. In lobbying to outlaw concubinage white women acted according to a particular view of the causes of Black Peril. In rejecting their demands male elites relied upon a contrary interpretation of sexual threat. Those differences formed one of the boundaries separating their constructions of racial politics.

SEVEN

DOMESTIC LABOR

By 1916 the Black Peril panics were over. With one exception the most important trials had been held and the worst offenders sentenced to death. And yet fears of Black Peril continued to haunt the white community. The story of Black Peril accusations is also the story of domestic labor. Most offenders were servants and discussion of how to end sexual threat harked back invariably to the recruitment and employment of domestic workers. Any discussion of servants always involved the issues of segregation and migrant labor.

In Southern Rhodesia segregation was based primarily upon land and labor policies. The Land Apportionment Act of 1930 precluded Africans from owning land in white areas and was consistent with the exclusion of blacks from urban centers that had been enforced from the first days of colonization. Blacks could live in towns only while employed and most who did so worked as servants. A large proportion of servants were "alien natives" from Northern Rhodesia, Nyasaland, or Mozambique. They were favored over Shona and Ndebele, the two major ethnic groups, because they were supposed to be better suited to such work. The system of migratory labor was always a compromise between competing interests. African laborers were discriminating. Men were willing to travel hundreds of miles to find the best pay and work conditions. They would withdraw their labor from a market the moment better opportunities arose.[1] Settlers wanted access to workers but were fearful of urban populations. Whites justified segregation by claiming that it preserved indigenous culture and was a panacea to racial tension. Missionaries were divided over the merits of such a policy. Some believed segregation protected blacks from the worst aspects of an alien culture and offered the best chance for African development. Others felt that it ruined the family life of black laborers. Regardless of the merits of either position, a model for segregation was found in the division of white households between masters and servants.

In nineteenth-century Britain the keeping of servants was important to the aspirations of middle-class families. In a provincial city like York almost one third of such households had servants.[2] Domestic service reproduced class privilege; one of the intangible benefits servants provided for employers was confirmation of their social achievement. Servants were a-ware of their subordination. In her 1925 study of domestic labor Violet Firth observed that to be a servant was painful to a young woman's self-respect: "A mistress does not demand of her servant work only," Firth reminded her readers, "she also demands a certain manner, a manner which shall clearly indicate her superiority and the inferiority of the woman who takes her wages."[3] It was for that reason that servants were expected to be socially invisible when they waited on tables. The subordination whites demanded of servants in colonial contexts was as profound, but for a vari-ety of reasons it was rarely achieved. Most settlers in Rhodesia were re-cruited from the middle and lower middle classes of Britain and South Africa and they brought with them well-developed traditions of subordin-ation. Those traditions included the ideal of "the great house," with its rigid hierarchies between servants and masters. In southern Africa that ideal was so important to the self-image of whites that the employment of servants was maintained even in times of labor shortage.[4]

In Africa, as in Britain, there were conventions governing the manage-ment of servants. The Federation of Women's Institutes of Southern Rho-desia (FWI) took care to instruct new arrivals on how to behave. A pamphlet based upon material supplied by the Federation was eventually distributed by the Department of Public Relations to ensure that white women immi-grants acted appropriately.[5] It informed new arrivals they must learn "kitch-en kaffir" and avoid indiscretions. Small daughters were not to be left alone or to appear naked in front of servants; women were to make their own beds and wash their own sheets. The slightest familiarity had to be avoided and women were never to appear in a state of undress. Public debate about the recruitment and management of servants was shaped by the moral pan-ics. But perhaps the most interesting questions which arise from the history of domestic labor are why so many servants were employed even dur-ing times of labor shortage and why male servants were not replaced by women.

DOMESTIC LABOR

Servants offered middle-class white women the chance to socialize and indulge in avocations such as painting and music.[6] That pattern was estab-lished early and persisted throughout the colonial period. On his arrival as a young man in Salisbury in the 1940s, Lawrence Vambe was surprised by the dependence of white families upon domestic labor: "Black servants were a necessity of life to every white person in his home, at his office and in every sphere except in his thinking. Black servants worked in white bedrooms, kitchens, dining-rooms and gardens. Black nannies, nursed, washed, clothed, and fed white children and also gave them the love and affection which their parents were reluctant to show them."[7] Servants were the only African males to enter white households. The idea that settler women were more racist than men emerged from the nature of their relationships with domestic workers. In *The Grass Is Singing,* Doris Lessing took up the theme that white women victimized their servants as revenge for their own demoralization in a world so dominated by men.[8] Both of those ideas were prominent in the explanations white males offered for concerns about Black Peril and both appeared in public inquiries into domestic labor.

In order to prevent cross-race physical contact a system of petty apartheid was used in restaurants, hospitals, hotels, railway carriages, and even jails. And yet the domestic setting was filled with African servants, cooks, gardeners, and nannies. Their presence meant that in white homes social distance came to have an even greater importance than it did in Britain.[9]

In both Southern and Northern Rhodesia (but not in the Cape) domestic labor was a male province and remained so into the 1980s.[10] Servants comprised the largest section of the urban labor force; they were the only group of African workers with whom all whites came into contact. The employment of male servants structured the composition of urban black communities; from 1893 the Salisbury municipality forbade Africans, with the exception of servants, to reside within the city limits. As the size of the labor force increased, that pattern became entrenched. According to the census of 1911 there were 6,300 African men in Salisbury but only 271 African women.[11] Domestic workers were privy to intimate details about the households in which they worked, knowledge which no doubt shaped the opinion Africans had of settlers.[12] In Rhodesia servants worked under the terms of labor laws which had their origins in eighteenth-century Europe. The Masters and Servants Ordinance of 1901 covered all aspects of the buying and selling of labor.[13] Under its provisions the term "servant" included domestic workers, farm laborers, and those employed in trade and manufacture. The only category of labor which fell outside its ambit was skilled work, which was reserved for Europeans. The ordinance provided the legal framework that bound workers to employers and laid down a variety of penal provisions for failure to comply with a contract. The ordinance specified twelve varieties of misconduct, including failure to commence work at a stipulated time, being absent or intoxicated, not perform-

ing work or performing it carelessly, making illicit use of a master's property, or disobeying a command. Clause eight allowed for a fine of 4 pounds
or one month's jail "if [a servant] shall be abusive or insulting, either by
language or conduct, to his master or his master's wife or children or to
any person lawfully placed by his master in authority over him."[14] In addition to jail and fines, penalties included a sparse diet and solitary confine-
ment. While the ordinance provided penalties for masters who withheld
wages, such provisions were rarely enforced. In Kenya, the Masters and
Servants Ordinance of 1923 contained a clause protecting black women
from molestation by male employers. However, the fine for the offense was
so small it was unlikely to have discouraged offenders.[15]

Under Rhodesian law there was no right of escape from a cruel or
unfair employer. After serving a prison sentence for failing to honor a contract, a servant was compelled to return to serve out that contract. If he
refused, another prison term was prescribed. The force of the law was enhanced by the pass ordinance of 1902, which made it compulsory for African males to carry an identification document bearing the holder's name
and employment history. When a worker entered or left a job his employer
signed and dated the certificate. If the pass was unsigned a worker was
subject to arrest. The pass laws worked in tandem with the management of
urban locations, but the system was never effective in regulating the movement of labor.

Their rates of pay and conditions of work meant that servants were a
privileged sector of the working class. In 1910 the average servant was
paid 15 shillings per month, which by 1920 had risen to 24 shillings; rates
for cooks were higher.[16] The monthly contracts that servants made were
also an advantage over the longer contracts used in mines and farms. Short
contracts made it easier for domestics to escape a bad employer. Throughout the early colonial period the Rhodesian economy was unstable, yet
the demand for domestic labor was almost insatiable. By 1904 there were
7,000 servants; seven years later there were almost as many servants as
laborers. From that time servants always represented at least the third largest sector of wage labor.[17] The transience of employment meant that in
addition to those who at any one time were employed there were many
more with experience of domestic work. In the period from 1904 to 1914
there was on average one servant for every two Europeans and after World
War One servants were in even greater demand.[18] Until the mid-1920s
white farms and mines were periodically stricken with labor shortages,
which made the presence of male servants in white households more significant. The author of a letter published in the *Rhodesian Herald* in June

1913 complained of the waste: "These natives should be at work in the mines and in the fields, instead of dusting the furniture, sweeping floors, making beds, and pushing perambulators. The houseboy has become a sort of maid of all work, and his physical energy is wasted in the performance of domestic tasks, which in most other countries and in the older and more settled parts of South Africa, are performed by women."[19] Such views were common, yet the pattern of labor remained unchanged.

White women often complained that their servants were lazy and inefficient, that they pilfered food and were insubordinate. They also complained that they spread disease. Despite such grievances servants offered some compensation for the hardships of colonial life. Their presence freed woman from heavy labor, which was important if white families were to enjoy an elevated standard of living. Servants also accorded whites a sense of having bettered themselves, for in Edwardian England only the privileged could afford domestic workers and of those only the wealthy employed male servants. The presence of servants allowed whites to express their superiority in a setting in which black males were disadvantaged through culture, experience, and gender. It is significant that male servants were expected to do female work which a white man would have felt uncomfortable in performing, a fact alluded to in the guide produced for new settlers by the Department of Public Relations.[20]

Servants were expected to possess a wide a range of skills. They were required to have an understanding of English and a good knowledge of white domestic arrangements. Their work included cooking, child care, cleaning, washing, and gardening. Duties also involved waiting at table— and standing at attention while doing so.[21] Work began at 5 A.M. and the only time off was usually a half day on Sundays. A minority of domestic workers were provided with accommodation in a "boy's" *kia* located behind the employer's home. Many *kias* had five rooms to house a cook, a gardener, a nursemaid, a housemaid, and a laundry attendant. Employers were free to enter a *kia* at will but servants were not free to have friends or relatives visit. Few servants were allowed to have their families live with them and as a result they saw their wives or children only during holidays. Most servants lived in locations, which lengthened their working days considerably. In addition they were faced with the danger of walking home at night. Servants had few fellow workers and their isolation increased their vulnerability at the hands of employers. The offenses for which servants were most severely punished included being late, burning food, burning clothes while ironing, or failing to set a table correctly. The *lingua franca* was chillapalapa, or, as white employers termed it, "kitchen kaffir." It was

a language of commands fabricated from Zulu, English, Shona, and Afrikaans. Servants were rarely called by their correct names and the use of
demeaning appellations such as "Sixpence" or "Lucky" was common. The
forms of address, the wearing of uniforms, and the use of "kitchen kaffir"
were but some of the devices used by settler employers to try to enforce
subordination. It was a wider repertoire than was available to metropolitan employers, but still it failed to achieve compliance.

The travails of settlers in dealing with servants were prominent in early
Rhodesian fiction. Gertrude Page, who achieved commercial success with a
series of novels published before World War One, wrote of the stupidity of
servants in misusing clothes, furniture, cooking utensils, and towels, all
objects associated with respectability. Page also wrote with candor about
the abuse of laborers. She has one male character beating a servant for
wiping his face on a tea towel in a passage that has no significance except
to emphasize the tribulations of pioneer life for whites.[22] We cannot know
how common such beatings were or how often they led to injury or death.
The evidence suggests that police, magistrates, and attorneys general were
loath to prosecute; few cases of assault reached court. Records do show
that a servant could be killed for a minor infraction. In February 1915, for
example, a preliminary hearing was held into the death of a servant named
Tom at Hillside, a Salisbury suburb.[23] Tom's employer, Mrs. Samuels, told
the court that he had been threatening to leave her employ and had been
making menacing gestures. To frighten him she fired her gun, accidentally
hitting him in the head. A charge of culpable homicide was issued but the
attorney general decided not to proceed and the case was dropped.[24] While
the circumstances of Tom's death may have been unusual, Mrs. Samuels's
attitude was not. In an early Rhodesian novel one main character describes
the qualities most valued in a servant: "A very stupid boy will often end by
making a good servant, because, his head being entirely empty of ideas,
becomes imbued with those you put into it, and he will therefore, with
parrot-like rigidity, perform regularly whatever you have taught him."[25]
Such contempt, like the behavior of Mrs. Samuels, was a flimsy disguise for
the remarkable dependence of white households upon black labor.

Servants used a range of strategies to protect themselves against employers. Resistance took the form of desertion, theft, sabotage, the defac-
ing of passes, and the temporary withdrawal of labor. Petty theft was common and it was often used as revenge. Women stole cutlery, dresses, food,
and sheets, while men were given to stealing bicycles.[26]

Despite its risks and hardships, domestic service was attractive to males.
Servants enjoyed a better diet than other workers and they were often given

rations such as milk and small amounts of meat. They also received cast-off clothes. The major appeal of such work, however, was that it was less hazardous than other forms of employment. Between 1903 and 1911 the numbers employed in mines increased dramatically.[27] Like farming, the profitability of mines was erratic. To cut costs, owners and managers reduced wages and the money spent on accommodation, medical care, food, and compensation for injury. Compounds were crowded, sanitation was poor, and there was a lack of properly cooked food, especially meat and vegetables. As a result the death rate among miners in Southern Rhodesia was higher than in South Africa. The major causes of death were not accidents, but illnesses such as tuberculosis, pneumonia, scurvy, and dysentery.[28] Charles Van Onselen has estimated that between 1900 and 1933 over 30,000 miners lost their lives, 27,000 of them from disease.[29] In addition to the threat of illness, workers had to cope with the isolation of most mines and the frequency with which "boss boys" and white managers assaulted them. In such a climate domestic service was an attractive alternative.

THE PANICS AND THEIR AFTERMATH

At the height of Black Peril panics newspapers were flooded with letters that criticized white women for their dependence upon servants. In January 1911 one correspondent told readers of the *Rhodesian Herald* that women should do manual labor as they would in England: "I have seen many cases of good, hardworking girls who, coming abroad to marry, have found the relaxation from the drudgery of the scullery or typewriter so pleasant, that they go to the other extreme and try to do nothing and do it well."[30] Another anonymous writer complained, "All right-thinking people will agree that the native engaged in domestic service is allowed too much freedom of action and, until it is curtailed, we shall have the unsavoury 'Black peril' in our homes."[31] One citizen suggested that if landlords were compelled to supply water to each household women could do without servants and there would be no threat of Black Peril.[32] Even men who otherwise supported women's rights condemned women for their poor management of servants. In May 1916 a meeting sponsored by the Girls Friendly Society, the Women's Franchise Union, and the Presbyterian Womens Association was held to protest the proposed immorality and indecency ordinance. Among those who spoke was the Archdeacon of Salisbury, the Rev. Etheridge. He told the audience that although he too opposed the legislation he was appalled by the criminal negligence of some women in their management of servants.[33] They would allow servants to serve them in their bedrooms and would even appear in a semi-naked state in front of male servants.

In its confidential report of 1916 the CID questioned the advisability of employing males.[34] The department suggested that since there were insufficient female workers available domestic service should be confined to married males, indigenous unmarried Africans, and boys under sixteen years. Certain jobs such as chambermaid, nursemaid, or laundrymaid should never be performed by men and in isolated areas only females should be employed, the CID argued.[35] The CID acknowledged that to enable women to live in locations or on white premises would require changes to both housing and sanitation. It would also have involved a reconstruction of urban social space. The CID was not the first to suggest the employment of female domestics as an antidote to so-called Black Peril.

Four years earlier a Native Affairs Committee had held an inquiry into social conditions in the colony. Most of the topics discussed, including taxation and the supply of labor, had commercial significance, but the committee also made comment on African marriage patterns and standards of morality. The Native Affairs Department feared that if left unsupervised African women would lapse morally and spread venereal disease: "The immorality of women, both married and single, in the vicinity of mines and other industrial centres, is a growing danger to the future welfare, both moral and physical of the native races."[36] To solve that problem the final report released in 1911 recommended that African girls be trained for domestic work in state-run boarding schools.[37] In Salisbury and Bulawayo alone there were over 6,000 servants and if such work were to be performed by women it would free men for productive labor.[38] There was no evidence to support the department's claims that black women were spreading venereal disease. At that time the incidence of infection among single black males living in urban locations was probably lower than that among servicemen in the British armed forces. Ironically, one of the most likely conduits for infection among black women was white males.

The committee found some support for their program and in July 1911 the chief native commissioner of Matabeleland, Herbert Taylor, suggested that farm schools be established to train African girls. "The girls are quite willing to learn domestic work," he wrote, "and for obvious reasons they are far more suited for work as servants, nurses, maids etc. than the male natives."[39] He was sure that if proper supervision and accommodation were provided there would be no objections from parents or guardians. Besides diverting women from a life of vice such a scheme would release male labor, which was sorely needed elsewhere. Although Taylor's suggestion was ignored, the debate continued sporadically for years. Behind such proposals stood the ever-present shadow of Black Peril. The management of servants was always associated with danger. Over time the perceived threat shifted from fears of Black Peril to the fear that venereal infection would be transmitted by domestic laborers.

White families were afraid of contracting diseases such as syphilis and gonorrhea from servants who handled crockery or cutlery. From 1910 there were repeated calls for government to monitor the health of domestics. The most tangible result of those demands came in the Natives Registration Ordinance of 1918.[40] Under the legislation, Africans applying for registration were subject to compulsory medical examination. Any person who failed to comply was liable to a fine of up to 10 pounds or three months' imprisonment. The ordinance, however, only applied in those municipalities where the administrator was satisfied that medical staff were available. Because of a lack of funds the provisions were not implemented for a further twenty years. During that interim the issue was raised repeatedly by women's organizations.

During the 1920s the threat black male servants posed to their white employers was raised by various public interest groups, including the Rhodesian Women's League and the Federation of Women's Institutes. A public meeting held at Gwelo in March 1925 that was attended by some two hundred white men and women demanded the introduction of a Native Servants Employment Act to combat Black Peril assaults.[41] Following that meeting, and another at Bulawayo in July, the Rhodesian Women's League wrote to the attorney general demanding an amendment to the pass laws. The League wanted all adult males seeking domestic work to have their fingerprints recorded; those free of venereal disease and who had not committed an offense against a white woman would have a mark to that effect entered on their pass.[42] The Bulawayo CID opposed the scheme. Fingerprinting had been used for some time with "alien natives" and had proven both expensive and difficult to implement; furthermore, according to the CID, there was no evidence that it had been effective.[43]

The early debates about servants were initiated by men who were critical of the failure of women to discipline domestic workers. By the early 1920s the terms of debate shifted as women took the initiative. The disciplining of servants became a battleground between white men and women. A letter published in November 1929 from a member of the Rhodesian Women's League complained of the impossibility of finding good servants, a problem the author attributed to the cohabitation of white men with black women. Servants were insolent because their respect for whites had been diminished by miscegenation; the author suggested that unless government addressed the issue it would suffer the penalty at the next election.[44]

THE FEDERATION OF WOMEN'S INSTITUTES

During the 1920s various women's organizations campaigned for the employment of female laborers. Women's groups had for some years been vocal about the threat of Black Peril and as the managers of households they had a special interest in the recruitment of domestic labor. The FWI, which was founded in 1927, took up the issue with enthusiasm and in 1930 compiled its own report on the subject. The Institutes were particularly concerned about the employment of African males in hospitals and hostels where white women were domiciled and it wanted a government inquiry into the practice. To that end it canvassed the opinion of various prominent men, including the mayor of Bulawayo, the Anglican bishop, missionaries, and members of parliament.[45] The FWI report was based on the fantasy that there was a pool of girls of marriageable age who were available for employment in white households. The report is indicative of just how little white women knew about indigenous society. Black women's labor was vital to the reproduction of rural communities: At the least the loss of their labor would have lowered food production. Besides, black women married at such a young age that there was simply no time between childhood and marriage for many of them to enter wage labor markets.

Reformers who hoped to convince women to employ female domestic workers used a variety of arguments to make their case, even as they pointed to some of the potential problems such change might bring. Like his Synod, Bishop Edwards opposed the use of males in hostels and he wanted an end to the employment of men in private homes. He acknowledged that such a change would take time and that an influx of black women into urban areas would have a devastating effect upon indigenous family life.[46] The mayor of Bulawayo, Mr. W. H. Peard, favored regular medical checks to ensure that servants were free of disease. Several of the FWI's respondents commented that domestic service would have a civilizing influence upon African girls. Mrs. C. Fripp, a leading spokesperson for the FWI, suggested that decent white employment would allow girls to see the advantages of a "white marriage" where a man and woman were partners.[47]

The strongest case in favor of change came from Tawse Jollie. Jollie agreed that the way to end the threat of Black Peril was to employ African women. Besides removing an immediate threat, there were psychological advantages in having female servants. "No native would attempt to rape a white woman if a woman of his own race was anywhere near," argued Jollie. "The presence of any of his own race would deter him not only for fear of detection but for psychological reasons but of course this protection would only be secured if the girl slept in the same house."[48] Jollie believed the rates of pay for males were too high and that women could be paid a lower wage. She had herself for many years used female servants who slept "in the large airy kitchen, have a sort of scullery where they change their clothes and cook their food on the kitchen fire or if convenient on a fire outside."[49]

A minority of those surveyed by the FWI opposed the use of female labor. C. L. Carbutt of Bulawayo, who two years later would chair a government inquiry into domestic service, was sure that Black Peril had its cause in male servants. Even so he was opposed to the employment of women because their immorality would degrade white men.[50] The Rev. Bertram Barnes of St. Augustine's mission, Penhalonga, agreed that girls were more strongly swayed by sexual desire than boys of the same age and were slower in adapting to white civilization. He believed that in the towns they would be open to many dangers and their parents had good reason to object to their entering wage labor.[51]

Like Carbutt and the Rev. Barnes, the native commissioner, Selwyn Bazeley, was concerned about Black Peril and although he supported the employment of women he offered what was the most forceful argument against them. Bazeley observed that some white women forgot that "native" males had strong sexual passions and so the obvious solution was to employ women.[52] Bazeley cautioned, however, that such a change would create further problems. "It is stated not without some show of reason that the native female is a mere animal as regards sexual morality. She is said to be non-moral rather than immoral. There is also the possibility of miscegenation. Some fear that the morals of the younger European men would be corrupted. It is pointed out that a native girl cannot be locked up at night. If she wishes she can always get out the window."[53] Bazeley argued that in the United States the use of female servants had not led to miscegenation and that "it is surely an illogical mind which regards this imaginary danger as equal to the real evil which we term Black Peril."[54] There was, he believed, no comparison between the terrible suffering of a white woman who had been attacked by a black man and the mild disapproval which arose when a black girl had a liaison with a white man. Besides solving the problem of Black Peril the introduction of female labor would increase the virility of African men and enhance their capacity for hard work. "It [domestic labor] tends to render them effeminate and to sap their physical and mental energy. It has been noted that on their return to their kraals they refuse to assist in the lands or any other heavy work."[55] Paradoxically, domestic labor made black men both sexually threatening and effeminate in the minds of some Southern Rhodesians.

Using a mixture of conventions about race, gender, labor, and sexual conduct Bazeley identified two possible vices arising from the employment of servants; there was Black Peril, which he saw as a real threat, and concubinage, which he did not. The connection between Black Peril and concubinage, a favorite theme of women's organizations, was rarely acknowledged by men and yet it was the point from which two different models of racial hygiene devolved. To Bazeley, as to most white males, the threat of Black Peril was more important than the consequences of concubinage, and for that reason he wanted women servants to replace men.

Many respondents referred to the need to supervise servants, who would lapse morally the moment they were left idle. However, there was little mention of urbanization. The FWI's correspondents were oblivious to the ways in which the rural economy subsidized urban male wages and allowed for the reproduction of labor. They also ignored the age of girls and their paths to marriage, which barred their entry into domestic service. Discussion of the need for social control was focused instead upon inherent passions and in particular upon the sexual desires of black men (Black Peril) and black women (concubinage). The FWI's informants agreed that it was the responsibility of the state, the churches, and employers to subdue sexual license. Sometimes the idea was applied historically to themselves (Europeans) who had achieved civilization and contemporaneously to Africans who had not. The impression conveyed by the FWI's report was of a frightening world in which the only defense against chaos was unrelenting vigilance.

The FWI identified two problems in the employment of female servants. First, the movement of young women to urban centers would have affected the structure of the family, thereby undermining the authority of patriarchs. Second, there was the sexual threat which the presence of African women in European households would pose to white men. In Victorian and Edwardian Britain the abuse of working girls by middle-class employers was common, but such offenders were rarely convicted of any crime.[56] That precedent gave the FWI reason to believe that miscegenation, an issue about which it had long campaigned, would follow the introduction of female labor. And yet not one respondent suggested that male employers would harass black women. In its final report the FWI chose to ignore that possibility.

THE CARBUTT INQUIRY

In 1932 the government finally conceded to the FWI's lobbying and held an inquiry, chaired by C. L. Carbutt, Superintendent of Natives at Bulawayo, into the employment of "native female domestic labor in urban white households." Hearings were conducted at Umtali, Bulawayo, and Salisbury. Over fifty witnesses were interviewed, including senior administrators, missionaries, medical officers, and a small number of Africans and Coloreds. The Institutes wanted to remove the threat of Black Peril from their homes; that ostensibly was the reason for the inquiry.

Neither the FWI nor any government department suggested setting up training programs for African males; yet it was always assumed that women would have to be trained. It was also assumed that women could not be housed in *kias* of the kind used for men. The churches and missions were concerned about the role they would be expected to play in the training of servants. There were also concerns about the effects that the employment of women would have upon indigenous society. The Rev. Sketchley of Bulawayo opposed the use of male servants: "We always have to remember," Sketchley commented, "the somewhat low position of women in native life, and I think there is a good deal, maybe subconscious, which rather tends to facilitate a dangerous contact between natives and white women."[57] Although the Rev. Neville Jones of the Hope Fountain mission was confident that female labor would solve the problem of Black Peril, he did not want the missions to become involved in training girls.[58] Similarly, Sister Lois of St. Monica's mission in Umtali had no objections to girls entering domestic service, provided that the conditions were right. She reminded the inquiry that the proper role of missionaries was to train young women to be good mothers and to raise the status of the African people; it was not to provide a labor exchange for white families.[59]

The Rev. Mussell of Epworth Mission believed it premature if not impossible for women to enter domestic labor. He reminded the inquiry that parents were opposed to their daughters becoming servants where they would be exposed to the dangers of prostitution.[60] Furthermore, because girls married between the ages of sixteen and twenty they would not be available for such work for any period of time. He suggested it would be best if white women did more work themselves. Two senior Anglican clerics, Bishop Paget and Archdeacon Christalowe, also spoke against the proposal, commenting that such an innovation would do great damage to African society. Paget observed that when two races came together there was a tendency for both to degenerate.[61]

The inquiry was established to placate the FWI, but women constituted a minority of those who gave evidence and they exerted little influence over the final report. Mrs. Fripp, a leading advocate of measures to combat Black Peril, gave both oral evidence and made a written submission.[62] She told the committee that the FWI wanted government to take control of native locations (which were administered by municipalities) and to establish suitable hostels and recreation centers for the training of girls. Those centers would provide education in domestic skills and English, thereby ensuring that women would replace men as domestic workers.[63] In her written evidence Mrs. Fripp commented that domestic work developed the "native's" mind and that it would bring money and employment to women which otherwise were available only through prostitution.

Fripp referred to the "constant repression" to which white women and girls were subject because of the presence of African males in white households. There was much syphilis in the black community and the FWI feared disease was being spread by servants. She told the inquiry: "Some women feel so preyed upon in their minds (I think many women feel this) that they suffer a constant nervous dread of such infection for themselves and their families and (knowing little about the subject) they are prey to terrors which are very unwholesome for their minds."[64] Fripp suggested that the threat of syphilis caught from cutlery or crockery would be lessened by the employment of women. She favored government control of the introduction of female labor with various functions being taken out of the hands of the municipalities. In Fripp's hands the chimerical threat of Black Peril was easily elided into the equally groundless fear of male servants spreading venereal disease. Even so, her speech was indicative of the anxiety about syphilis within the ranks of the FWI.

In Southern Rhodesia, as in contemporary Britain, such ill-informed views about the transmission of venereal disease were commonplace. What was notable in Fripp's speech was the slippage between Black Peril and the idea that male servants could infect innocent white households. In reality black men were the least likely conduits for bringing syphilis into white homes. A far greater threat was posed by illicit sexual relations between the husbands of FWI members and black women. And yet even the most vehement members of the FWI, including Mrs. Fripp, never acknowledged that possibility.

In spite of the professed altruism of the participants there was a venal quality to much of the testimony. Employers wanted domestics who could perform a range of complex tasks, live in poor housing without access to their families, and do so without complaint. Mrs. Stewart, the wife of a medical officer, told the committee, "I employ one girl as a nursemaid. I leave the girl in the house, locked in, if I go out at night, and I go out any time during the day and leave the girl in the garden with the children."[65] Mrs. Russell of Bulawayo complained that servants wanted excessive wages and were not satisfied with a diet of ground maize, or mealy meal.[66]

Among those who supported a change was the assistant native commissioner of Bulawayo, Mr. Stead. He commented that white women were often left alone with male servants and so the recruitment of women was necessary for their protection. The employment of females would also release African men for work on farms and mines. He wanted the government to create separate townships in place of locations which would see part of each town set aside for blacks.[67] Mr. Lanning, who was the superintendent of natives at the Bulawayo location, supported the replacement of all males whom he believed were dangerous by virtue of their gender and race.[68] He also commented that African families were reluctant to have their daughters enter domestic service because of the threat to their moral welfare. He avoided any mention of the prospect of sexual exploitation by employers.

The hearings, like the earlier report by the FWI, involved a deft inversion with regard to the moral order of colonial society. One of the most obvious problems in introducing female labor was the sexual behavior of white men, yet the problem was not mentioned by any witness nor was it cited in the final report. Its place was taken by discussion of the bad influence of African women on white children, their interest in seducing white men, and the problems of preventing them from falling into prostitution. As was the case with Black Peril, the supposed vices of blacks became a medium for demonstrating the virtues of whites.

During the hearings there was much comment on the effects of close contact between domestic workers and white children. Several witnesses remarked that such contact impaired the child's development and should be stopped but they were unsure about what effect the presence of female servants would have. Mr. C. Bullock of Salisbury told the committee: "It is platitudinous to state that the association of nurse and child must have enormous psychological results. There may be no deliberate inculcation but if the nature of the nurse is of an immoral or even non-moral type the child will assimilate without direct instruction. That is an immediate danger."[69] For that reason he believed males were preferable. The practice of sending children to boarding schools or to Britain for education was common among parents who could afford to do so. Besides the educational advantages, it precluded white children from learning vernacular languages. Even a child as intellectually independent as Doris Lessing never learned Shona. Children who could not speak Shona or Ndebele were, like their parents, effectively sealed off from indigenous society. They were also unlikely to undermine parental authority by colluding with servants.[70]

Many witnesses wanted more control exercised over locations and were critical of municipalities for failing to better regulate urban populations. But there was no suggestion that an influx of African women would make matters worse. That was because neither missionaries, native commissioners, nor private citizens considered the possibility that married or single women would live at locations; they all assumed that females would live on employers' premises. There remained the practical questions about the age at which girls were to begin work and how the issues of marriage, rural labor, and *lobola* (bride price) were to be negotiated. Discussion of those problems was carried out in a social vacuum. Instead of referring to the delicate balance between rural and urban labor patterns the proposal was framed in terms of two abstruse questions: Did the presence of black male servants induce white girls to White Peril and would the presence of black female servants encourage white boys to concubinage?

The colonial administration tended to be inept and it was common for legislation to be amended because of some glaring technical error. The same was true of government inquiries. That does not mean that the committee was confused about its political purpose; when the final report was released in October 1932 the document was inelegant rather than aimless.[71] The report, like the transcripts, shows that the inquiry was held by white males for a white male constituency whose perceptions differed markedly from those of the FWI.

The committee found it undesirable for government to encourage females to enter service because the disadvantages of close contact between black women and white families outweighed the benefits. It also found that the movement of African women to towns had already begun and the replacement of males by females was inevitable. The committee wanted that flow to be controlled by the state. The report recommended a registration system to bring prospective servants into contact with employers and the establishment of hostels to house them. In those cases where females lived on the premises it advised that employers provide suitable accommodation in a room close to the main house protected by a lock and barred windows.[72] Such measures were to prevent prostitution, protect the virtue of white males, and assuage the concerns of patriarchs about the safety of their daughters.

In handing down its report the committee tried, unsuccessfully, to appease the various parties with an interest in the inquiry. Missions saw domestic service as part of the emancipation of African women, African patriarchs wanted to retain control over the labor and *lobola* of wives and daughters, and the FWI wanted an antidote to Black Peril. In the process the committee sought to avoid forcing government to accept responsibility for the cost of training servants or the miscegenation which it believed would follow an influx of black women into white households. As a consequence the report was filled with anomalies. It suggested, for example, that government encourage African and Coloured girls living in locations to enter service because they were familiar with European mores and better able to resist moral dangers.[73] That suggestion ran against the prejudice shared by white women, police, missions, members of parliament, and administrators that Coloureds and urban Africans were immoral. The FWI proposal that government guarantee a supply of female servants gained only limited support from missions. Although the churches welcomed any policy which eroded the authority of patriarchs they did not want a flood of girls into the towns. Government was wary of assuming responsibility for locations, which was a difficult and expensive task. It was even less enthusiastic about providing training and accommodation for girls.

It would have been unthinkable for Carbutt's committee to have trivialized the threat of Black Peril. To avoid criticism from the FWI he asked the Salisbury CID if the employment of female servants had led to a rise in immorality, if the increased number of "houseboys" had led to more cases of Black Peril, and if there was any evidence of sexual assaults upon female servants. Although the CID's reply is unknown it is significant that the final report made no mention of sexual assault.[74] To reconcile the contradictory interests which dominated the hearings, the issue of Black Peril, which was paramount in the FWI document and was the reason why the inquiry was held, was simply erased in the final report.

Carbutt's report was a success. Prime Minister Moffat agreed that it was unnecessary for government to encourage the entry of females into domestic work because that process had already begun and should be left to run its course.[75] This would solve the problem of Black Peril in time, he felt. The process of change that Moffat and the inquiry identified was a mirage and for the next half century domestic service continued to be a male domain.[76] During the economic depression of the early 1930s white employers decreased wages and as a result many males chose instead to work at mines or farms. Consequently there was an increase in the number of women entering service, especially in Bulawayo, but they never represented more than 10 percent of the labor force.

CONCLUSION

Although each Black Peril panic had its own politics, each panic used the exact same ideology of black male sexuality. The stereotypes of black men were immutable and gave the ideology of Black Peril a timeless quality which disguised its contingent nature. That is why social theorists and even some historians have tended to see all moral panics as the same. The panics of 1908–1912 were directed by white males against imperial authority. In 1919 women gained the vote and in 1923 responsible government was achieved. Following those changes women took up the issue of Black Peril as a weapon to challenge the position of white males. The politics of the two periods were distinct.

White males had various justifications for their opposition to female servants such as the cost of training, the disturbing influence of girls upon white households, the reluctance of African patriarchs to relinquish the labor of girls and women, and the threat of miscegenation. What they failed to acknowledge, which was far more important, was that the introduction of female servants would have fractured the system of migrant labor upon which the colonial economy was based. The Carbutt inquiry did not discuss the material constraints preventing the employment of women, most notably the need to reproduce labor on the reserves. On the contrary, its members behaved as if the colonial state had control over indigenous society and that the choices facing white employers could be determined by themselves alone.

As early as 1911 it was officially acknowledged that the employment of male servants ran against the economic interests of settlers. Four years later the CID observed that servants were the major cause of Black Peril. It is remarkable that the presence of male servants was tolerated. In the past decade historians have offered two explanations. According to one explanation women were kept out of domestic service by an alliance between white administrators and black patriarchs who wanted to retain control over African women. Another explanation is that black women were perceived by whites as being disruptive and therefore unsuited for domestic work. As Teresa Barnes and Elizabeth Schmidt have shown, such explanations obscure the importance of female labor in rural areas, without which the colonial economy could not have functioned.[77] Because it was underwritten by the unpaid labor of women the employment of male servants involved little disadvantage for whites. The labor shortages on farms and mines was due to the reluctance of workers to accept poor wages and conditions and it is uncertain that the employment of women would have driven men into other forms of wage labor. The choices of employees were carefully made and depended upon levels of taxation, rates of pay, and conditions of work. As Ian Phimister and Charles van Onselen first showed more than twenty years ago, labor was more discriminating than capital.

There was a third element, however, which was invisible to both the Carbutt and FWI inquiries. Although Black Peril ideology made domestic service dangerous for African men, it was safer than work in mines or on farms, where mortality rates from illness were so high and the casual violence of white managers so prevalent. It also offered advantages in terms of shorter work contracts, higher pay, and better food and clothing, which males wished to keep for themselves.

The presence of servants helped to confirm the middle-class pretensions of white families and in particular their quest for respectability. The number of "grass widowers" meant that there were relatively few white households consisting of a husband, wife, and children supported by a male breadwinner. That in turn heightened the demand for paid domestic workers. Within the domestic sphere the model for authority was provided by the masters and servants ordinances and yet the management of domestic labor was wracked with conflict, desertions, and resistance. The domestic sphere was also the site for incidences of Black Peril, which shaped discussion of sexual hygiene both in the FWI report and in the evidence presented to the inquiry of 1932. Like Selwyn Bazeley, the authors of those documents understood domestic service in terms of sexual pathology rather than in terms of political economy. As a consequence the debates about servants exposed a range of self-contradictory interests in white society; in particular the chronic conflicts between men and women.

In Southern Rhodesia segregation was constructed around race and gender: Black families were excluded from urban locations, the white community was divided by class and ethnicity, white children were sent away to boarding schools, and public spaces and labor sectors were segregated. The entire social landscape was riven by fine racial distinctions. Yet white households were filled with black servants.

BLACK WOMEN

After 1918 African women began to leave villages in significant numbers. Their movements into towns and mine compounds reshaped patterns of rural and urban labor and the payment of *lobola,* or bride price. The new-found mobility of women became entangled with other issues, among them Black Peril. The morality ordinances always had a wider context than sexual crime. By providing a model for colonial relations as a whole they drew the black community within their ambit; they influenced debates about adultery in the black community. What had begun within white society as a means of challenging imperial authority in time came to influence discussions of gender and labor relations for the country as a whole.

In the histories written during the colonial period African women were all but invisible. That has now changed and a new generation of scholars, including Teresa Barnes, Diana Jeater, and Elizabeth Schmidt, has begun to research issues of labor, gender, and power.[1] With that change has come a new set of controversies about the mobility of women, the pass ordinances, and the relationship between rural and urban labor. Such work has also made the connection between Black Peril fears and gender politics more accessible.

The colonial state was sensitive to what it perceived as "native immorality," a broad category which included beer drinking and sexual liaisons outside marriage. The state and its largely male constituency were particularly sensitive to the misconduct of women and to their role in the social conventions which arose from wage labor. They often attributed to biology or to tradition forms of behavior which the colonial economy itself had made possible. Although African women played no immediate part in the Black Peril scenarios whites constructed, they were central to a number of disputes which brought indigenous society and the state into conflict. The behavior of women influenced the ways in which the moral panics were understood. The panics in turn influenced the state's response to women's mobility.

In the period from 1910 to the mid-1920s African women shed a number of their conventional roles. They were also blamed for many of the ills

afflicting traditional society. Those ills included adultery, the spread of venereal disease, and a crisis over the payment of *lobola*.[2] Every gain by African women involved some loss to African men and in seeking economic
independence women defied male authority.[3]

Denying African men and women access to social space was an important element of the colonial system. The places where they enjoyed mobility were villages, reserves, and, to a lesser extent, urban locations. Other
spaces designated as white could only be entered under special circumstances.[4] The movement of men in and out of urban areas was controlled
by a system of pass and location ordinances. The Native Urban Locations
Ordinance of 1906 stipulated which men were allowed residence and imposed fines of up to 10 pounds or three months' imprisonment for offenders. The ordinance gave broad powers to administrators to control entry,
fix rents, and issue passes. The ordinance also allowed servants to live on
employers' premises. Over time the system was refined so that eventually
all men were required to carry an identification certificate which also served
as a record of employment.[5] A pass was needed to enter a town or to be
outside a location during designated hours. Women were exempt from
those provisions.

Locations were segregated on the basis of gender; according to official
estimates men outnumbered women at Salisbury and Bulawayo by as much
as ten to one. But, as Teresa Barnes has shown, the censuses were unreliable.[6] Because census takers counted only the women who were engaged in
wage labor, they greatly underestimated the female population. Evidence
that many men had female partners also suggests that the census returns
were flawed. At Salisbury women lived at the location and in the town
proper; some lived on employers' premises while others lived on white
farms on the town's outskirts. Some women also lived on the municipal
commonage. The numbers themselves are less significant than the rigor
with which the exclusion of women was pursued by the state.

Only a minority of women in locations were married or in wage labor.
Before 1910 beer selling, especially near the towns, was more profitable for
women than laboring or domestic service was for men. The destruction of
the beer trade through the ordinances of 1909, 1911, and 1915 undercut
women's economic independence and so they turned to other activities.[7] In
1914 90 percent of the stands in the Bulawayo location were rented by
women who used the opportunity to generate income through subletting,
trading, and prostitution.[8]

Black men had contradictory attitudes toward women. Married men
wanted their wives to remain in villages because the right to land was de-

pendent upon continuous cultivation. They also wanted women to provide a home during periods of non-wage labor. All men wanted access to the sex and domestic services women provided. In addition men did not want to compete in the labor market for work as servants.[9] The attitude of white administrators was just as ambivalent. In assessing settler reactions to women's mobility it is necessary to distinguish between missionaries and the state, which was itself fractured along various lines of interest.

MARRIAGE AND ADULTERY

During the first decades of colonization missionaries and native commissioners felt it was their duty to rescue black women from oppressive male authority. Consequently the settling of disputes between men and women took up most of the time of local courts and negotiating marriages and divorces dominated the work of native commissioners. Missionaries sought to strengthen the institution of marriage. Initially their protective attitude toward women drew them into conflict with both black patriarchs and the white state. Over time the outlook of missionaries and the administration changed. Black women who were not immediately subordinate to black men came increasingly to be seen by the state as a threat to social order.

In the period from 1901 to 1917 a number of ordinances regulating African marriage were introduced. The earliest of those laws suggested a largely benevolent attitude. The Native Marriages Ordinance of 1901 stipulated that a native commissioner had to be satisfied that the *lobola* was correct and that the girl had given her consent to marriage. Over the next ten years the principle of consent was maintained. The Native Marriages Ordinance of 1917 made the registration of marriages compulsory and prohibited the pledging of children. It also decreed that the consent of the woman had to be clearly established. The ordinances were in part designed to protect the rights of women in choosing a partner and to regulate the payment of *lobola* for their benefit.[10] Such laws embodied a different set of principles than those found in the correspondence of the Native Affairs Department and the CID. Those departments identified two categories of women; the subordinate and the refractory.

A wife's earnings belonged to her husband, as did property within marriage. As legal minors women had no independent access to land or housing and in forcing them to find a patron both customary law and state regulation intended to bolster male authority.[11] Yet that policy was undermined by the social and economic forces it was intended to control. Husbands wanted their wives to stay at home and grow crops while they sought work in mines or on farms.[12] Single males in towns wanted women to cook for them and provide sex, needs which were often met by relationships outside of marriage. Mine owners were willing to allow single women into compounds with the knowledge that their skills in cooking and brewing beer would attract labor and reduce rates of illness.

From as early as 1910 native commissioners were concerned that black women were undermining the stability of village society. Promiscuous women could disrupt lineage arrangements more easily than promiscuous men and it was in that context that adultery and prostitution were judged. "Alien natives" were especially attractive as patrons to Zimbabwean women; generally they earned higher wages and as temporary residents they were less able to exert control over their partners. The appeal of such men also meant that in cases of adultery aggrieved husbands rarely received compensation. The refusal of some women to marry designated partners; their adulteries; and their flights to missions, mines, and locations confounded male authority. Their transgressions were made more significant by the absence of effective mechanisms for dealing with such behavior. African patriarchs petitioned native commissioners to criminalize adultery not because they though it immoral but because it threatened their power. The perspective of white administrators was rather different.

Adultery was a crime in Natal and also in British India and before the occupation of Rhodesia it had been an offense under customary law.[13] From as early as 1900 cases of adultery came before native courts and by 1914 protests from chiefs and elders about unruly women were common. Native commissioners were concerned about the number of women leaving their husbands to live at compounds and the matter was discussed at length in official correspondence.[14] One commissioner who wanted the procuring of another man's wife made an offense pointed out that since no compensation was paid there was much bitterness among jilted husbands.[15] Patriarchs wanted legal sanctions placed upon girls who ran away from their villages and women who left their husbands.[16]

In 1911 the report of the native affairs committee of inquiry was tabled.[17] Many of the subjects covered had commercial significance but the inquiry was also concerned with moral questions. Its findings were cited frequently during Black Peril debates in the Legislative Council. The report was replete with paradoxical intentions, the most obvious of which was the contrast between moral purpose and commercial advantage; where possible the committee conflated the two. As the number of Africans who contracted Christian marriages increased, men began to complain that marriage had been weakened and that wives were being lured away from their husbands. The committee also heard many complaints about the impetuous behavior of girls. Some girls ran away from home and took refuge at missions; others defied the authority of their fathers and the Christian churches.[18] The committee agreed that the possibility that wives would commit adultery while their husbands were absent was a problem which discouraged men from entering wage labor and recommended that it be made an offense for men and women.[19] In so doing the committee hoped both to enhance the sanctity of marriage and increase the supply of labor.

The report of 1911 was full of contradictions. The most notable was an image of traditional society as both pristine and degenerate.[20] According to the committee, African marriages had been more stable before the advent of wage labor and prior to white settlement African prostitutes had been practically unknown. Paradoxically, it noted that even among blacks remote from white settlement sexual immorality was common in children as young as twelve. The report concluded: "From the evidence of many of the witness it would appear that the natives have degenerated in some respects, and that contact with civilisation has had a retrograde effect, especially in regard to sexual immorality and in the lack of respect for parental and tribal authority."[21] That judgment helped to strengthen an alliance between white administrators and black patriarchs. Teresa Barnes has attacked the idea of such collaboration, claiming that because women often remitted part of their earnings men had a vested interest in their continued employment.[22] That argument is contradicted by the work of Elizabeth Schmidt and Diana Jeater and by the archival record, which documents the demands of patriarchs for state intervention.[23]

In December 1914 the chief native commissioner's office recommended legislation which it believed had the full support of the black male community.[24] The commissioner believed that if adultery were to be made illegal for both men and women it would stem moral degradation and the spread of syphilis. The number of married males willing to leave their villages would rise, thereby easing the labor shortage on white farms. Such a proposal, which combined moral purpose with economic benefit, eventually proved irresistible. On May 15, 1916, two morality ordinances were introduced into the Legislative Council: a white slavery bill, the Criminal Law Further Amendment Ordinance; and the Immorality and Indecency Suppression Ordinance. On the following day the Natives Adultery Punishment Ordinance was brought to the table. The rationale behind all three bills was the same: to control women. The timing of the adultery ordinance was particularly significant. Under Roman-Dutch law, adultery had ceased to be a criminal offense for whites in 1914.

Under the Natives Adultery Punishment Ordinance any man who committed adultery with a married woman or who induced such a woman to leave her husband was liable for a fine of up to 100 pounds or one year in prison.[25] Such a fine represented at least four years' income for a skilled worker. In moving the second reading Attorney General Tredgold observed that legislation was necessary because the whole of African life was being undermined by the conduct of women. While the behavior of single women was regulated by the *lobola* system, married women had "crossed the line."[26] In justifying the legislation he repeated the reasons given by the chief native commissioner's office in 1914, which emphasized the need to encourage men to enter wage labor. With some justification elders claimed that the state had taken away their power to regulate marriage and that the ordinance was necessary to allow them to control women. Tredgold explained that the legislation was not intended to make people moral. On the contrary: "The basis of the law was to preserve certain economic and social conditions."[27] Where the offender was an alien it was impossible to gain damages and the only remedy open to a husband was divorce.

There followed a debate about the survival of the settler community, access to labor, the stability of African society, the threat of miscegenation, and fears that the ordinance would be applied to white men. The issue of Black Peril was discussed at length, which seems odd in an ordinance about the infractions of black women. There was also discussion of the rebellion of 1896, which, according to one member, had been triggered by the sexual predations of white males. In general members of the council had little difficulty understanding indigenous marriage in terms of property and lineage. But whenever the issues of marriage and black women's mobility were refracted through moral imperatives debate tended to became inchoate.

Charles Coghlan was sure that the future loyalty of Africans depended upon curtailing the misbehavior of black women and he supported the bill. But he was not prepared to see the legislation extended to the white community.[28] John McChlery was alone in opposing the ordinance. He wanted a law which also protected unmarried black girls and he was particularly critical of the fact that the ordinance ignored the sexual misconduct of white men.[29] In reply to McChlery, Mr. Cripps argued that Africans did not expect to be treated as equals and it would be dangerous to treat them so. With disarming candor he reassured his colleagues that "[i]n a great number of instances the native was proud that the white man should take their women."[30] The ordinance was passed with only McChlery dissenting.

The issues which aroused the most intense debate were concubinage and the possibility that the legislation could be applied to white males.

Both of those questions turned the ordinance back to Black Peril fears. Given the disingenuous nature of debate the final ordinance was surprisingly unambiguous. But it failed to solve the problem of independent black women and complaints from patriarchs continued.

John McChlery was persistent in his opposition to the morality ordinances and in May 1921 he moved that illicit sexual intercourse between white men and black women be made a criminal offense. McChlery told his colleagues that the ordinance of 1916 which made adultery an offense for black women but not for white men had augmented the Immorality Suppression Ordinance of 1903.[31] In so doing he re-interpreted both laws in terms of the sexual misconduct of white males, a strategy which can hardly have pleased his colleagues.[32] McChlery claimed that the adultery legislation was opposed by many settlers because it required such a high standard of morality from blacks. He reminded the council that while white Rhodesian women wanted legislation to make white men and women equal before the law what they received instead was the Criminal Law Further Amendment Ordinance of 1916, a white slavery act.[33] Not surprisingly, the motion was defeated unanimously. McChlery enjoyed speaking unpalatable truths and by linking the adultery ordinance with miscegenation he maintained his opposition to the morality legislation.

In the early 1920s reduced access to land, drought, and high rates of inflation left many black women without a means of subsistence.[34] Some found a solution in selling beer, vegetables, and sex to men living at locations and mines. As their numbers grew the administration ceased supporting black women in their defiance of male authority and instead endorsed initiatives for harsher controls over their movements. At that time a similar pattern of change occurred in Northern Rhodesia, where declining conditions in reserves attracted women to urban centers.[35] The state feared the disintegration of rural communities and by tying women to villages it hoped to stabilize both urban and rural workforces.[36] As the result of the appropriation of land by white farmers, lobola had become a major source of wealth for lineages, thereby increasing considerably a young woman's value. Her residence in a town lowered her price and therefore her family's assets. That shift in wealth heightened the importance of the contests for authority between women, the state, and patriarchs. It also drew missionaries into the dispute.

MISSIONARIES

Missionaries wanted African girls to become good mothers. They were reluctant to teach girls academic subjects—especially English—because they believed intellectual work would only hinder their proper vocation. Instead, girls were taught domestic skills; their unpaid labor was often a major source of mission income.[37] In general missionaries viewed the mobility of black women as socially disruptive. But in some circumstances they actively encouraged young black women to leave their villages.

In the period from 1910 until the mid-1930s there was incessant conflict between missionaries and the state over the administration of African society. Missionaries wanted the state to exercise greater control over the consumption of alcohol and sexual license while the state was usually reluctant to become involved in domestic life. Missionaries were also brought into dispute with the state over the recruitment of girls as novices. Missions were keen for young women to leave their villages and join the Church, as such recruits were a measure of their success in spreading Christianity. Novices also provided missions with much-needed labor. As early 1910 a number of African parents complained to the Committee of Inquiry into Native Affairs that their daughters were being held against their will at mission stations. In its final report the committee objected to the practice of harboring. Although the attorney general favored legal compulsion against missions which encouraged young women to join the Church he found little support and in April 1912 the administration decided not to make harboring a criminal offense.[38] As a compromise missionaries were reminded of the committee's recommendations.[39] That made little difference and the practice persisted.

From the early 1920s the files of the chief native commissioner contain many cases of young women who chose to enter the Church in opposition to their fathers' wishes. Native commissioners wanted to defend parental authority while missionaries were keen to recruit novices. Such disputes called into question the status of traditional law and the degree of intervention which the state was willing to make. It was not unusual for disputes to be referred to the attorney general's office for legal opinion. A typical case was that of Theresia Mushangagzi from the Driefontein Mission, Rusapi. In October 1930 the chief native commissioner ruled that if a woman could not be forced to marry against her will (as laid down in the ordinance) she also had the right to choose not to marry at all.[40] In the following year, despite her father's opposition, Theresia chose to join the Native Sisters. Her father claimed that he needed her *lobola* to pay off a family debt and the mission loaned him money for that purpose. Eventually the case was referred to the superintendent at Fort Victoria for a ruling and the girl remained with the sisters.[41]

The story of Theresia Mushangagzi was but one of many and in August 1931 a native affairs advisory committee met at Salisbury to consider a remedy. The committee was aware that such disputes were part of a wider conflict in which the issue of *lobola* was paramount. It was also aware that over time cases of young women seeking work as teachers or nurses would become more common.[42] In the view of Charles Coghlan, when a girl reached the age of twenty-one she was a free agent and could make her own decisions. The attorney general and his department believed, however, that a court would have to be satisfied that the refusal of a parent to grant a daughter consent to join a mission was unreasonable and contrary to the girl's interests. He did concede that under certain circumstances a guardian was entitled to compensation.[43]

Apart from the conflict between European and traditional law, such cases posed practical problems. It was often difficult for a native commissioner to decide the extent of a girl's understanding of her own interests or to determine the rights and interests of her parents.[44] In the end the committee opposed any legislation which would enable unmarried girls to enter the Church against their fathers' wishes.[45] That decision was a defeat for the missions, which expected state support in their endeavors to rescue black girls for Christ. It was not the only issue about which the missions and the state differed.

Missionaries were offended by a number of indigenous practices including "night dances." Mrs. Anderson, the wife of the head of the London Mission Society (LMS) station at Lonely Mine was troubled by immorality at the compound. In July 1928 she wrote to the Prime Minister asking for some action to be taken over "tea meetings."[46] She explained that at those meetings beer was drunk and girls and women were auctioned for the night to the highest bidder. Consequently many illegitimate babies were born and women were encouraged to leave their husbands to work as prostitutes. Mrs. Anderson claimed to have seen motor trolleys filled with young girls driven by "half-castes" and Indians plying between the Bulawayo location and the compound. Mrs. Anderson's letter, which followed allegations by her husband, was investigated by the native commissioner at Inyati. He found tea meetings there which resembled the cabarets favored by Europeans. There was no evidence of prostitution and he strongly denied the Rev. Anderson's suggestion that auctions of girls were held with the approval of his office.[47] The Andersons were not the first to protest against innocent entertainments and they were not the last.

In August 1930 the chief native commissioner at Salisbury advised his officers where possible to suppress night dances and tea meetings. His circular followed resolutions taken by the Southern Rhodesian Missionary Conference which believed the dances encouraged drinking and prostitution. Commissioner Hudson was aware that intervention would antagonize Africans but would buy the good will of the conference—a meager benefit. As he had probably hoped, his circular resulted in a flood of correspondence which gave missionaries little comfort. The majority of commissioners believed that night dances were an innocent entertainment and that to ban them would cause bitter resentment. The native commissioner for Mrewa argued that they were a very old institution and that beer was rarely drunk. The officer at Mtokohe had attended several hundred dances while on patrol and had never seen beer served.[48] Another observed that such gatherings were akin to a dance on Saturday night at any British pub which ended with a quotation from Robbie Burns.[49]

Several officers held contrary opinions about the causes of immorality. According to the commissioner at Inyanga the loose habits of girls were due to the undermining of traditional authority by mission schools.[50] Schools taught girls to read and write and so enabled them to correspond with dissolute young men. The missionaries also taught daughters to look upon their parents with contempt. Another wrote: "There is no doubt in my mind that the immorality on the part of the young native girls is principally due to the gradual destruction of parental control, and the Missionaries who could do much to assist parents in regaining such control, though I fear that they fail to realise that in many cases their teaching tends to have entirely the opposite effect."[51]

In contrast to missionaries, who tended to view the social landscape in terms of moral order and sin, native commissioners were often more knowledgeable in their observations of the changes sweeping indigenous society. The officer in charge at Bindura observed that the distribution of labor was such that men were concentrated in towns or mine compounds while women remained in villages. Virtuous girls were left to a drab existence while their less chaste sisters could enjoy a life of luxury without damaging their chances of marriage.[52] After reading the correspondence Commissioner Hudson concluded there was no substance to the missionaries' complaints and the subjects of night dances and tea parties were dropped.[53]

Missionaries were committed to moral order but it was of a different kind than that favored by the Native Affairs Department. The churches were willing to support a girl's defiance of parental authority so long as that choice was framed in terms of Christian commitment. They did not support in principle the rights of women, an issue about which the white community was itself deeply ambivalent.

THE TRAVELING PROSTITUTE

In the 1920s, when the departments of health and native affairs came to consider why syphilis was so common among African males they soon arrived at an answer: Just as white prostitutes caused Black Peril, so, they believed, again without evidence, that black women, and in particular "alien native women" and "traveling prostitutes," spread syphilis and gonorrhea. Of all the vices for which whites blamed black women syphilis was the most damning. It was a vice believed to directly threaten the safety of white families. The alien native woman and the traveling black prostitute were poorly distinguished and often merged into a broader category of the refractory female. That figure combined the sins of avarice and sexual gluttony and reinforced the idea that social calamity was gendered. In explaining the spread of syphilis administrators could draw upon the precedent of the British purity movements which held prostitutes responsible for the infection of middle-class society. But the figure of the European prostitute was never quite so demonic as her African counterpart.

The Department of Public Health believed venereal disease was promoted by the improved means for travel, a slackening of moral standards, and the ease with which prostitutes could earn money. The traveling prostitute was seen to be the major source of infection, a view shared by the white public at large. In the eyes of the administration a prostitute was a woman not under the control of a husband, father, or patriarch. Any woman who moved between village and location was likely to be so classified. However, the state was constrained in its attempts to suppress prostitution. The movements of women were almost impossible to regulate. They were exempt from carrying passes and without compromising their independence single women could gain a male protector. Such arrangements fell outside of African and imported notions of marriage and women who entered "*mapoto* marriages" (marriages of the cooking pot) were usually looked upon by native commissioners as prostitutes. Those who understood location life knew that such liaisons were a way of providing domestic support for urban labor and contributed to the stability of the workforce. Many white men believed that the services offered by prostitutes to segregated males decreased the threat of Black Peril and that suppression of prostitution would create discontent in urban centers.

In her study of colonial Nairobi, Luise White found that prostitution was a form of migrant labor for many women.[54] Some invested their earnings while others remitted money back to their villages, thereby preserving the integrity of households. Teresa Barnes has found the same pattern in

Southern Rhodesia, where prostitution was so lucrative in the 1920s that some women earned as much as ten shillings per customer. One of Barnes's informants claimed that she could make the extraordinary sum of 10 pounds a month.[55] In few cases was prostitution a full-time occupation and there were no clear boundaries separating such work from marriage.[56]

Despite those realities African women were blamed by the state for spreading disease and discontent among black males and thereby threatening the colonial economy. In November 1917, for example, a farmer named Cooper complained to Medical Director Fleming that "alien native" prostitutes were encouraging his men to squander their wages.[57] Such complaints were so common that under Fleming's direction the Department of Public Health eventually kept records of all women treated for venereal disease. In a number of cases the department obtained from the native commissioner the name of the woman's headman (or village chief), how long she had been absent from her village, her marital status, and the names of relations to whom she could be repatriated.[58]

Fleming was unconvinced about the threat posed by syphilis but he readily accepted the prevailing view about its agents of transmission. In 1919 he proposed that special wards be established at the major hospitals to treat prostitutes.[59] During the 1920s native commissioners in northern districts frequently voiced their concern about the influx of women, many of whom were the wives or reputed wives of miners. According to one officer, although they were fickle and spread syphilis, they also helped to make the workforce more stable and thereby minimized the threat of Black Peril.[60] Such statements suggest that some native commissioners were blissfully ignorant of indigenous labor patterns in which the work of women was so vital to food production and the access to wage labor that males enjoyed.

In its annual report for 1927 the Department of Public Health claimed that the main reason traveling prostitutes resisted treatment was to avoid the loss of income. Such women often changed their names and the department, the CID, and mining companies made some effort to trace them.[61] Their mobility, however, made it impossible to enforce a system of medical checks.[62] According to another annual report, "[p]robably the worst feature of this evil [syphilis] is the ease with which these women make money and their comparative wealth which is attracting a large number of women and young girls from the neighbouring reserves and villages."[63] That idea, which became a feature of settler discourse, was never challenged nor was it substantiated. The causes of infection within the African community were complex and were made less visible to the state by the specter of the traveling prostitute. Other explanations such as the impact of wage labor and urbanization and in particular the system of segregated locations were ignored. Missionaries, native commissioners, members of the Women's Institutes, and health department officials believed that syphilis was the price paid for sexual incontinence. For that reason the cause of infection had to be an African woman, the person identified by settler culture as most driven by greed and sexual desire.

The belief that prostitutes spread disease in locations was a common theme throughout the 1920s. When Fleming met with a delegation from the Bulawayo Landowners and Farmers Association in October 1928 it was one of the topics discussed. A delegate named Hay claimed that only months earlier twenty infected women had come into Bulawayo and had to be ordered out of town. He wanted women subject to examination. Another delegate, Mrs. Bloomhill, commented: "One diseased woman is more dangerous than twenty diseased men. I have it from a very able private practitioner that the danger to the Europeans lies not so much from native men as from contagion through native women."[64] Mrs. Bloomhill wanted a clinic established to which women would report on arriving in town. They would sleep at the ward and would be supervised and medically examined. Fleming explained that compulsory examination of female servants was impossible. There was no woman doctor in the territory to carry out such work and it was department policy that European nurses were not to treat black female patients. The department assumed that such women did not object to examination by a male; besides, an African orderly could always be present.[65] That view was not shared by district surgeons, some of whom opposed the suggestion because it would have increased their already heavy workloads.[66]

Five months later the Chambers of Commerce held a congress at Bulawayo at which venereal disease was discussed. Delegates claimed that infection was a threat to white families and protested that the government was doing little to solve the problem. In response Fleming argued that local councils were themselves to blame because they failed to control stray women in municipal compounds. "It is common knowledge," he told delegates, "that groups of these women rent houses in the location for the express purpose of carrying out their profession."[67] The only safeguard was to encourage the infected to seek treatment and for councils to deter prostitution.

The most significant aspect of the controversy was the ease with which a discussion of public health could turn into a debate about venereal disease and then to the sexual behavior of women. The Chamber of Commerce described an imaginary cycle of infection through women in reserves, into locations, and then into white homes. Transmission was sexual until it reached the stoop of European households, from which point it was spread by non-sexual means. It was unimaginable to white males that they could be a conduit for spreading syphilis into their own community.

THE SALISBURY LOCATION

Locations provided settlers with access to labor, but locations also made them apprehensive. Whites viewed locations as reservoirs of infection and the most heated debates about controlling the mobility of women focused on location life. In April 1929 Miss Waters, who was an instructor with the Department of Native Education, prepared a report on conditions at Salisbury.[68] She estimated that there were some six hundred women in the location, many of whom worked as prostitutes. Birth rates were abnormally low, a fact she attributed in part to the prevalence of syphilis. The municipality provided facilities for the diagnosis and treatment of venereal disease in men but not, as Miss Waters noted, for women. She suggested: "It would be an additional safeguard to the health of the white population, if the diagnosis and treatment of these diseases were put on a sound basis."[69] Like many of her contemporaries, Miss Waters was under the delusion that syphilis could be contracted by children or adults via spoons or cups; she believed that since Africans were employed in preparing food in white homes there was danger of infection. The Welfare Society for Native Women and Children, which had been formed in 1928, proposed that a VD clinic be established at Salisbury. The idea was rejected by the municipality, whose chief officer explained: "Affairs were probably so bad at the Location as regards venereal disease, that if investigated they would probably need a Native hospital, and that this would involve a huge expenditure." He also noted that "prostitutes at the location were a necessity as a safe guard for the white women."[70]

In 1930 public inquiries were held into conditions at the Salisbury, Bulawayo, and Gatooma locations. The inquiries covered a range of issues, including alcohol and housing and the indiscipline of black women. At the Salisbury inquiry a large number of witnesses were called, including health officers, superintendents, members of the CID, representatives of the Rhodesian Natives Association, and a number of men (but no women) who lived at the location.

The municipal health officer, Dr. Hurworth, commented on the absence of a settled married life, which made it difficult to control venereal disease. If there was evidence that a particular woman was infected she was forced to have treatment and placed in the *lazaretto,* or isolation ward. Hurworth acknowledged that although there was no legal sanction for such a practice he believed it to be justified.[71] According to the CID there was no organized pimping but there was a feeling of disgust among residents about the number of prostitutes.[72] Evidence from male residents suggested a deep-seated resentment of black women. One told the inquiry: "Prostitution is rife in the location. The women rule the men. They chose their man and he books the house. If the girl tires of the man she sends him off and takes another and she sends him along to register the house in his name."[73] He suggested that a black woman should not be allowed into a town unless she had a husband. A number of witnesses commented upon the traveling prostitute who dressed well and by example enticed other women into a life of immorality. Another resident, Mr. John Muketsi, complained that 75 percent of the female residents were prostitutes.[74]

During the inquiry at Bulawayo, Major Blundell of the CID explained that prostitution had always been a part of location life and that reports of immorality had been common since 1915.[75] It was widely believed, he said, that prostitutes attracted men to wage labor and also served to protect white women from the threat of Black Peril. Col. C. L. Carbutt, Superintendent of Natives, acknowledged that there was some prostitution but that he did not believe it could be controlled by legislation. The Mayor, Mr. H. Peard, commented "that to endeavour to stamp out prostitution entirely might re-act on the number of black peril cases which arise."[76] Missionaries wanted prostitutes removed from locations. However, according to one member, Mr. Bazeley, of the Native Affairs Advisory Committee, which debated the issue in August 1931, such a policy would have caused great harm. In the locations there was a large number of single adult males with strong sexual passions who were habituated to using prostitutes. If deprived of their services those men would cause trouble to the wives and daughters of respectable blacks and increase the threat of Black Peril.[77] Like many of his contemporaries, Bazeley believed in the hydraulic model of sexual crime, namely that rape is the product of frustrated lust. It was an argument used repeatedly by male officials who opposed the suppression of prostitution in locations.

The inquiries were woven around two propositions: that in spreading venereal disease black women were ruining the labor supply; and that by providing domestic services black women stabilized the workforce. Some members of the Legislative Council believed the first and some the second. Missionaries did not like mobility except when it benefited them directly and were quick to condemn women for ruining village life. Native commissioners were worried about adultery, which they attributed to women's mobility. Municipal officers in charge of locations along with some mine managers understood the importance of women's labor and opposed any further moves for segregation. Some also saw the presence of black women as an antidote to Black Peril. The moral imperatives which invariably arose in any discussion of location life obscured the powerful political economy which underlay the mobility of black women. That economy became visible whenever proposals were made that, like black men, black women should carry passes.

PASSES

There were two schools of thought about the best way to prevent black women from moving into towns. Some administrators argued that parents should exercise control over their daughters and that husbands should control their wives. Others favored state intervention. From the turn of the century pass ordinances were used to regulate male labor but it was not until 1927 that the introduction of passes for women was seriously considered.[78]

Most members of the Native Affairs Advisory Committee (1931) opposed the use of passes for women. The policy was anathema to black leaders and there was also the problem that native police might use the opportunity for sexual harassment.[79] (No mention was made of possible transgressions by white officers.) At a meeting in August Mr. Howman pointed out that both in towns and in the countryside there was strong feeling against passes. "I think first of all that it is rather hard lines on a respectable girl if she has got to parade at the town pass office and ask for a monthly contract. She is sent over to the medical man and she has to strip off and be examined to see if she is suffering from venereal or some other disease."[80] The committee was aware that such a system had been tried in Johannesburg and had led to a strike.

In August 1931 the police asked native boards to help enforce the vagrancy act, especially with regard to young women. Citing various laws, including vagrancy and immorality acts, the department suggested that to avoid accusations of sexual harassment native officers should not be employed in arrests unless under the supervision of a European.[81] After that it was common for police to round up girls and take them before a native department official who returned them to their villages.[82] A list was kept of offenders and if found again in a town they were prosecuted.[83] The

Bulawayo CID compiled dossiers on alleged prostitutes which included the woman's name, her tribe, kraal, chief, marital status, and remarks about her activities. The lists were used to distinguish between a class of so-called habitual prostitutes and young vagrant women. There is no indication of the means used to identify prostitutes and it is probable that the only criteria was that a woman was independent of male authority. The system was never successful and women found various ways to avoid detection. They could not be prosecuted if they did not enter towns and so they would stay at private locations, market gardens, or industrial sites.

The chief native commissioner supported the program but instructed his officers that because of problems of jurisdiction non-indigenous black women should be left alone.[84] The policy clashed with the principle that a girl had the right to chose her marriage partner. But the commissioner and the CID were confident in their ability to distinguish between a woman's right to marry and her choice to live an "immoral" life. The matter was discussed again by the Native Affairs Advisory Board in November 1931, which decided that there was no need for further legislation. Instead officers were to encourage parents to report the unauthorized departure of any girl from her village.[85]

The Salisbury, Umtali, and Bulawayo CIDs filed quarterly returns on the "immorality of native girls." But only flagrant cases were prosecuted and in general women who formed relations with single men were left alone.[86] The ratio of those prosecuted to the number "living by doubtful means" was about one to ten.[87] Over time prosecutions fell to almost zero while the numbers of women designated as living by doubtful means remained steady at around six hundred in Salisbury and three hundred in Bulawayo. The returns were taken as proof that surveillance had suppressed immorality, yet the evidence suggests otherwise. In May 1935, for example, the Matabeleland Home Society, which represented residents of the location, wrote to the Bulawayo police. The Society asked the CID to close the town to immoral women through inspection of marriage certificates. It requested that a public meeting be held at which the superintendent of natives would explain the meaning of the Native Adultery Punishment Ordinance.[88] Carbutt refused.

The mobility of women was a serious issue for the government. But that did not prevent it from being subject to self-parody. In 1934 one settler approached Prime Minister Huggins with a remedy he was certain would succeed. Mr. Laing of Bulawayo pointed out that every girl's morals were known to her community and that her reputation affected the amount of *lobola* she attracted. As a first step he suggested that government remove the influence of missions. The missionaries had done their best to wreck customary law and they were the main cause of girls "going to the dogs." According to Laing the government could solve the problem for a sum of 3,000 thousand pounds.[89] He proposed an annual beauty contest in each district. Girls would be judged by a panel of their own people that was supervised by native department officers and any missionary who wanted to attend. Each girl would have to be voted moral by her community before she was allowed to enter the contest. The winner would receive 10 pounds and there would be separate sections for married and single contestants. Laing had talked the idea over with some reliable missionaries who suggested the contest be used in conjunction with a fund-raising pageant. "Give them three years of beauty contests," he wrote, "and the indunas a bit of real power and you will have real virgins once more in savage S. Africa."[90] Although Huggins ignored Laing's scheme, within eighteen months government and local councils took further steps to restrict the movement of women.

The belated introduction of the Native Registration Amendment Ordinance of 1936 heralded a change of policy. It also suggested some diminution in the emblematic power of Black Peril. The ordinance presumed that married women were under the tutelage of husbands and so they could stay in locations without the certificate required of single women. In November, Mr. C. Bullock, secretary of the Native Affairs Department, wrote to all town clerks explaining that the Act had two objectives: to safeguard African society (especially women) and to discourage undesirables from crowding into towns. "In regard to the difficult question of native sexual life there can be no doubt that we must aim at the elimination of immorality, and I am authorised by the Prime Minister to ask your council to agree to measures in furtherance of this policy."[91] Where a couple lived together pressure was to be applied to ensure they married; women who engaged in a series of unions were to be excluded from locations. The principle on which the policy was based was clear: "It is not thought that sexual intercourse is a necessity for young bachelors who mostly work in the towns for comparatively short periods if facilities are provided for games and recreation."[92] Ten years earlier there would have been an uproar in the Legislative Council at the suggestion of such an act because denying single black males sexual release would have been seen as promoting conditions in the locations conducive to Black Peril assaults.

There were a number of reasons why the state did not force women to carry passes or seek to exclude them from urban spaces.[93] Pass laws did not work with men and there was no reason to believe they would have been any more effective with women. There was such opposition from the black community to passes that it was never a serious option for government. The exclusion of women from locations would probably have fomented direct resistance to the state.[94] There was also the problem of imperial censure; Whitehall would have opposed passes on ethical grounds. The most common justification for tolerating women in towns was that they were a safeguard against the threat of Black Peril.[95]

CONCLUSION

The controversies over adultery, syphilis, locations, and passes were all related to the mobility of black women. That cluster of issues was apparently far removed from Black Peril. Yet all were viewed by the state and missionaries as moral issues and so finally all were drawn within the ambit of the moral panics. The adultery ordinance of 1916 was passed at the same session of the Legislative Council which passed the major Black Peril ordinances. Members saw the ordinances as analogous and discussion of one flowed over into the other. The contests for authority between African patriarchs, missionaries, and the colonial state were played out against a backdrop fashioned from the moral panics.

Patriarchs criticized black women for undermining their authority and thereby destabilizing village life. Native commissioners condemned them for being slothful, immoral, and uncivilized. They blamed black women for the rising incidence of adultery and venereal disease and for the reluctance of black men to enter into wage labor. Missionaries made the same criticisms, adding that black girls were more difficult to educate than boys. Paradoxically, it was their value to both the indigenous and colonial economies which made black women so vulnerable to the machinations of patriarchs and the state.[96]

Teresa Barnes has shown how women often congregated in spaces beyond the control of the state. In Salisbury there was a legal white city of families and bachelors and an illegal black city of trespassers, vagrants, squatters, and prostitutes.[97] Although women were a disruptive element, the domestic services they provided to men were recognized as important to urban stability. They were also recognized as a panacea to Black Peril. Even so, authorities were relentless in their condemnation of black women. The imagery they used was to a degree the obverse of the asexual imagery associated with white women. During the 1932 inquiry into female domestic labor Selwyn Bazeley spoke with malice about the vices of African women.[98] Four years later in his annual report the native commissioner for

Goromonzi commented: "Whether or not they (the women) have benefited from this freedom must be a matter of opinion, but whatever the cause may be sexual immorality is rampant in the Salisbury native reserves. That the women are brazen and shameless is emphasized by the fact that during the last six months a daily average of three cases of erring wives came up for arbitration."[99] Such comments found their apotheosis in the figure of the traveling prostitute.

In the minds of many white men and women, the traveling prostitute was a nameless, deracinated, and infertile woman who had no guardian or father, no home or family. She was driven by a craving for sex and money and if infected with syphilis would avoid medical treatment rather than interrupt her income. Such women would pass on disease to many men, yet somehow remain themselves undamaged. They seduced men, taking their hard-earned wages, and encouraged other women to fall into a life of vice. They destabilized indigenous society and damaged labor relations, thus depriving white farmers and mine owners of income. The traveling prostitute was a nightmarish figure who made it unthinkable that a black woman could be an innocent victim of syphilis or that a white male could be responsible for spreading disease. And yet there were countervailing forces which justified the presence of women in locations. The CID and the Department of Native Affairs wanted to make wage labor more attractive to men. They also wanted to erase the threat of Black Peril. As a consequence the mobility of black women formed the centerpiece in a confused set of motivations.

After 1920 the fading of Black Peril coincided with the imposition of harsher controls against mobile black women. The influence of the moral panics did not disappear completely and Black Peril continued to be cited into the 1940s as justification for the presence of black women in locations.[100] If white women were responsible for Black Peril, black women were to be the antidote.

NINE

SYPHILIS

THE CONTEXT

Infectious disease was one of the major hazards facing white settlement and although by the turn of the century housing and sanitation had improved, the threat remained.[1] In 1902 rabies broke out in Matabeleland; in response the Bulawayo council ordered the destruction of 60,000 dogs. Despite such measures outbreaks of rabies were intermittent and Dr. Loir, a nephew of Pasteur, was appointed to head a local Pasteur Institute.[2] Each year the rains brought dysentery and gastroenteritis and in 1904 there was an outbreak of typhoid fever. It was presumed that disease was spread by Africans but proposals made in council to provide latrines for blacks were rejected as too expensive.[3] Between 1900 and 1904 bubonic plague threatened a number of major South African centers, including the port cities of Cape Town and Port Elizabeth. The hasty removal of Africans to urban locations was deemed necessary to protect whites from infection. In Salisbury the threat of plague was used to justify the establishment of the first urban location.[4] But diseases such as plague and rabies never exerted the kind of imaginative force that were associated with syphilis and gonorrhea.

In Edwardian Britain it was commonly believed that syphilis could be passed on from wet nurses to infants or caught from a dentist's drill, a barber's razor, or a lavatory seat. World War One increased the spread of infection and provoked the eugenic nightmare of healthy men dying in the trenches while the *heredos,* the hereditary syphilitics, multiplied. Between the wars there were fears of butcher's hands, the hairdresser's comb, hotel sheets, and office implements. Because syphilis was sexually transmitted its avoidance was presumed to require moral action. The young were expected to restrict their sexual activities while the state focused its intervention on the suppression of prostitution.[5] Fueled by popular novels and plays warning of the dangers of incontinence, the fear of syphilis declined only after the invention of penicillin in 1929.[6] Colonial administrations were haunted by the specter of syphilis.[7] Infection among blacks in east and central Africa was believed so common that it was used to explain the labor short-ages which plagued mines and farms. Infection among urban black com-munities and particularly among domestic workers was assumed to endan-ger white families.[8]

Throughout the nineteenth century prostitution was a feature of life in the Cape. A combination of poverty and an imbalance in the numbers of white men and women ensured that the industry thrived. Pressure to con-trol both prostitution and the spread of syphilis came initially not from the local white community but from the War Office, which was concerned about the health of British troops.[9] The Contagious Diseases Act, passed in the Cape in 1868, was based upon British legislation and provided for com-pulsory medical inspections and forcible detention. In less than a year an abolition campaign had begun and by 1871 the act had fallen into disuse. As in Britain, much of the opposition came from the Christian churches, which believed the law condoned vice.[10] Within a decade a movement had begun in rural areas for legislation to curb what whites believed was the spread of disease from African workers to white families.

Almost exactly a year before the repeal of the last of the British acts in 1885 the Cape parliament passed the Contagious Diseases Prevention Act.[11] One part covered the registration and medical inspection of prosti-tutes, the other dealt with the spread of syphilis in rural areas by granting surgeons the power to detain those who were infected.[12] Like the British acts it proved difficult to enforce. Physicians were unable to distinguish between syphilis and yaws, a skin disease endemic to the Cape, while few women worked consistently as prostitutes, which made their identification as a class impossible.[13] Before the invention of the Wassermann test in 1906 the diagnosis of syphilis was unreliable and prior to the development of Salvarsan in 1910 there was no cure. The principal treatment was mercury. But the effective dose was so close to being fatal that untreated syphilitics probably had a lower mortality rate than did those who were medicated.[14]

In 1892 a review of Cape legislation found that although its impact had been limited there was one immediate benefit: "Since the introduction of the Act, farmers and employers of labor generally are beginning to intel-ligently suspect diseased servants, and insist on their being treated."[15] Cit-ing a case from Humansdorp, where the young daughters of a white farmer were supposed to have innocently contracted syphilis from a black servant, the report warned of the dangers posed by domestic labor, emphasizing the need for vigilance with regard to cooking utensils, spoons, and kissing.

We now know that syphilis is a fragile organism which cannot survive long outside the body. At least 95 percent of infections are transmitted through sexual contact.[16] The clinical symptoms vary greatly, as does the effect of the disease upon the patient's general health. In only a minority of untreated cases does a patient develop neurosyphilis and many of those infected can live comfortably for years. The tropical disease yaws, or framboesia, is seriologically indistinguishable from syphilis and blood tests for syphilis are positive for yaws. The diseases also provide a strong cross-immunity so that people living in areas of endemic yaws are less likely to contract syphilis. Unlike syphilis, the means of transmission of yaws are non-sexual and the primary symptoms are a pimple which occurs at the site of contact. As the disease progresses multiple blisters will appear on the skin, including the face, which, if left untreated, can be disfiguring. During the colonial period yaws and syphilis were often confused, as in the Humansdorp case, and even an experienced physician would have difficulty in distinguishing between them. Among laypersons that ignorance contributed to the fear of infection which in British Africa was sufficiently important for it to find its way into colonial fiction.[17]

Settlers in Rhodesia brought with them from Britain and South Africa a fear of sexually transmitted diseases. They believed syphilis to be so common among blacks and the disease so infectious that the handling of cutlery, crockery, or even sheets by servants was sufficient to infect an entire household. Those fears were present from the beginning of colonization. Megan Vaughan has argued that in British Africa the fear of disease reflected tensions arising from urbanization and the spread of wage labor. Within that context syphilis epitomized some of the dangers of colonial life.[18] However, urbanization and industrialism are broad categories and while there is merit in the parallels Vaughan draws between the administrative responses in Uganda, Kenya, and Southern Rhodesia there are also notable differences.[19] From the early 1920s there was a perceptible shift in Rhodesia between Black Peril and syphilis as the principal focus for settler anxiety; as one faded the other became more prominent. That shift occurred at a time when the tide of medical evidence showed venereal disease was not a threat and when the availability of Salvarsan had provided the first effective treatment.

MANAGING DISEASE

By 1900 the lay communities of Salisbury and Bulawayo had arrived at an explanation for the transmission of syphilis. Infection was due to the lax morals of the Matabele and Shona and was spread by African prostitutes and miners returning from Kimberley.[20] It was commonly believed that venereal disease threatened the supply of labor. Over the next two decades those assumptions were repeatedly challenged by the health department and in particular by its director, Dr. Fleming.

During the first twenty-five years of settlement the Public Health Department was dominated by Andrew Fleming. The son of a Scottish clergyman, Fleming was educated at Durham and Edinburgh Universities. He became medical director of the Public Health Department of Southern Rhodesia in 1897. He was a forceful and independent thinker who was prominent in public debate. Despite his strengths and his obvious clinical skills in regard to venereal disease, Fleming was at times overwhelmed by the sheer force of public opinion and in particular by the prejudices of town councils and farming and mining interests. The intensity of debate was such that it brought into conflict the departments of public health and native affairs. On at least one occasion it involved the Colonial Office.

During Fleming's tenure there was a prolonged struggle between central and local authorities about who should pay for the treatment of infected Africans. That question dominated policy making and fueled the constant stream of complaints from councils and concerned citizens. Most important, the threat of venereal disease influenced the regulation of labor and the management of locations and reserves. To whites such disease had two distinct settings: an urban context of domestic servants and a rural context of farm and mine workers. Each had a different constituency and each evoked a different imagery.

THE RURAL SETTING

In November 1906 Fleming attended a conference of principal medical officers in Cape Town at which the issue of venereal disease was discussed. The consensus among South African physicians was that syphilis spread principally from mining centers such as Kimberley and, on occasion, from servants to the members of white households.[21] Although Fleming accepted that orthodoxy he changed his mind several times about the best means for prevention and treatment and it took some years for his department to establish a firm policy. Late in his career Fleming observed that there were two schools of thought about the way to control disease. A state-enforced legislation was, he believed, inefficient and he favored a decentralized approach in which the role of the state was largely advisory.[22] In arriving at that policy Fleming had to reconcile the pleas for protection from a fearful public, the demands of employers and churches for assistance, and his department's lack of resources.

By July 1907 a number of white farmers in the Victoria, Belingwe, and

Charter districts approached the health department, claiming that syphilis was threatening the supply of labor. In response Fleming made an extended tour of Victoria during August and September. He found no evidence that the rate of infection was 60 percent, as had been suggested; he believed it was probably closer to 10 percent. Even so syphilis was more common in those districts than elsewhere. According to Fleming, its prevalence was due to living conditions: "The spread among the native population," he wrote, "cannot be ascribed to immorality but is rather direct infection from one member of a family to another; a mother infecting a child, and a child a brother or sister or playmate."[23] What Fleming had seen was yaws, not syphilis. Because of expense the use of lock hospitals, the ideal method to halt the spread of infection, was out of the question and Fleming held little hope of suppressing the disease.

During the early colonial period state services were minimal and the introduction of European medicine came principally from the Christian churches. Missions made frequent requests to the department of health for drugs, claiming the treatment they provided to their congregations imposed a financial burden they could ill afford.[24] Fleming was concerned that most missionaries were unskilled as medical practitioners and initially he opposed supporting medical stations on reserves.[25] If one such station were established, he argued, then other missions would demand assistance because offering medical care was one of the means they used to proselytize.[26] Circumstances eventually forced Fleming to change his mind. The department had no resources to appoint more officers to rural districts and in 1912 Fleming reluctantly agreed to fund posts and dispensaries that used the services of missions and municipalities.[27] Eventually that led to a system under which district surgeons supplied medicine and gave instruction to native commissioners, assistant native magistrates, and missionaries, who then treated the infected. In those areas where there was no surgeon or mission, drugs were supplied free of charge to employers.[28] The scheme appealed to missionaries because it attracted converts. For the department it was a cheap means to provide medical care and placate the white community. Although missionaries clamored for Fleming's support, mine managers and farmers were often more successful in demanding medical supplies. They were better connected than the missions and had strong support within the Legislative Council.

There was no proof that syphilis was a major problem. Fleming's change of mind was due largely to pressure from farming and mining interests. The health department lacked the funds and staff to do what the white community demanded, namely to place the labor force under surveillance and quarantine the infected in lock wards. The dispensaries were a compromise. The department was well aware of the scheme's limitations: Laymen were unable to distinguish between syphilis and yaws. Lack of knowledge was sometimes a problem within the department itself. A farmer named Cooper, for example, wrote to the medical director seeking advice on prophylactic treatment for his workers. He was concerned about the loss of labor because of sickness and the threat to public health; "It is not pleasant to think," wrote Cooper, "that infected natives are milking one's cows especially when the milk is sold in Bulawayo."[29] Cooper recalled an ointment which prevented infection that had been used during his time as a soldier. The director recommended a mixture of calomel and lanoline and he sent Mr. Cooper a sample pot which was to be applied before intercourse. Cooper was pleased with the results.[30]

The Chamber of Mines was adamant that syphilis was the cause of labor shortages; it blamed traveling prostitutes for spreading infection in compounds.[31] At the autumn sitting of the legislative council in 1923 Minister of Mines and Works H. U. Moffat proposed on behalf of the Chamber a system of compulsory medical checks of mine employees. Under existing legislation resident medical officers were obliged to examine workers every fourteen days and forward a monthly report to the compound inspector.[32] The Chamber was aggrieved that infected Africans were treated at the expense of its members while in the Transvaal the cost was borne by the public.[33] Although few mines provided adequate medical care some of the larger mines did; the Chamber wanted the cost shifted to the state. It also wanted all women who visited compounds to be forced to carry a health certificate.[34]

While Moffat's proposal met with a sympathetic hearing, testimony from the medical director ensured that the debate soon collapsed. Fleming informed the council that their concerns were unjustified because the returns for mines showed a rate of infection of less than half of 1 percent.[35] He suggested that if a contagious diseases act were introduced it should also be applied to whites, an idea he knew was abhorrent to members.

Under existing regulations if a mine discharged a sick employee without treatment it could be proceeded against under the Masters and Servants Ordinance or the native labor regulations.[36] Although that was rarely done, mine managers and their supporters continued to complain of the costs incurred in treating infected workers.[37] In fact, under the terms of the Public Health Act of 1924 mine owners had the right to bill their employees for treatment. A number of mines, including the Globe and Phoenix, one of the largest and most profitable gold mines in the country, charged its workers forty shillings for a course of injections, thus enabling the company to make a profit.[38]

Estimates about the prevalence of syphilis and gonorrhea in rural areas varied greatly. Much of the evidence was anecdotal. In order to provide reliable data district medical officers were asked in July 1924 to file returns on the incidence of disease. The returns covered all districts, but without accurate estimates of the size of the African population and some certainty that distinctions were being made between syphilis and yaws, the figures in themselves meant little. Those who were willing to make a guess estimated that between 1 to 15 percent of rural blacks were infected. T. J. Williams, the medical officer at Ndanga, examined 416 adults and children and found only one active case of syphilis. In passing he acknowledged that Africans in Ndanga used one word—*djovera*—to describe both syphilis and yaws.[39] Such evidence had no impact on public opinion. During the 1920s concern about the rate of infection turned gradually into a conviction that the country was in the grip of an epidemic, forcing Fleming to act. In so doing he found his department in conflict with the Department of Native Affairs.

Following claims that infection was rife in the Uzumba reserve, a meeting was held in June 1926 between Fleming and the native commissioner about the erection of a temporary hospital.[40] It was agreed that the medical department would pay for medication and food while the Native Affairs Department would construct the buildings and supervise the facility. At the meeting Fleming called for close cooperation between the two departments. However, within a month relations had broken down over the issue of funding.

The Department of Native Affairs believed that syphilis was a major problem and in 1926 conferences on the subject were held by native commissioners at Salisbury, Bulawayo, and Victoria. They wanted all cases to receive free treatment and, where necessary, accommodation at government expense. At the superintendents of natives and native commissioners conference of 1927 a number of resolutions were passed, including a demand that the government provide adequate funds for the segregation of lepers and syphilitics.[41]

Conflicts over jurisdiction between departments were common but this dispute reflected important differences in perspective. The Native Affairs Department was concerned about the changes sweeping African society and wished to preserve village life. The department was worried about the breakdown of marriage and increased promiscuity, which it viewed as proof of the social disintegration. Those fears were not shared by health officials, who also wanted social order but of a somewhat different kind. Native commissioners had direct access to black communities but they had little clinical knowledge. They were as likely as any layperson to confuse syphilis with yaws and imagine that the skin disease was proof of a calamity facing rural Africa. They also represented the one arm of the state which was dedicated to preserving "native interests." For those reasons commissioners tended to agree with missionaries and farmers that a pandemic was sweeping the countryside.

In the first three decades of colonization many farms and mines were unprofitable. Settlers tended to blame the shortcomings of labor rather than to reflect upon their own inadequacies.[42] In January 1928 a meeting of the Bulawayo Landowners and Farmers Association was held to discuss the shortage of labor. One member named Mitchell had raised the issue of a syphilis epidemic with the government only to be informed that the rate of venereal infection among wage laborers was less than 1 percent. He told his fellow delegates, "Anyone who would believe that would believe anything. It did not help persons who were suffering from this horrible disease and who were spreading it throughout the country." The African laborer was, he said, "often nothing less than a walking reservoir of disease."[43] Mitchell's comments and the meeting's recommendations were reported in the *Rhodesian Herald,* adding to the stream of invective directed against the health department and forcing Fleming once again to seek the opinion of district medical officers. Their reports contained an imagery found also in discussion of Black Peril: Towns were a source of corruption where prostitutes infected migratory workers, who then returned to their villages bringing disease with them. At Sinoia, Dr. G. Barratt judged that while venereal disease was not prevalent there, prostitutes in mine compounds were the main source of infection.[44] J. S. Liptz of Enkeldoorn wrote that in a two-year period he had seen only seventeen cases of syphilis, every one of which he could trace to the towns and mining camps. But he cautioned that many Africans would claim a history of syphilis to avoid having to meet payments under the native tax ordinance.[45] P. Wallace of Filabusi believed the disease had become concentrated in compounds and towns. Blacks entered wage labor for a few months, contracted the disease, then returned to their villages to infect others.[46] Even at such low estimates the rates of infection were probably inflated by the high incidence of yaws. During the 1920s yaws was so common, especially in the Zambesi valley, that the medical service was incapable of dealing with the problem.[47]

In rural areas the politics of syphilis was fractured between a number of competing and sometimes contradictory interests. The issue was fought over by missions and the Native Affairs Department, both of which feared social decay, and miners and farmers who wanted access to labor. The health department sought to work within its limited budget yet placate criticism of its policies from a fearful and ill-informed public. Members of the legislative council mostly supported the interests of the farming lobby.

On the surface the demands by mine owners for state intervention appear benign. In reality they served to disguise the brutal fact of compound life, where the prospect of contracting venereal disease was the least of the hazards facing workers. The moral force with which employers railed against sexual vice and syphilis contrasts with their silence over the causes of pneumonia and scurvy. To minimize overhead costs managers saved on rations, housing, and medical care and, where possible, worked labor to exhaustion. The consequences were scurvy and pneumonia, which until the 1940s took a massive toll of life.[48] The claims about a syphilis epidemic excused the deplorable labor conditions in mines in Rhodesia, which, if anything, were worse than those in the Transvaal.

THE URBAN SETTING

In the period from 1910 to 1920 claims of a pandemic in rural areas were promoted principally by farmers and mine managers. With the inflation that followed World War One labor became more plentiful and people began to fear that syphilis would spread from the countryside into towns.

Although syphilis threatened the capital of farmers and miners in the countryside, in the towns it was seen to threaten the survival of white society itself. In speaking of the danger settlers drew upon an imagery of pollution, sexual license, and social disintegration of the kind associated with Black Peril. By 1920 only Fleming and a minority of his department doubted that disaster was imminent. The origins of those fears can be traced back almost a decade. As early as 1911 a conference of native superintendents found that "the presence of syphilis among natives in European centres is not receiving adequate attention and that it is a matter calling for immediate action."[49] Its recommendation that a lock ward be established at hospitals in each of the major towns was rejected because of the cost and Fleming's doubts about the extent of the problem. Over time the fears expressed by native superintendents became commonplace.

During 1917 the Salisbury town council made several appeals to the administrator's office. In May of that year the council passed a resolution that all Africans entering the town be detained for medical inspection.[50] The council pointed out that while there were inspections at mines there were none in urban centers: "The consequence is that many natives suffering from loathsome and contagious diseases are allowed to go about towns possibly spreading the germs among European families."[51] The council proposed "[t]hat all natives should on arrival in town to seek work be obliged to go to a Central depot where they would be vaccinated, obliged to have baths, wash their clothes etc and undergo a medical examination."[52] Since government already collected taxes from employers and from Africans it should bear the cost, which the council estimated at around 700 pounds per annum. In August a similar demand was made by the Bulawayo municipality. The administrator, while sympathetic, was concerned about who should pay for the scheme.[53] The issue of medical certificates also came into conflict with existing ordinances controlling the movement of labor.[54] Legal opinion suggested that new legislation would be necessary and since it would discriminate between Africans and settlers it would have to be ratified by imperial authorities.[55]

The council supported its case with testimony from Dr. F. Appelyard, an experienced Salisbury physician. Appelyard had treated many cases of syphilis and although he could not recall infection passing from a servant to an employer that did not mean such infection had not occurred. In his experience most Shona, including a large proportion of servants, suffered from infections such as scabies, but his most frightening evidence was anecdotal. He referred to a case he had heard of from a Cape Town physician in which a white infant was infected with syphilis by an African nurse. The baby in turn infected its mother and another child.[56] Appelyard was certain that the same risk existed in Salisbury.[57] The case was a variation on the Humansdorp story but although it contained the predictable elements of a dissolute servant and defenseless children, it confused yaws with syphilis. Appleyard's testimony was supported by the CID, which documented four instances of domestic workers who were found to be suffering from venereal disease.[58] The council demanded that medical inspections be comprehensive because "a great deal of disease might be carried in a native's clothing and blankets and it is our intention to provide a steam disinfector and baths where natives should cleanse themselves before medical examinations."[59]

The pressure applied by the councils was such that the attorney general, at the request of the administrator, prepared an ordinance called the Medical Examination of Native Servants (Urban) Ordinance of 1918.[60] The draft allowed for compulsory examination and treatment by local authorities of all prospective servants. Non-compliance was to be punishable by a fine of 10 pounds or one month's imprisonment. Although the ordinance contained everything the Salisbury and Bulawayo councils wanted, it was never debated in the legislative council. Instead it was replaced by the Natives Registration Ordinance Amendment Ordinance. The amendment enabled the administrator to authorize the compulsory medical examination and vaccination of Africans who applied for work. Significantly, the ordinance made no mention of urban areas or of municipal authorities; it merely gave greater powers to the administrator. During debate there was some confusion about the duties of Fleming's department and much concern about who was to pay for the scheme. It was commonly believed, for example, that the government was obliged to treat free of charge all cases of venereal disease. That, however, was not the case and although destitute men or women could be referred by a magistrate to a government medical officer where the patient (black or white) was employed, he or she had to pay for his or her own treatment.[61] After clamoring for such a scheme the Salisbury council announced that it would not bear the cost of treating those who failed a medical test.[62]

The fears of councils were heightened by the influenza epidemic which arrived in central Africa during the final months of World War One. The first case of Spanish influenza occurred at Bulawayo on October 12, 1918, and within two weeks it had spread throughout the territory.[63] Economic activity was brought to a standstill. The administration initiated a massive campaign to limit the spread of infection which involved the native and health departments, missions, and traditional authorities. A prohibition forbade Africans from traveling by train and chiefs were instructed to keep their people confined to their villages. Many Africans deserted the mines and fled north. The state requisitioned cattle and petrol supplies. Almost ten times as many whites perished from influenza as had died in the *chimurenga*. By mid-November the crisis had passed as quickly as it had begun, but the effects were to be felt for many years. The official explanation for the epidemic was the same used to explain the spread of syphilis—the infection had been carried from South Africa by migrant workers.[64] It reminded whites of their vulnerability and fueled their fears of being surrounded by a immense but invisible pool of infection.

Before the Spanish influenza, Fleming had ridiculed claims that venereal disease was a threat to settlers. By the beginning of 1919 he had come to believe that many servants were infected and were exposing European families to risk. The problem for the department of health was how to respond to such a threat. There were no special hospital facilities and such patients were unsuited for general wards, which, moreover, were under the charge of European nurses.[65] But the main problem for the department was the expense.[66] A single treatment for syphilis cost 6 shillings and the cost per patient was around 1 pound.[67] Because of distance in many cases, in-patient care was necessary, thereby increasing the expense.

In his public pronouncements Fleming was sympathetic to settlers, but he was often annoyed by their hysteria. In October 1922 he told the police commissioner; "I know it is popular opinion that our natives suffer greatly from venereal disease, and therefore it may interest some people to know that in the many years I have been in medical charge of the BSA Police and the BSAN Police, I am sorry to say that a far higher proportion of venereal disease occurs amongst the white trooper as compared with the native."[68] In 1923 his department surveyed the incidence of infection among black males resident at Salisbury, Belingwe, and at mine compounds. It found that the rate of infection was less than 0.6 percent, which was probably only slightly above the rate for the African adult male population as a whole.[69]

The annual report of the Department of Public Health for 1923 noted that due to a lack of funds and an appropriate legislative framework there was no systematic policy of treatment or prevention. It was in part to provide such a framework that the Public Health Act of 1924 was introduced. The act, which included an entire chapter devoted to venereal disease, was focused specifically upon urban areas and was designed to protect settler families.[70] While the legislation was welcomed by the white community the provision to make vaccinations compulsory for whites proved unpopular. Those who did not want to be vaccinated were exempted.[71]

The legislation gave a wide range of powers to physicians and local authorities to regulate the movement of men and women in and out of urban areas. It empowered officers to forcibly examine any African, to disinfect his or her clothes, and, under certain circumstances, to destroy domiciles.[72] It also obliged schoolteachers, employers, and heads of families to give notice of any contagious disease. The definition of risk was left to medical officers and in effect allowed for the removal, isolation, or internment of any person seeking employment. The act also stipulated that an infected person who continued in employment in a shop, home, factory, hotel, or restaurant was guilty of an offense; it made treatment compulsory and the failure to seek treatment a crime. The minister for health was given the authority to designate an area as one prevalent in venereal disease and to order the medical examination of all its black inhabitants.

The act was a model for the division of social space which, when read against the history of the later colonial period, has sinister connotations. Other legislation provided rules for the regulation and surveillance of labor but the act of 1924 was unusual in permitting the confiscation and destruction of property. The legislation was also notable for the extent to which it was motivated by the threat of syphilis and by the lack of reference to that disease in the debate surrounding its drafting.[73]

The immediate effect of the act was to increase the amount of time and money spent in identifying and treating the infected. Within twelve months the municipal medical officer at Salisbury reported a rise of almost 100 percent in the number of cases.[74] However, because many of those cases had come to town specifically for treatment that increase was not in itself significant.[75] Health officers noted that Africans would readily present for treatment and were impressed by the speed with which lesions could be healed. But the act did not halt the flow of complaints about the threat to white families. Settlers wanted the disease to be controlled among blacks. They also wanted it rendered invisible and the provision of clinics only made them apprehensive.[76]

Conditions at rural clinics were poor and reflected the rationale which lay behind the program. In one report, the clinic at Shamva was described in the following way: "The building is of Kimberley brick with thatched roof and calico ceilings. The outside walls are crumbling away with age, the laths of the ceiling have rotted and the ceiling is falling down, there is a large hole in the thatched roof through which rain pours. Generally the place is unfit for habitation."[77] There was also frustration among medical staff because the legislation proved so difficult to administer.[78]

The act did little to assuage the fears of whites. In October 1928 Fleming met with a delegation from the Bulawayo Landowners and Farmers Association. The association wanted reform of the local hospital and increased funding for health care. It also wanted a bacteriological laboratory established in the town. Most of all, the association demanded that the department conduct a comprehensive survey of the African population.

The association was a powerful group which Fleming could not ignore, no matter how fanciful its claims. He patiently explained that syphilis was prevalent among urban Africans because most were young males who were divorced from family life while they were employed.[79] According to the 1926 census, there were 110,041 African males in wage labor and only 2,908 females living in urban or mining centers. The statistics for urban Africans included those in jails, members of the Native Police Force, patients under care at government hospitals, miners, and railway workers. The rate of infection among those groups was between 2 and 3 percent. The rate for those seeking employment as servants in Bulawayo during 1926 was less than half of 1 percent.[80] As Fleming pointed out, those figures were far lower than for the British armed services.[81]

To conduct a medical survey would, according to Fleming, have cost between 100,000 and 150,000 pounds and have involved the forcible examination of men and women. In political terms alone such a survey was unacceptable. Furthermore it was difficult to distinguish between syphilis and leprosy, while in the tertiary stage it was almost impossible to discriminate between syphilis and yaws. Fleming reminded the delegation that clinics had been established at Bulawayo, Salisbury, Gatooma, Umtali, Que Que, Ndanga, and Mnene and that Rhodesia was doing better than were authorities in England in controlling infection. He reassured the association that the health department was tracking down prostitutes who traveled the country spreading disease.[82] No survey was conducted but Fleming's careful explanations did little to halt demands for intervention.

In April 1929 the Chambers of Commerce held a congress at Bulawayo at which the issue of syphilis was discussed. According to one participant the matter was raised because "all delegates employed blacks and therefore such health matters had commercial significance."[83] The meeting passed a number of resolutions demanding greater control over labor. It wanted more clinics and a guarantee that no woman would be allowed employment as a servant without a medical certificate. There was strong feeling that the government was not doing enough and that as a result white women and children were at risk. The Rhodesian Women's League, which had supported previous council initiatives, wrote to the Colonial Secretary demanding that a clinic be set up in the Salisbury location to examine African women as well as those males who were seeking domestic work.[84] The Colonial Secretary referred the matter back to the municipalities.

Throughout his struggles with employers' associations and the Salisbury and Bulawayo councils Fleming sought to minimize the costs incurred by his department. His position was made more difficult because there were many within his own administration who believed that syphilis was a threat.[85] What finally turned the tide against Fleming were fears for urban populations, behind which lay the specter of Humansdorp.

In May 1930 the Salisbury council demanded that a *lazaretto* be built on the Salisbury commonage.[86] Fleming rejected the proposal as too expensive and pointed out that the council stood to reap 550 pounds per annum out of the scheme.[87] He was also concerned that the council wrongly believed it had authority to forcibly detain infected Africans. Despite the expense and the lack of powers to enforce treatment, within six months the Native Isolation Hospital or, as it was later called, the Native Venereal Diseases, Fever, and Isolation Hospital was established.[88] It had taken eighteen years of political agitation to force the state to act. At no time was there medical evidence that such action was necessary.

While the issue of controlling the disease among blacks dragged on for almost three decades, provision for the care of whites was resolved within a matter of weeks. In October 1927 the Salisbury town council requested that a small clinic for Europeans be established as part of the government hospital. Within two months a ward was operating at Salisbury.[89] Most of those treated were private patients who, because of the stigma attached to venereal disease, were too embarrassed to go to a specialist clinic.[90] The white community was much smaller than the black community, which in part explains the ease with which the issue was resolved for Europeans. There was also the fact that among whites venereal disease had little resonance with the maintenance of racial boundaries, state power, or economic advantage. The provision of care was therefore largely a technical matter.

CONCLUSION

Farmers and mine managers wanted the state to treat disease, guarantee a supply of cheap labor, subsidize their costs of production, and prevent further armed resistance. They also wanted to be free from state regulation so that they could do what they liked with their workers. Those two sets of wishes were irreconcilable and drew employers into conflict with the Native Affairs Department and the departments of mines and health. Part of that conflict was played out through the issue of venereal disease.

There were rather different reasons why mine owners, farmers, missionaries, and some district commissioners wanted state intervention. Town councils also wanted intervention but only in urban centers. All demanded access to the health department's limited resources. Because of Fleming's instrumental attitude the conflict dragged on for more than two decades. It was part of a wider process in which can be seen the formation of the Rhodesian state.

The Southern Rhodesian state was racialized in terms of its administration, personnel, ethos, and purpose. It was also racialized with regard to the laws it produced. Its officers were to a marked degree preoccupied with questions of morality and sexual conduct, which were themselves boundary issues about race. The legitimate role of the state included passing laws to make citizens and colonial subjects more moral. It is not surprising that the morality legislation of 1903 and 1916 set a precedent for the Public Health Act of 1924.

The white population was so small and the settler state so rudimentary in scope that the actions of individuals were sometimes important. That was so in the case of Andrew Fleming. The delays in bringing in legislation to control venereal disease were in large part due to Fleming's resistance.

Without him those initiatives would have been made earlier and the syphilis panics and Black Peril would have run side by side instead of being sequential.

How the history of venereal disease is written depends upon which sources are used. Megan Vaughan relies upon the annual reports from the department of public health. In so doing she fails to see what lay beneath those documents, namely the pressure which local councils, the Native Affairs Department, and missions exerted on the Public Health Department and its director.[91] The stance taken by public health officials was moderate, but public debate was not. That fact eventually pushed Fleming into adopting policies he did not want. The annual reports were distilled from a range of interests and were in part designed to conceal intra-departmental conflict. In using only those sources the temper of public debate is lost, as are the reasons for the interventionist policy of the 1920s.

Labor shortages were a problem for farmers and miners but there is no evidence that venereal disease had any impact upon the economy. In 1906 a native labor committee was established to inquire into the reasons for the periodic shortages of labor and to determine the best means to collect and distribute workers. The final report made no mention of venereal disease.[92] Four years later the Native Affairs Department committee of inquiry into the conditions of the African community concluded that syphilis was prevalent but found no evidence that that prevalence was relevant to the labor supply.[93] In 1927 the rate of infection among Africans who worked for Europeans in Salisbury and Bulawayo was around 1 percent.[94] Those who were best informed, such as Dr. Fleming, knew that venereal disease had no commercial significance. He also knew that the source of infection lay in the migrant labor and segregation which were the foundations of the colonial economy. In light of the low rates of infection, what explains the importance of syphilis to the white community? The answer is complex and leads us back to fears of Black Peril.

The origins of Black Peril fears were so diffuse that it is impossible to identify a simple causal chain leading, for example, from sexual anxiety among white elites to the morality legislation. For that reason I cannot prove there was a causal relationship between the panics over Black Peril and syphilis. But there was at the least a strong correspondence. The components of the fears were similar: The body was at risk, the cause was vice, a racial boundary was breached, and the innocent suffered. In both cases white families were at risk. In the case of syphilis, even more so than in the case of Black Peril, there was no proof of a threat.

Apprehension about syphilis was common to metropolitan Britain and to colonial administrations such as the one in Uganda.[95] But the ways in which administrations reacted varied from place to place. In Kenya, in the period from 1907 until 1919 there was a steady fall in the number of Africans treated for syphilis. However, after 1920 that changed dramatically and in response to a rise in the number of patients in 1925 two venereal disease clinics were opened in Nairobi.[96] It is not clear why a sudden increase occurred but it is probable that the reason lay in the provisions of the new public health act and in the greater willingness of Africans to seek treatment. There was also at that time a dramatic rise in the reported cases of yaws. According to the annual report of the Public Health Department for 1921 the economic importance of that disease could not be overestimated.[97] To an extent the prominence of yaws in Kenya, and the willingness (or ability) of physicians to distinguish between yaws and syphilis, diminished the importance of venereal disease. The situation in Southern Rhodesia was very different.

In the Zimbabwe National Archives there are several hundred files dealing with venereal disease. The files document the panics which swept civil society and the state. Community groups, professional associations, and local councils all pressured the department of health to combat a threat which did not exist. In the Kenya National Archives there are references to syphilis and gonorrhea in district commissioners reports and in the correspondence and annual reports from the departments of health and native affairs. Those documents show that the rates of infection in the two colonies were similar. They also show that in Kenya syphilis was considered less important than yaws or plague or malaria. There was no panic among medical officers or the white male public about the prevalence of syphilis. Nor was venereal disease of concern to groups such as the East Africa Womens League.[98] There was no suggestion that infection among Africans had any economic importance or that it posed a threat to the health of Europeans. It is significant that in Kenya fears of Black Peril were less important.[99]

Between 1902 and 1916 Black Peril was a major issue in Rhodesia. There was also concern among farmers and miners about the impact of syphilis upon the supply of labor. For more than a decade Fleming was successful in opposing demands for state intervention by financing missions and employers to treat the infected. From 1920 to 1930 fears of Black Peril waned and Fleming and his department were finally overwhelmed by lobbying from town councils and missions who claimed the country was in the grip of an epidemic. In the countryside syphilis evoked images of a declining economy, capital gone to waste, fallow land, and rusting machinery. In the towns settler fears were focused upon servants and the threat to families: In the minds of settlers locations were reservoirs of disease and domestic workers its conduits.

The panics over syphilis, as Megan Vaughan has shown, were in part a metaphor for changes that were sweeping indigenous society. Those changes, which the churches and the state viewed in essentially moral terms, included the spread of wage labor and the increasing economic independence of black women. Missionaries and native commissioners were alarmed by what they believed was the disintegration of rural communities. However, there was little agreement about the best way to prevent infection. After 1920 an expanding economy ushered in a period of urbanization that increased the number of women in locations. Fears of an urban epidemic corresponded to the introduction of the theme of "unruly women"; the traveling prostitute joined the infected servant as the focus for settler fears.[100]

The most obvious solution to Black Peril was to replace male servants with females. As we have seen, there were a number of reasons why that was not possible. Similarly, given the theory of the traveling prostitute, the obvious means to combat an epidemic in urban areas was to introduce compulsory medical examinations of women, as was done in Buganda during the 1920s.[101] Because of opposition from male urban workers, black women, and traditional authorities, administrators in Salisbury knew that such a scheme was out of the question. It would also have exhausted the limited resources of the health department. Under Fleming it was department policy that male physicians should not examine African women because of fears that such a practice would have exposed them to temptation or blackmail, ideas borrowed from the moral panics.[102] At a more prosaic level, physicians opposed compulsory examinations because that would have increased their already heavy workloads.[103]

The panics over Black Peril and syphilis shared a number of elements. Neither had much basis in fact and the anxiety they provoked appears in retrospect to have been out of proportion to the actual threat. Both were sexualized and involved the corruption of otherwise healthy bodies. Both evoked ideas of degeneration and racial decline; rape could result in half-castes, syphilis create a class of *heredos*. Because both had their origins in the sexual domain both were invested with particular moral force. The panics over Black Peril and syphilis involved contests of authority between different factions of the state. They were also the issues over which criticism of the state was most bitter. Reformers wanted more police in order to control locations and regulate mine compounds. They wanted surveillance of servants and constraints placed on the mobility of women. They attacked the state because it could not protect white women from assault or prevent the spread of infection. The main issue in both panics was a perceived threat to white families. In the case of syphilis the danger was more insidious.

The ideology of Black Peril set a precedent for an inclusive vision of sexual threat upon which fears of an epidemic could be built. It expanded the scope for state intervention and conflated the issues of moral order and the safety of families. The phobias differed in that they involved a shift in gender from black men to black women as the source of danger. That shift can be explained by changes to the colonial economy and to the increased mobility of black women in particular. It was the importance of those factors to white men which allowed the panics over syphilis to become so widespread and to survive for so long.

TEN

COLOUREDS, POOR WHITES, AND BOUNDARIES

Black Peril assaults aroused intense feeling among white men because symbolically at least they involved the violent breaching of a racial boundary. Such crimes were unusual and voluntary sexual relations between white women and black men were probably even rarer. The panics tended to disguise the points at which the differences between whites and the subaltern races blurred. Even though legislators spoke as if Black Peril was the major threat to racial integrity, in practice racial boundaries were often compromised by other means. The most significant were the sexual transgressions of white men, the demands by Coloureds for civil liberties, and the presence of poor whites.

Colonial authority rested upon administrative, military, and economic advantage. It also rested upon the assumption that Europeans made up a natural community which was clearly distinguished from Africans, Coloureds, and Asiatics.[1] That, however, was not the case; neither physical appearance nor material circumstance were adequate markers of identity. Whiteness was acquired rather than inherited: Birth was not the only point of entry to the white community nor death the only exit. The most common reason for exclusion from white society was poverty. Many settlers were barely middle class and the category European included junior clerks, subaltern soldiers, nurses, domestics, and the unemployed. Racial taxonomies were made more problematic by Coloureds who could pass as European. When it needed to decide who was white the state was often forced to fall back upon the identification of particular psychological traits. Consequently the attorney general and the Department of Education were faced with incessant problems in assigning the privileges of citizenship.

The first Coloureds who arrived in Southern Rhodesia in the 1890s were skilled or semi-skilled artisans from the Cape.[2] The mixed-race population of the new colony soon grew as settlers formed permanent relationships with local women and took wives under customary law. There were no legal impediments to a white man having sex with a black woman and

in the first twenty years of settlement the social costs were negligible. From
the turn of the century Salisbury's Coloured community lived in squalor in
a haphazard collection of houses between the railway line and the *kopje*.[3]
The term half-caste denoted a first-generation person of mixed race while
the term Coloured meant those who belonged to a second or later generation. Coloureds were members of a community; half-castes were isolated
individuals usually living with their mothers. The definitions of Coloureds
used by the state were essentially negative; they referred to a class of persons who were neither European, African, nor Asiatic.[4] No matter what
definition was used, in practice the distinction was always aesthetic and
judgment could vary from one official to another. Prosperity elevated the
economic status of some Coloureds while bad luck, personal failings, or
economic recession reduced a minority of whites to poverty. The ambiguous status of the Coloured community was compounded by the variations
of skin tone which could occur even within a single family. Segregationist
policies directed against Coloureds were not confined to physical proximity but involved the management of information, the suppression of attitudes, and the frustration of any sense of equality.

It is difficult to estimate the size of the Coloured population in Southern Rhodesia. According to the census of 1911 there were 2,042 people of
mixed race in the territory, which represented a rise of almost 50 percent
from 1904.[5] Yet according to official estimates, after that date the Coloured
population barely increased. In 1926 it numbered 2,100 and by 1936 it
had risen to only 3,200.[6] From the early 1930s it was government policy to
discourage Coloured immigrants, which probably reduced the eventual size
of the mixed-race population.[7] But that alone does not explain the census
returns. There were no objective criteria for judging race, and the eager-
ness of Coloureds to be classified as white meant that their numbers were
often underestimated.[8] It is also probable, as Ibo Mandaza has argued, that
some prominent whites fathered half-caste children, which gave administrators further reason to conceal the incidence of miscegenation and the
size of the Coloured population.[9]

Coloureds were perceived by the administration as an ill-defined threat
and segregation was designed to control both their mobility and aspirations. In an attempt to separate Coloureds from whites a policy of exclusion eventually touched upon most aspects of social life. It was evident, for
example, in jails, hospitals, and schools or where access by non-whites to
information about whites and their conventions was deemed unsafe. Public employment was closed to Coloureds and various justifications were
used for the segregation of housing and education. The principle of exclu-

sion was applied also in contexts in which no white person was present.[10] In 1928 one Umtali resident warned the native commissioner of the need for a comprehensive policy: "If left to develop under the present lack of system, it [the Coloured community] will inevitably tend to degrade into a criminal class."[11] Such views were commonplace.

MISCEGENATION AND CHILDREN

Sexual relations across racial boundaries were common but marriages between white men and black women were rare. The permission of the Native Affairs Department was required for such unions and in those rare instances when a man contemplated marriage every effort was made to dissuade him.[12] The first Christian or civil marriage between a white man and an African woman did not take place until 1920, and the event was viewed with disquiet by the Native Affairs Department.[13] Such marriages caused fewer problems for the administration than did the children of sexual unions between white men and black women. Shifts in policy toward half-caste children are a good point from which to survey the placement and maintenance of racial boundaries.

By 1910 the Salisbury CID had begun collecting information on miscegenation and had developed a series of rationales about the circumstances under which transgressions were likely to occur. According to department files miscegenation was most common in isolated areas adjacent to native reserves. Infractions were mostly the result of "sexual opportunity."[14] It noted that a large number of the fifty-five men listed as offenders in 1913 were Jewish and Greek shopkeepers of "a low type." Because such behavior was legal the CID could only charge such individuals with a minor offense such as being in a location at night.[15] The Bulawayo CID also kept records, noting the occupations of offenders, the frequency of intercourse, and whether the man was known to suffer from syphilis.[16] The CID identified three types of offenders. There was a small minority who lived openly with "native" women, a larger number who regularly visited women at their huts, and a majority who had promiscuous sex with prostitutes. The activities of the first group was held to be the most damaging because of the openness of their behavior and the number of half-caste children they produced.[17]

It is difficult to gauge the incidence of miscegenation for the country as a whole. Between February 1916 and June 1930 the Bulawayo CID identified only seventy-seven offenders. Those cases, however, involved cohabitation as distinct from commercial sex, which was certainly more common.[18] One estimate from Gwanda suggested that around 10 percent of the white male population either cohabited with black women or engaged in casual sex.[19] White men who formed enduring relationships often faced conviction for a minor offense, which was the means the CID used to intimidate them. The African men who acted as messengers or go-betweens were charged with the more serious crime of procuring. The Department of Native Affairs had a rather different perspective; it was most sensitive to cases involving its own officers or cases in which a mission had made a complaint.[20] Even so, from the beginning of World War One the Department required headmen and chiefs to report any white man who was interfering with local women.[21]

The conventions governing sexual relations between white men and black women were ambiguous. There was official censure of concubinage and casual sex but until the late 1920s such activities were tolerated so long as offenders were discreet. When a sexual assault had been committed against a black woman the CID usually took little interest and it was rare for a white man to be brought to trial, let alone convicted.[22]

From as early as 1913 the native commissioner, working in conjunction with the CID, kept records of the number of mixed-race births and from the 1920s compiled biannual returns for every district. Although those records were part of a wider monitoring of miscegenation, in most cases the name of the father was not recorded.[23] The Native Affairs Department and the CID made every effort to prevent mixed-race marriages and applied pressure to men who lived openly with African women. A more ruthless policy was used in deciding the fate of the children of such unions.

Between 1910 and the 1920s women's organizations and the churches appealed repeatedly to the attorney general to act on the plight of mixed-race children. According to Native Affairs Department estimates, by 1930 there were 182 half-caste children under the age of five years, 289 between the ages of five and ten, and 255 between the ages of ten and fifteen. Those figures were at odds with both the census returns and the presumption that miscegenation was a thing of the past.[24] The question of what to do with such children was complex. Some administrators and women's groups wanted fathers to be forced by law to accept responsibility. But any program of assistance to half-castes would have involved if not the identification of offenders then at least some admission of the sexual misdemeanors of white males. As the result of persistent lobbying by the Rhodesian Women's League (RWL) in July 1930, the premier decided to save such children "from being thrust back into the lower culture of their mother's people, by whom they are not welcomed, and where neither tribal nor Location custom makes any provision for them."[25] He was equally determined that their mothers should in no way benefit.[26] In August the prime minister's office wrote to Mr. F. L. Hadfield, a leading Bulawayo businessman, to ask for his views on the subject.

Hadfield had for many years worked among Coloureds and was considered an expert on their needs. He had also served as a member of the education commission of 1924 when the issue of the education of half-caste children was discussed. According to Hadfield, such children fitted in nowhere and even the Coloured community despised them. "If they go right into kraal life" he wrote, "it is generally with a sense of being degraded by doing so, especially the young men, and if they persist this consciousness degrades them still further. They not infrequently become leaders of viciousness. They refuse to work as a native and cannot work on the level of their fathers."[27] Hadfield warned the prime minister that half-castes often developed a strong sense of bitterness and grew up to become a menace to the white community. The only solution lay in religious instruction and practical training that would give them the means to earn a living. Without such training "strong hereditary tendencies to sexual indulgence and excess will drag them down and nothing but a very wholesome life with sincere Christian teaching can combat it."[28] In an aside which would have pleased no one, he observed that some white children would also benefit if removed from the care of their parents. After reading Hadfield's report, Prime Minister Moffat recommended that separate schools and hostels be established and that children, if necessary, be forcibly removed from their mothers.[29] But because of the high costs involved no hostels were built and cases continued to be resolved on an individual basis.

In practice the fate of mixed-race children was determined not by the conditions under which their mothers lived but by the attitude and wishes of their fathers. If a father chose to have a child educated it was removed from its mother's care and she was not allowed to visit the child or to have any further say in its upbringing. Under a policy which had precedents in the United States, Canada, and Australia, most children taken from their mothers were over seven years of age.[30] A typical case was that of Ann, the daughter of James Tweedie and Mary Chambasi. Tweedie acknowledged paternity to the native commissioner, A. G. Yardley, and agreed to pay for Ann's care in an institution. Yardley welcomed the decision because it avoided "the objectionable consequences to be apprehended in the case of a half white child growing up among natives in the care of a mother of loose morals," as Ann's mother was described.[31] A Catholic orphanage agreed to accept Ann so long as funds for her care were guaranteed and Chambasi had no further contact with her daughter. The church wanted Ann removed at once so that the ill-effects of "kraal life" could be minimized.[32] The

major obstacle, Chambasi's reluctance to give up her daughter, was over-
come by Yardley, who told her "[t]hat she has a duty to the child and must
allow her to be taken over by the sisters of St. Johns completely. She is of
course heartsore but I anticipate no difficulty over this question. I have told
her that she will not be allowed to see the child hereafter."[33] Ann was delivered by her mother to St. John's, at Avondale. At the nuns' insistence Chambasi left the grounds immediately and to their knowledge never saw her
child again. It is unclear what was being rescued in this story—Ann's father's reputation, Ann's future, or the genetic material she represented. From
the point of view of the state, each of those possibilities masked the more
fundamental issue of miscegenation.

There were many tensions surrounding proposals to rescue children
such as Ann. A minority of members of the Legislative Assembly, along
with the churches and women's groups, wanted men held responsible. By
November 1930 the premier was determined to suppress miscegenation
and in particular the activities of "southern European storekeepers," thereby solving the secondary problem of the offspring of such unions.[34] Moffat
was keen to distinguish between men who lived with African women and
those who occasionally transgressed. Purely sexual encounters could be
tolerated but not relations that were sentimental.[35] Hadfield held similar
views, suggesting that permanent unions gave much offense to white women.[36] The issue occupied the attorney general's office for some months,
but because of difficulties in arriving at a definition of cohabitation no
legislation was drafted.

In 1933 the director of education, Mr. Foggin, chaired an inquiry into
the education of Coloureds.[37] Like most sections of white society, the committee felt some discomfort over the plight of half-caste children.[38] It also
feared any solution which would have exposed to scrutiny the sexual misconduct of their fathers. Several witnesses argued that because half-castes
were abhorred by both African and white communities it was necessary
to proscribe miscegenation. That proposal was rejected on the grounds
that legislation would merely create opportunities for blackmail, a specter
which harked back to fears related to the issue of Black Peril.[39] Some witnesses wanted children removed forcibly from villages and educated at special schools. The committee, however, opposed coercion because it would
have involved transferring the cost of the children's upkeep to the state.
The committee also feared that if all children were removed it could lead to
the formation of a new racial group, Rhodesian half-castes and their de-
scendants.[40] Given those factors it decided that while a few children could
attend Coloured schools the best outcome would be the absorption of the
majority into native society. Their superior mental powers meant that they

would act "as the leadership of the more enlightened section of African opinion."[41] The decision as to which children should be "saved" was to be decided by circumstance.[42] The committee confirmed that sexual relations between white men and black women were common. Surprisingly, its findings were never cited by women's groups in their demands to change the immorality ordinances.

Any public discussion of half-caste children made male legislators uncomfortable. The Foggin inquiry, like the earlier proposal by Moffat, exposed a number of tensions between white men and white women over the question of sexual opportunity. If a law were to be passed there would be no guarantee that prosecutions would be confined to Greek and Jewish storekeepers. In the view of the administration the prestige lost through such revelations could well have been worse than that associated with the presence of mixed-race children living in villages. That was why children remained with their mothers and the CID did not record the names of their fathers.

The issue of what to do with half-caste children became prominent at the end of the 1920s. By that time miscegenation had become less palatable to male elites. There was a more expansive state apparatus and the demographic imbalance between white men and white women had shifted. In 1919 women had gained the vote and access to employment in the civil service. By 1931 the Black Peril panics were a memory. But the same contests for authority between white men and white women continued. Women's organizations wanted fathers to take responsibility for their children; missionaries wanted the state to show charity toward the offspring of illicit unions; the administration wanted to maintain racial boundaries. Those who favored change always ran up against the weight of the morality ordinances which blamed women for sexual transgressions.

The Foggin report contained two distinct voices. One argued that half-caste children were proof of illicit sexual relations and therefore should be rendered invisible; the other that they represented good genetic material and should be rescued. Foggin decided that the best outcome was for children to be absorbed into village life, thereby endorsing the education act under which a person living as a native was ineligible for entry to a Coloured school.[43]

SCHOOLS AND TAXONOMIES

The presence of Coloured children in European schools caused the Department of Education endless trouble. While it was a simple matter to exclude dark-skinned children, the light-skinned progeny of Coloureds often gained entry. Coloured parents were keen to send their children to white schools because it bestowed an European identity upon the child and its family. That was why when the first exclusively Coloured schools were opened they failed to attract children of fair complexion. The presence of pupils suspected of being Coloured angered white parents, who usually threatened to withdraw their own children. Those parents were the department's most important constituency and in general it did what they wanted. The department was also accountable to the colonial office. Whitehall tended to view exclusion as improper because it frustrated the Coloured community's attempts at social betterment and on more than one occasion it questioned the practice.[44]

St. Cyril's, the first school to accept Coloured children, was opened at Bulawayo in 1900. It was classified by the Department of Education as both a white and Coloured institution.[45] The government preferred to support missions like St. Cyril's rather than establish special schools. That policy may have continued indefinitely but for opposition from white parents. The presence of children whose skin color allowed them to pass as white necessitated government aid to mission schools and later the establishment of Coloured schools operated by the state. The Education Ordinance of 1903 allowed for the creation of separate schools for Coloured children.[46] It also gave the director of education the right to ban or expel a student for any reason he saw fit. The purpose of that clause was to justify the exclusion of children whom the department suspected of being Coloured.

The first school to be established at Bulawayo under the ordinance was the Church of Christ Coloured School, which opened in 1907. In deference to the wishes of parents the principal barred African children. By September the school had more than sixty pupils but because many parents could not afford to pay fees the mission was left to bear the cost.[47] Over the next ten years state grants increased, as did the willingness of the Department of Education to consider taking over the school's operation. Those policies were counterbalanced by protests from white parents over proposals to have Coloured children attend white schools. Whites believed the Coloured community was vice-ridden and that Coloured schools were reservoirs of crime. One of their most common criticisms was that because Coloureds lived openly in sin they exerted little control over their children.[48] The department held much the same view and the Church of Christ Coloured School was dogged by controversy.

For a family which considered itself European the exclusion of a child was a calamity. It lowered the family's status and denied the child access to a decent education. Over a period of fourteen years the sons of Mr. Pearmain of Bulawayo, whose wife was from St. Helena, were rejected repeatedly from white schools. Because the family mixed only with whites, Pearmain refused to send them to the Church of Christ school and appealed to the chief inspector. School authorities would not accept the children and eventually a special grant was made for Pearmain to have them educated in private. While exclusion was common the solution in the Pearmain case was unusual.[49] Only a handful of such decisions were made by any school in a given period, but because such cases were so difficult to resolve they caused a persistent problem for the administration.

The nomenclature of race was clumsy. In the absence of a clear definition the decision to omit or accept a child was often problematic. The director of education, Mr. Foggin, recognized those difficulties and from 1908 he used the method employed in the Transvaal; the decision was left to local school committees.[50] Evidence that a family mixed with Coloureds was taken as proof of identity and in general no matter how light-skinned a child was, if one parent was deemed to be Coloured the child was barred.[51] In February 1911 the secretary of Bulawayo schools, G. Brownhead, wrote to the department asking for an unambiguous definition of identity. He feared that if mixed-race children were allowed to enter primary schools as fee-paying students they would eventually have a case for admission to high schools.[52] The policy was difficult to apply and in some instances one child was excluded from a school while a sister or brother was accepted.[53] When children were excluded parents would appeal to the department or even to the administrator.[54] During 1911 the principal of Umvuma school, Miss Brownlee, rejected the children of a Mr. Jenkins because they were of dark complexion and Mrs. Jenkins appeared to be Coloured. As she explained to Foggin, "Had I admitted these two children it would have meant the withdrawal of at least half the pupils of the school."[55] The department upheld Miss Brownlee's decision and with it the local community's power of veto. Running parallel with the exclusion of mixed-race children from white schools was the exclusion of black children from Coloured schools. That policy was demanded by parents who hoped to improve their children's prospects. It was sanctioned by the Department of Education because it helped justify the purification of white schools.[56]

The passage of time did not make the department's task easier. Neither did it help those children, such as Grace Maggio of Ardbennie, who were ostracized by their classmates. Mrs. Maggio admitted to authorities that her grandparents were Cape Coloured but she attached greater importance to the fact that her husband was serving in the army as a European. She wanted Grace to remain in the school she had attended for almost a year. After assessing the case the department advised the minister for education: "Whatever decision you may reach on the question of colour I suggest that the over-riding consideration is the unfortunate child whose life is being made a misery by the other children at Parktown."[57] Mrs. Maggio declined the offer of a place for her daughter at a Coloured school with the comment that "[w]e think it will be a disgrace to the British to put a child of English and Afrikaner persons into a Coloured school."[58] Thus Grace Maggio's schooling ended.

For the period from 1910 until the 1940s the files of the attorney general and the director of education are filled with such stories. The indeterminate boundaries between poor whites and Coloureds and the lack of any objective criteria for allocating identity allowed some cases to drag on for years. The judgment of race was aesthetic and could vary not only between one school committee and another but also over time with regard to the same child. The parents of May and Gustavus Lottering wanted them admitted to the European school at Shabani, an asbestos-mining community northeast of Bulawayo. The principal refused, fearing the reaction of other parents. Mr. W. Richards, the local magistrate, was called in to adjudicate. He visited the family and met Mrs. Lottering, of whom he wrote: "If I may say so without prejudice, [Mrs. Lottering] has the appearance of having a considerable admixture of Hottentot or similar blood in her."[59] The director of education ruled that the children were not to be admitted, observing that on a number of occasions the father had tried to have them enrolled in white schools. There followed a lengthy correspondence between Lottering and the director, who eventually sought information from the police as to the family's social standing. The CID reported strong opposition from white parents and the director instructed all schools to exclude May and Gustavus. That, however, was not the end of the matter. Five years later, in 1929, Mrs. Lottering wrote to the director pointing out that May and Gustavus had attended white schools in the Transvaal: "I can cite innumerable instances of children now attending Govt schools whose claims to PURE European descent are nil. May I be informed if the children of a Jew born in Asiatic Russia are eligible? You may also like to inform me how it is that my grown sons are registered voters?"[60] Her appeal was again rejected, although the director did ask for the names of the children she had referred to in her letter. In 1936 Mr. Lottering succeeded in having his two youngest daughters enrolled at Kingsdale on the understanding that if other parents protested they would be removed. There was only one objection, so the principal kept the children on. There were in all nine Lottering siblings and it is probable they differed considerably in skin tone. That would explain their varied success in gaining entry to white schools. It also explains the embarrassment that is obvious in much of the department's correspondence.

The story of May and Gustavus is a good example of the brittleness of racial taxonomies. The story also raises the question of what it meant to be Coloured. Coloured schools were poorly funded and few in number. As a result many children received no formal education. An excluded child also lost a number of future civil liberties, including the right to vote and to seek employment in the public sector. In appearance children such as May and Gustavus were white, but in some other senses they were not. The Department of Education did not discuss the principles which were at stake in deciding their case because those principles were considered self-evident to the department's officers and the white parents they served. Racial identity meant something more subtle and profound than social or material attributes. It involved temperament and, in particular, the supposed tendency of Coloureds toward criminal behavior. Children such as May and Gustavus were assumed to have a racial inheritance which made their misclassification a danger to their classmates.

WHITENESS AND POVERTY

Settlers were ambitious people. The 1913 inquiry into the cost of living noted that most arrived in Rhodesia expecting to become rich. However, the speculative capitalism of the BSAC and the nature of the colonial economy it helped to create meant that financial success was achieved by only a few. Besides those whose failure reminded others of the precariousness of the economy there were many more who endured shabby gentility. Doris Lessing and her parents arrived in Southern Rhodesia in the early 1920s. Many of their neighbors in the Banket district struggled to make ends meet and in the first volume of her memoirs she writes bitingly of those who assumed that all whites were rich. Lessing attributed the poverty she lived with as a child to the abstract workings of the economy and not to the failings of her parents or their neighbors. In such a setting the maintenance of racial boundaries became more important.

Whiteness referred to membership in a community and to an ensemble of cultural practices. But because whiteness flowed along more than a single axis, codifying membership was no simple matter. There were positive attributes such as language, lifestyle, dress, dedication to work, thrift, Christian beliefs, sexual continence, family forms, and personal hygiene.

Conversely, there was the absence of vices associated with non-whites such as poverty, drunkenness, shiftlessness, and sexual indulgence. The conventions for maintaining identity were gendered. White men could at little cost engage in sexual relations across racial boundaries; white woman could not. Whites could buy land and live where they chose and they had access to the best jobs, education, and health care. They also had access to the segregated social spaces of hospitals, railway carriages, and amusement parks. They could own firearms and drink alcohol on license premises. As employees they could work where they chose and they were free from the kinds of violence sanctioned under the masters and servants legislation.[61] In such an environment whiteness should have been easy to construct. It was not. The settler community was ethnically divided and many whites lacked the material success which should have distinguished them as a class.

The term poor white was first used in South Africa in the 1890s, when it referred to the economic and social retrogression of a part of the white rural population. By 1930 the class had broken into two factions: *bywoners,* or hired men who worked on farms, and unskilled urban laborers. A commission funded by the Carnegie Foundation to look into the plight of those men and their families published its findings in 1932. It concluded that while there were problems in defining a white standard of living, a survey of schools suggested that more than 17 percent of families lived in poverty.[62] In most cases their decline had been caused by an inability to adapt to modern economic conditions. A minority suffered from the eugenic failings of low intelligence and defective social hereditary. The problem of white poverty was never so extensive in Southern Rhodesia but the presence of poor families still caused government some concern.

The connection between poverty and low levels of education was recognized early and under the Education Ordinance of 1903 grants were made to assist poor families. As a result the number of European schools rose from eight in 1901 to fourteen in 1904. However, many children still received no formal education and in 1907 24 percent of children were not at school. Those who did attend often performed poorly.[63] Literacy continued to be a problem and the Hole inquiry of 1908 had as one of its principal findings the need to improve the standards of education.[64] After 1923 expenditure on white education increased but there was still criticism that the system contributed to poverty.

With responsible government the problem of poverty became more pressing and in 1924 a select committee was appointed to inquire into poor relief.[65] The committee, whose members included Tawsie Jollie, met with representatives of various church and voluntary organizations and prepared a report for the Legislative Assembly. Although the committee found it difficult to estimate the number of those in need it did manage to identify a group of poor whites. The committee argued that they were a discrete class whose existence was due not to economic circumstance but to moral failure. The class consisted of families impoverished by drink, women deserted by their husbands, and those rendered unemployable through lack of education, training, or intelligence.[66] The committee found that many children left school prematurely, thereby "creating a near criminal class of unemployed and shiftless poor."[67] Their numbers were small but because they could not compete against blacks for unskilled work they were bound to become a burden on the state. The remedy lay in the development of the middle-class virtues of thrift, hard work, and education and in the absorption of the poor into government work programs. The committee made no mention of eugenics or feeble-mindedness but its explanation of white poverty could easily have come from the writings of Francis Galton, Karl Pearson, or H. H. Goddard.[68]

Like his colleagues, Prime Minister Charles Coghlan believed that poverty eroded the boundaries separating whites from the subaltern races.[69] To solve that problem he proposed a labor colony or gulag for unemployables in which each man would be set to work communal land. There would be no black labor and surplus produce would be sold to help maintain the colony. A special school for the children of the poor would also be provided. Only poor whites would be admitted and Coghlan warned: "It should, however, be quite clear that those who can be admitted to the Labour Colony but prefer to wander about the country haunting Kaffir kraals, or to loaf in the towns will be dealt with as vagrants and imprisoned. The same fate should befall those who are expelled from the Labour Colony for mis-conduct."[70] Because of the costs involved Coghlan's scheme was never implemented, but in 1928 a work gang was established in the Mtao forest for unemployed men. They were paid a minimum wage and provided with rough accommodation.

Once the benign economic conditions of the 1920s had given way to the Great Depression the problem of poverty became more pressing. The state used various strategies to shelter whites from competition in the labor and commodity markets. The Land Apportionment Act of 1930, for example, precluded Africans from owning land in designated areas, thus protecting white farmers from more competent African producers. It was soon followed by the Industrial Conciliation Act, which reserved skilled work for white artisans. Neither proved sufficient to eradicate poverty. In 1934 the government established an inquiry, chaired by Commissioner of Labour G. E. Wells, into unemployment and relief for the destitute. He identified 825 unemployed men, of whom the majority were farmers, clerks, or salesmen and their dependents. Among their ranks were a sizeable number of carpenters, bricklayers, and mechanics. In an industrialized society, Wells observed, such men would have taken menial work, but in Southern Rhodesia a white man who could not find skilled employment was likely to free-fall through the class system.[71] The inquiry took pains to distinguish between the decent but unfortunate poor and poor whites whose circumstances were due to their own failings. Of the almost 1,000 unemployed and their families only 105 were so classified. Wells observed, "It is by the standard of living and by the psychological traits, more than by the actual financial position, that the class is identified."[72] The committee warned that as Africans became more skilled there would be even less place for unskilled Europeans. An increase in their ranks could only be prevented by expenditure for training and education and the reservation of certain classes of work. Wells also recommended a policy of restricted immigration which was eventually implemented. Like the "social refuse" of North America identified by Goddard and Terman, the presence of poor whites threatened to corrupt what whites believed was "decent" society.[73]

Interest groups such as the Coloured Community Service League (CCSL) were anxious to have the matter of racial definition resolved. The League was formed in 1931 to fight discrimination in government employment and housing. It also campaigned resolutely for the right of its members to buy alcohol and for children to have access to white schools.[74] The League argued that Coloureds were a distinct community of Afro-European origin and it objected to the inclusion under that title of individuals who were of mixed Asiatic and African parentage.[75] The CCSL's major concerns were with access to education, government employment, and housing and for that reason it persisted with the issue of definition. The CCSL was not the only organization which wanted clarity and in July 1939 the secretary to the education commission wrote, without success, to the medical director asking him for an objective test to decide borderline cases.[76]

During that year the Department of Education debated at length the question of race and the medical inspector of schools, Dr. Baker Jones, set out his thoughts on the subject. According to Dr. Jones, neither appearance nor blood was an adequate guide to racial identity because even siblings could have a different skin color. He warned that if a scientific judgment were applied the result would be disastrous. "I feel sure," he wrote, "that a very considerable group of children would be excluded from European schools on the grounds of color if there were any certain test, including a certain number who were born in Europe of 'pure European stock.'"[77] For that reason he opposed the Cape system, the method used by the department, of deciding on the basis of the child's or parents' appearance. What was important, according to Baker Jones, was not racial inheritance in the form of physique but racial tradition as cultural achievement. It was achievement which determined identity.[78]

In effect Baker Jones believed identity could be acquired. Not surprisingly, Dr. A. P. Martin, the medical director, viewed his comments as heretical. Martin supported fully the Cape system and so long as a child was believed to be white and as long as "its external appearance does not attract any impertinent scrutiny" it should be accepted into a white school. However, if the issue of race was raised just once the child should be removed, which in fact was department policy.[79] The administration wanted racial identity to embody fixed oppositions between civilization and savagery, sexual vice and continence, immorality and virtue, poverty and wealth.[80] That wish for symmetry was frustrated in a world where some Africans wore hats, some Coloureds lived in decent houses, and some whites were poor.

Public debate about poor whites and Coloureds had precedents in the discourses about degeneracy that gathered pace in the metropole during the first decades of the twentieth century. The eugenicists believed poverty and criminality were inherited. They also feared that the white race was degenerating because the worst stock were reproducing fastest. In colonial Africa that meant poor whites. The belief was used in Britain in a variety of ways and drew patronage from across the political spectrum. It found most support among Fabians and, in particular, among some women who were enthusiastic about the prospects for social improvement. Enthusiasts were generally upper-middle-class men and women with an interest in public affairs and science.[81] They were far better educated and socially more progressive than settlers in Rhodesia.

Fears about the future of the white race had wide currency in colonial Africa. Yet in Southern Rhodesia the science of Galton and Pearson was rarely mentioned in discussion of Coloureds or poor whites. Eugenics was a modernizing ideology which ran counter to the economic conditions of colonial life and the feudal social order about which prominent Rhodesian intellectuals dreamt.[82] It was also closely associated with first-wave feminism and socialism, the two ideologies the white male elite most abhorred. It was probably for that reason that eugenics was ignored by legislators even when they were justifying ordinances based upon its central tenets. By contrast, according to Ann Stoler, in the Dutch East Indies eugenics was an important element in public debate. It provided a language for whites to express their anxiety about the maintenance of racial boundaries.[83]

The racism of white elites was practical. They borrowed most of their discriminatory legislation from South Africa and they had no interest in racial science or in making grand statements to justify their political dominance. One of the reasons is to be found in their relatively low levels of education and cultural achievement. Whites showed little interest in the rich Shona culture that surrounded them except to dispute the origins of Great Zimbabwe, which is one of the world's great monuments. In the face of overwhelming scientific evidence that Great Zimbabwe was built by the Shona, settlers clung tenaciously to the idea that the ruins were the product of Phoenician or Portuguese builders. White males in particular had little familiarity with avant-garde sciences or arts. The paintings and fiction produced in Southern Rhodesia could not have been further removed from the contemporary work of Picasso or James Joyce. Colonial society was conventional and inward looking and it remained so. In the late 1940s Doris Lessing fled from the philistinism of Salisbury, which even after World War Two had remained impervious to innovation.

CONCLUSION

The introduction of the death penalty for rape in 1903 and the immorality ordinances that followed were as much intended to maintain racial hygiene as to protect women from the threat of assault. The moral panics and their attendant legislation sealed off women's bodies as an entry point to white society. There were others point of entry which, although less dramatic, were far more important. Coloureds clamored for admission to white society and poor whites were in danger of exclusion. Those tensions were not easily resolved. Poverty among whites was due mainly to the nature of the colonial economy. No man could hope to decently support a family by unskilled labor and there was never sufficient skilled work for all. The Coloured community was persistent in its demands for civil liberties.

The placement of racial boundaries either granted or denied access to civil rights, education, and work opportunities. For that reason Coloureds had better reason than whites to be aware of the points at which one race graded into the other. Various groups, including the Rhodesian Coloured Society and the Coloured Community Service League, represented the interests of Coloureds. Interest groups were as much concerned about prestige as about civil liberties and among the issues pursued by the League were the provision of separate accommodation for Coloured passengers on trains, segregation at race courses, and the right of entry to amusement parks.[84] They also sought to fortify the barriers separating themselves from blacks. In 1931, for example, the Eurafrican Association protested to the attorney general about the mixing of Coloured prisoners with black inmates at Salisbury jail. The association complained that "[a]ll the Coloured people of Salisbury have native servants in their homes. That the natives find themselves classed with those Coloured youths in gaol will teach these natives to belittle the Coloured people."[85]

Coloureds sought to emphasize their affinity with Europeans and for that reason their demands made whites all the more apprehensive. The League's activities were monitored by the police, who attended its meetings and kept dossiers on its members. The attorney general's office, like the CID, was unsympathetic toward Coloureds. Official correspondence about Coloureds was often derisive and contempt was the usual response to demands from the CCSL for civil liberties. In seeking to attach themselves to the dominant culture Coloureds adopted the habits, dress, and avocations of the ruling minority.[86] English was the medium of instruction in Coloured schools and Afrikaans was frowned upon. In response, Europeans were determined to exclude Coloureds from white social space, be it schools, railway carriages, or race course pavilions. The attitude of the administration, like that of the white community as a whole, was fueled by contrasting desires: to make Coloureds invisible and to emphasize their difference. The desire for invisibility was obvious in the decision to leave half-caste children to be absorbed into village life; the wish to accentuate difference found expression in discriminatory legislation. Behind each was a desire to make racial boundaries inviolate.

The Rhodesian press rarely mentioned Coloureds and it is possible to read the *Rhodesian Herald* for a period of thirty years without being aware of the existence of such a community. The labor of Coloureds had little commercial significance and it was only the efforts of organizations such as the CCSL which made them visible. Because their numbers were so small, Coloureds were never perceived by whites as a physical threat and Coloured males played no part in the Black Peril hysterias. To whites, they were the embodiment of sexual corruption rather than its instigators, and their failings formed a contrast to the hyper-sexuality associated with black males. Within colonial discourse Coloured males were often feminized and the vices ascribed to them were analogous to those identified by misogynists; like women, Coloured males were supposed to be deceitful, cunning, vain, and petty. Even so, the Coloured community was important in the wider sexual politics of the early colonial period. Half-castes were proof of the sexual transgression of white males and they became the focus for a protracted conflict between white men and women over concubinage. Coloureds made whites more aware of the positioning of racial boundaries, reminding them of the fragility of white identity, which had to be constantly repaired and re-asserted.

ELEVEN

CONCLUSION

Under British law the history of rape is simple. Most women who are assaulted never report the matter to police. Many guilty men who are changed are acquitted. The proportions may vary from place to place and over time but the principle remains. In contrast, in Southern Rhodesia almost all the accused in Black Peril cases were severely punished. As many as twenty men were executed while another two hundred were imprisoned and flogged. Many of those men were at worst guilty of petty theft or common assault. How was it possible for innocent men to be found guilty of rape when throughout the British Empire guilty men so often walked free? What kinds of social forces were capable of overturning such a powerful convention?

It is tempting to follow in Ronald Hyman's footsteps and to see only consistencies in the sexual politics of empire and to assume, as Hyman does, that the play between sex and power was more or less the same everywhere. Sexual assault, for example, has been an important theme in colonial fiction. It has provided the leitmotifs for three of the most famous novels: Doris Lessing's *The Grass Is Singing*, E. M. Forster's *A Passage to India*, and Paul Scott's *Raj Quartet*. Each author explores the contradictions between liberal creeds of equality and the realities of racial dominance, themes which are in a sense universal. Black Peril itself was exported to the far-flung colonial society of Papua New Guinea, where the same term was used for sexual threat and a law based upon the Rhodesian legislation of 1903 was enacted. The White Women's Protection Ordinance of 1926 prescribed the death penalty for the rape or attempted rape of a European woman or girl.[1] The legislation was unique in two respects: It made specific reference to race (which the Southern Rhodesian legislation did not) and it allowed no alternative to the death penalty. At the time the ordinance was passed no white woman in the territory had been raped. Ann Stoler has suggested that the empire's sexual discourses filtered back into the metropoles, helping to define bourgeois subjectivity.[2] The White Women's Protection Ordinance of 1926 suggests that there was also a complex trade in legislation across the periphery. But that ordinance does noth-

ing to suggest that the politics of sexual dominance were in any way uniform across the imperial world.

Sexual mythologies about black men and women may have been common in Western science, popular literature, the fine arts, and medical illus-
tration. But the stereotypes of which Sander Gilman has written were never
in themselves sufficient to produce Black Peril fears. The moral panics of
Salisbury, Umtali, and Bulawayo were contingent on particular alignments
of class, race, gender, demography, labor relations, state formation, and
imperial authority. Even where the legal systems, the recruitment of settlers, and the imperial centers were much the same, as in Kenya and Southern Rhodesia, there were major differences in the behavior of male elites
with regard to race and sexual threat.

In the period from 1903 to 1922 Zimbabwe changed from a frontier
society of mines and scattered farms to one of permanent settlement. By
the 1920s settlers had some economic success and they shared, however
equivocally, in the ownership of an imperial culture.[3] They also enjoyed a
monopoly over the legitimate use of violence. The BSAC was powerful but
it had little authority over important aspects of the economy. At no time
was the state able to regulate the movement or supply of labor. Medicine
and education were largely in the hands of missionaries who were often
hostile to company policy. The pass system, the location ordinances and
the masters and servants legislation failed to control the movement of workers or to subvert their rational economic choices. Black Peril was itself
symbolic of the fragility of the state.

THE LAST TRIAL

In the years between the world wars missions had difficulty finding
suitable staff for their schools. Because of a lack of local candidates the
Anglican and Methodist churches often recruited teachers from South Africa. Such teachers were important figures within an emerging African leadership. Their presence was a measure of the success of the churches in producing a Westernized elite. One teacher who was recruited in 1934 from
South Africa was named Ndachana. He was to be the last man executed
for a Black Peril crime.

Ndachana was born at Uitenhage location in the Cape and at the time
of his arrival in Rhodesia he was twenty-two years of age. He had been
educated in the Cape at St. Matthew's School and spoke four African languages and was fluent in English and Afrikaans. However, he was ill-pre-
pared for the social conventions of Rhodesia and in particular for the

kind of subordination expected of him. Ndachana was originally engaged through the director of native education to work at Domboshawa, a training college outside of Salisbury, where he began teaching in March 1934. The principal, Mr. J. Mylne, found him to be a willing worker and above average for a teacher of his type; yet after only twelve months Ndachana was dismissed.[4] Ndachana was reluctant to accept orders without question but Mylne believed that once away from the temptations of town life he would do well. At the beginning of April 1935 Ndachana was appointed as an assistant teacher to St. David's Mission, Rusapi. Less than two months later he was charged with the rape of Miss Bessie Dobbs, a white missionary who was his immediate superior.[5] The trial took place at the end of the Great Depression. In South Africa the Nationalists had recently formed a coalition government with Smut's South Africa Party. The land issue in Rhodesia had been resolved to the benefit of the white minority and responsible government was over a decade old. The Black Peril panics had long passed, and the penalties imposed by courts on black men for sexual assault were in general less severe than the death sentences common fifteen years earlier.[6]

According to the trial transcript the crime was committed at Bonda on May 19, 1935.[7] On that evening the staff attended a religious ceremony before retiring to their sleeping quarters. Miss Dobbs was staying temporarily in a hut some hundred yards from the compound while her own quarters were being refurbished. On entering her room she found the accused drunk and asleep on her bed. She reported the matter immediately to the mission head, the Rev. Lawrence, who had Ndachana carried to his own quarters. Miss Dobbs had returned to her room when she heard a noise: It was the accused, who tried to grab her through the window. She screamed and attempted to close the window, catching Ndachana's fingers with such force that the frame broke. As she tried to escape she was grabbed by the throat. A violent struggle followed before she was raped. The accused threatened to kill her and Miss Dobbs was so afraid that she did not report the attack until the morning. During the assault there was a four-month-old baby in the room asleep in a box.[8] The child did not cry.

After her assailant left Miss Dobbs wiped herself with a sheet which she later handed to Mrs. Lawrence, the director's wife. When informed about what had happened the Rev. Lawrence did not contact the police nor did he dismiss Ndachana. Instead he went to Salisbury, where he reported the matter to the church dean. The dean saw the accused the following day and told him to be off the mission within the hour. Ndachana went directly to Salisbury, where he left his belongings at the Anglican cathedral. He made no attempt to escape. When arrested there were stains on the front of his trousers which he claimed were from beer. Under cross-examination Ndachana appeared confused and could not explain either the sequence of events on that evening nor his role in them. When asked if what Miss Dobbs had said was true he replied, "I cannot really say. I do not know."[9]

May Bloomfield, the matron in charge of the boarding girls at Bonda, told the court that the morning after the assault she was handed a bedsheet by Mrs. Lawrence. "I put it in to soak because," she informed police, "I did not want the native girls who do the laundry to see it."[10] In fact she placed it in a bucket of Lysol and water, where it remained for twenty-four hours.[11] The sheet was later handed to police and formed the basis of the forensic evidence against Ndachana. The combination of Lysol and water would have destroyed any evidence of a stain. A sheet is a large object and to microscopically test such a surface for an invisible stain would have been virtually impossible.

Apart from Miss Dobbs, the two key prosecution witnesses were Dr. Blackie, the director of the public health laboratory, who examined the sheet and Ndachana's trousers; and Dr Edward Rowlette, the government medical officer who examined Miss Dobbs and the accused. Surprisingly, Dr. Blackie found that the sheet tested strongly for semen. Semen was also supposedly present on the inside of the blue trousers belonging to the accused.[12] Dr. Rowlette examined Miss Dobbs and found bruises on her arms, knee, and foot. Her genitals showed no evidence of bruising or other injury and her hymen was intact. He told the court, "In my opinion penetration of a male organ has not taken place."[13] He also examined Ndachana and found no injury to his hands. Defense counsel did not pursue the issue of penetration because that would have subjected Miss Dobbs to scrutiny, neither did it challenge the forensic evidence which formed the basis of the Crown's case. The possibility of a pre-existing romantic relationship between the accused and his victim was not raised because it would only have antagonized the jury. The only strategy used by the defense was to question Miss Dobbs's identification of her assailant.

The trial was shaped by a cluster of competing interests. The police wanted the case prosecuted as they would prosecute any Black Peril assault. In the view of the CID, Ndachana's lack of a criminal record made his crime all the worse.[14] The white community as a whole cared little for missions and less for mission-educated blacks and it probably wanted Ndachana hanged. The Bonda mission wanted the matter covered up, hence the dean's decision to have Ndachana dismissed rather than call the police. That decision, which the prosecutor found so reprehensible, was due perhaps to the Rev. Lawrence's sense of culpability in failing to prevent the assault. For missionaries as a whole the case was a test of their policy in fostering a Western-educated elite. For the black leadership in Salisbury the trial was a blow to their claims for civil rights.

As he passed the sentence, Justice McIlwaine commented that it was one of the most serious cases to have come before his court, made worse because it involved an educated Christian African. He found that the accused had committed rape as defined by law, a verdict incompatible with the forensic evidence, and he was critical of mission authorities for having endeavored to let Ndachana escape. Rejecting the claim that at the time of the offense the accused was drunk, he found Ndachana guilty and sentenced him to death.[15] On the passing of sentence Ndachana replied, "I have nothing to say, my lord, except I still say that if it had not been for drink I should not have been here."[16]

Although there was nothing unusual about the quality of the forensic evidence, the inconsistencies in the Crown's case were flagrant. There was the baby who did not cry, a rape without proof of penetration, the absence of bruising on the victim's throat, and the lack of bruising on her assailant's hands. There was also an assailant who did not attempt to escape and a mission head who did not contact the police. Those inconsistencies made a verdict of rape rather than attempted rape necessary in order to prevent an outcry in London. Under the circumstances, British authorities would no doubt have viewed the death penalty for the crime of attempted rape as racist.

While awaiting execution Ndachana wrote a letter which was sent to the High Court as part of an appeal.[17] He claimed that Sister Dobbs had tried to seduce him, thus using the habitual defense of men charged with sexual assault. It is possible that Miss Dobbs had been attracted to Ndachana or that her kindness had been seen by him as sexual interest. Perhaps he convinced himself subsequently that such was the case. He may also have simply been lying. The surviving documents make it impossible to tell. The High Court no doubt viewed the letter as a cynical attempt to shift the blame to Miss Dobbs, and the appeal was rejected. The trial transcripts and Ndachana's appeal exposed the kind of sexual politics typical of rape trials, which until that moment had been noticeably absent from Rhodesian courts. The case is disquieting because it is so familiar in ways in which other Black Peril cases are not. It is also disquieting because it suggests how little we know about relations between black men and white women.

In the weeks preceding the execution numerous representations were made on Ndachana's behalf. In pleading for clemency missionary Arthur

Shearly Cripps and five colleagues told the governor: "The convict Edwin was cruelly placed in a teacher's post of much trust and much temptation, a post for which his past record had shown him to be utterly unfitted."[18] The vicar general and the director of missions both approached the minister of internal affairs. The case also attracted attention in Britain. The Anti-Slavery and Aborigines Protection Society reminded the governor that since the law in Southern Rhodesia would not lead to the death penalty in the case of a white man the legislation was racist.[19] Others, such as the Rev. M. J. Rusike, a prominent African cleric, argued that on account of his age Ndachana should be reprieved.[20] When it was certain that Ndachana was to be executed the attorney general had a psychiatric assessment carried out by Dr. Rodger, the superintendent of Ingutsheni asylum. Rodger found the prisoner calm and coherent and he detected no evidence of mental illness.[21] Nine days later Ndachana was hanged at Salisbury jail. Hundreds attended his funeral, at which the Rev. Rusike gave the oration. During 1935 seven men were executed; all were Africans and with the exception of Ndachana all had been found guilty of murder. In a sense his death brought the story of Black Peril to an end. Although fear of sexual assault continued, the climate of panic never returned nor did the ritualistic killing of black men for sexual crime.

Ndachana's trial had great significance for the black community. It is the only Black Peril case which has been written about at length. Stanlake Samkange and Lawrence Vambe agree, I believe correctly, that Ndachana was punished by the state as a demonstration of settler power over Western-educated Africans.[22] The trial was certainly very different from those held twenty years earlier. Ndachana gave evidence on his own behalf, and his testimony along with that of other witnesses accorded him an identity at law which men like Singana and Bonali were denied. His relationship with Miss Dobbs was unusual in that it included equalities and exchanges which would have been unthinkable in another context. The reason why he had gone to Miss Dobbs's room on the night of the assault was to borrow a copy of Charles Dickens's *A Tale of Two Cities*. That fact no doubt further alienated an already unsympathetic jury. The jury was composed of white men who had little formal education and only the most rudimentary grasp of a middle-class culture. All would no doubt have heard of Charles Dickens, although it is unlikely that many would have read his novels. To be confronted with a young African man more familiar than themselves with British culture would probably have made them angry. Even Ndachana's nickname, Edwin, was the name of a person rather than a belittling appellation. His trial and execution became the kind of symbol that earlier Black Peril trials did not create.

SOME DYNAMICS

Black Peril dramatized many of the problems settlers faced in maintaining racial boundaries. White elites were under pressure from Coloureds, who wanted civil liberties and access for their children to white schools. They were even more embarrassed by the presence of poor whites. Settlers did not talk about boundaries as such but they talked incessantly about the need to maintain their community's prestige.

Prestige was gendered in the sense that it was owned by white males but could be compromised by the behavior of white women.[23] It was a quality no African or Coloured person could possess. Good works did not increase prestige and the activities of missionaries were more likely to diminish prestige than otherwise. In character prestige was closer to the scrupulous exercise of power than charity, but unlike charity it was secular. Prestige was similar to the middle-class virtue of respectability but it could not be accumulated in the same way. White employers could cheat or assault African workers without compromising their status; white men could have sexual relations with black women so long as racial dominance was maintained. In Britain there were clear rules for acquiring respectability and rules for its decline. The loss of respectability by individuals did not endanger decent society; on the contrary, it reinforced social standards. There were various ways in which prestige could be threatened and it was of those dangers that new settlers were cautioned by old hands. Most especially it could be jeopardized by any suggestion of equality between a European and members of the subaltern races. By bringing indigent settler families into social proximity to Coloureds and Africans, poverty diminished the prestige of the white community as a whole. The distinction between decent whites who through no fault of their own were in difficult circumstances and poor whites who were temperamentally flawed did nothing to lessen that danger.[24] In defense of prestige male elites made sure that white women were hedged in by the morality laws, vilified in the Legislative Council, and denied ready access to social space.

Settlers were in general recruited from the lower middle classes of Britain and South Africa and they tended to be sensitive about their status. They were much concerned with the cultivation of the bourgeois virtues of temperance, industry, cleanliness, and chastity. Male settlers were anxious to avoid being associated with vice, especially the vice of unmanliness. Manliness was particularly important in a frontier society. It was also integral to the configuration of Black Peril ideology.

The creation of the public school system ran parallel with the growth of the British Empire. Within that system the idea of Christian manliness linked virtue with physical prowess and bodily discipline.[25] The most disliked qualities in a man were sentimentality, intellectualism, and a lack of sexual control.[26] One of the principal tasks of a gentleman was to offer protection to women, which barely disguised one of the doctrine's most enduring qualities, its misogyny. This construction of masculinity was taken up with enthusiasm by the middle classes. It grew from a number of sites and over time it came to be an almost universal marker of manhood.

In Southern Rhodesia the boundaries between hegemonic and subaltern masculinities were drawn according to race. Black males were supposed to be lazy, dishonest, and hyper-sexual. Those attributes made the employment of black men to do feminized work under the command of white women all the more curious.[27] There were complex reasons why white households were filled with male servants. The most important were to do with the structure of labor markets and the conditions for their reproduction. The quest by whites for civility and status was both reinforced and compromised by their dependence upon male domestic labor.

The concept of the individual is both institutionalized and historically specific. The obvious tensions between societies which demand conformity from their citizens and the doctrine of the sovereignty of the individual has been a theme in intellectual debate since Max Weber.[28] In colonial Africa, as in Europe, discourses about individuality were important in the defining of boundaries between the public and private domains. They were also influential in the allocation of the rights and obligations of citizens.

The connection between patterns of internal governance and the pacification of populations has been theorized in the work of Max Weber, Norbert Elias, and Michel Foucault.[29] The central thesis in Norbert Elias's study of European manners is the connection between the growth and extension of state monopolies over the means of violence and the tightening self-controls over the passions of ruling classes. "The peculiar stability of the apparatus of mental self-restraint which emerges as a decisive trait built into the habits of every civilised human being, stands in the closest relationship to the monopolisation of physical force and the growing stability of the central organs of society."[30] According to Elias, where strong centralized states emerged in western Europe they were usually accompanied by a change in personality among the nobility: The growing complexity, differentiation, and interdependence of social formations led to increased levels of the self-control expected of individuals. The process took place first among the nobility and then spread to the lower strata: Where it was most advanced self-restraint became habitual. As new capitalist and trade relations developed, both the nobility and the "industrious classes" began to condemn idleness, stress discipline, and exalt work. Writing in the 1930s, Elias traced that development through the spread of "manners"; in the 1960s Foucault described the same process in terms of surveillance and internalized authority.[31]

The notion of internal governance, be it in the form of civility (Elias), or work (Weber), or surveillance (Foucault), has depended upon the existence of bureaucratic states, production for exchange, universal wage labor, and incorporated populations. For each of those theorists obedience involved the establishment of modern forms of subjectivity and the idea of freely given rather than forced compliance. While such a process may have occurred in Western Europe it was foreign to colonial Africa, if only because the disciplines of the marketplace and the authority of states were so ineffectual. Colonial systems were violent and fragile. State violence was used to contain armed resistance and to enforce compliance from labor. Although the moral order of settler society was very different from that found in Britain, the demands for civility were the same. The Black Peril trials were, among other things, pageants celebrating the fiction of the self-control of white males and the lack of control among black men. Hidden from public scrutiny was the violence of white men against black laborers. Concubinage with black women was also hidden. The tensions between those ideals and colonial practice erupted in the moral panics.

The political economy of Southern Rhodesia was riven by contradictions. The state was weak and the economy unstable, the ruling elite was divided, and there were profound demographic imbalances between men and women and between whites and blacks. The moral economy was equally flawed. White males engaged in miscegenation while blaming white women for breaking ranks; there was great emphasis upon civility in a community where many families were barely middle class. There was also the chronic problem of segregating Coloureds and rendering poor whites invisible. It was a brittle system which was constantly being eroded from within. Its surface was broken by the reprieves of Singana and Alukuleta, the indiscretions of Mrs. Cromer, and the brutalities of Sam Lewis, William Laidlaw, and the miners of Battlefields. Whites sought comfort in segregation that divided social space to their advantage, yet even that failed to provide them with security.

The Black Peril panics represented key moments when the boundaries of race, class, and gender were being established. The panics were both an expression of the problems of constructing a white identity and the means by which it was temporarily achieved. During the first decades of colonization there were various barriers to the creation of a settler identity; perhaps the most important were the economic obstructions to family life. White identity needed to be constantly repaired and re-asserted and so the panics were repeated. The trials of 1908–1912 were directed against urban blacks as a class, while the execution of Ndachana in 1935 was an assertion of white supremacy against Western-educated Africans.

Settlers in Southern Rhodesia wanted to create a middle-class existence for themselves and in so doing they hoped to recapture the vitality and heroism of some mythical British past. Those aspirations touched the lives of most whites and were of particular importance to men. The quest for bourgeois virtue found its apotheosis in Black Peril ideology. Unfortunately, settlers gained little solace from their endeavors and the purity they sought was as pitiless and barren as their pursuit of wealth and social advantage.

Most of the archival materials cited here are from the National Archives of Zimbabwe in Harare. Sources from South African archives are identified individually.

I. INTRODUCTION

1. *Rex versus Singana,* trial transcript, Salisbury High Court, November 11, 1908, Series S628, No. 425, p. 2.

2. Ibid., p. 3.

3. Rev. John White to the Resident Commissioner, November 19, 1908, RC3/3/20.

4. Dispatch: High Commissioner Selbourne to the Resident Commissioner, November 12, 1908, RC3/3/20.

5. Report of Attorney General H. C. Tredgold to the Administrator, January 13, 1909, RC3/3/20, p. 3.

6. Ibid.

7. Report of Justice Watermeyer, January 4, 1909, RC3/3/20, p. 1.

8. Native commissioners and the Native Department to which they belonged were the bureaucratic instruments through which the BSAC sought to exercise control over the indigenous population. Native commissioners were in general appointed from the ranks of failed miners and prospectors. In the first two decades of white settlement they were in effect labor agents who supplied workers to mines and farms. Although many of the early appointees were unable to speak an indigenous language they were presumed to be experts on native affairs. See J. J. Taylor, "The Emergence and Development of the Native Department in Southern Rhodesia, 1894–1914," Ph.D. diss., University of London, 1974; and M. C. Steele, "The Foundations of a Native Policy: Southern Rhodesia, 1923 to 1933," Ph.D. diss., Simon Fraser University, 1972.

9. Report of Mr. Hulley, Part 1, Native Department, Umtali, January 29, 1909, RC3/3/20, p. 1.

10. From the first days of white settlement urban centers were segregated according to race. The area of a town reserved for blacks was called a location. In March 1892 the first location was opened in Salisbury: Others soon followed as white settlement increased and towns appeared. Locations were run by municipal authorities with the central government retaining certain powers. The system was intended to control the movement of black labor. On entering a town a worker was obliged to report to the Registry Office, then find an employer who would either supply accommodation or arrange for housing at the location. Rentals were high and often were close to one-third of average monthly earnings. See Tsuneo Yoshikuni, "Black Migrants in a White City: A Social History of African Harare, 1890–1925," Ph.D. diss., University of Zimbabwe, 1989, pp. 38ff.; and Steele, "The Foundations of a Native Policy," p. 470.

11. Report of Mr. Hulley, Part 2, Native Department, Umtali, January 31, 1909, RC3/3/20, p. 3.

12. Ibid., p. 5.

13. Miss Falconer to the High Commissioner, March 19, 1909, RC3/3/20.

14. There are obvious parallels between Miss Falconer's experience and the assault upon Miss Quested in E. M. Forster, *A Passage to India* (1924; reprint, London: Penguin Books, 1970), p. 189.

15. In New South Wales at that time only one in five cases brought to trial led to a conviction. See Judith A. Allen, *Sex and Secrets: Crimes Involving Australian Women since 1880* (Melbourne: Oxford University Press, 1990), pp. 120–121. For a history of rape in British society see Anna Clark, *Women's Silence, Men's Violence: Sexual Assault in England 1770–1845* (London: Pandora, 1987).

16. See the Criminal Law Amendment Ordinance, No. 3 of 1903. Although the ordinance makes no reference to race, the death penalty was never imposed on a white man for the crime of rape or attempted rape.

17. It is difficult to be certain how many men suffered the death penalty for accusations of Black Peril; Lawrence Vambe's figure of thirty executions between 1903 and 1933 is probably exaggerated. See Lawrence Vambe, *From Rhodesia to Zimbabwe* (London: Heinemann, 1976), pp. 107–128.

18. According to a confidential CID report written during World War One, Black Peril cases were those in which actual rape of white females or any assault with intent to commit rape on white females occurred. The definition included indecent assaults, acts, or overtures and molestation of white females for the purpose of exciting or satisfying "bestial" assaults. Black and White Peril in Southern Rhodesia, Special CID File, 1915 or 1916, S1227/2.

19. The murder of the three van Rensberg children is such a case. In October 1924 the children were killed by a farm laborer named Chakawa, who was employed by the children's father. Chakawa became disturbed after a prolonged quarrel over the payment of his wages. After killing the children with an axe he made no attempt to escape. He was tried in Salisbury High Court, found guilty of murder, and hanged. See Series S628, Case No. 1731, October 15, 1924.

20. See Amirah Inglis, *Not a White Woman Safe: Sexual Anxiety and Politics in Port Moresby, 1920–1934* (Canberra: Australian National University Press, 1974). See also Chilla Bulbeck, *Australian Women in Papua New Guinea: Colonial Passages, 1920–1960* (Melbourne: Cambridge University Press, 1992).

21. Jeremy Krikler, for example, argues that in South Africa repressed fears arising from the Anglo-Boer War erupted in irrational fears of a black uprising and of Black Peril. See Jeremy Krikler, "Social Neurosis and Hysterical Pre-Cognition in South Africa: A Case Study and Reflections," *South African Historical Journal* 28 (1993): 63–97. See also John Pape, "Black and White: The 'Perils of Sex' in Colonial Zimbabwe," *Journal of Southern African Studies* 4 (1990): 699–720.

22. Under the Immorality Suppression Ordinance, No. 9 of 1903, any native who had illicit sexual intercourse with a white woman or girl with her consent would upon conviction be liable to imprisonment with hard labor for a period not exceeding 5 years. Illicit intercourse was defined as sex outside of marriage. The ordinance was rarely enforced and after 1930 it seems not to have been applied. It was finally repealed in 1962 by Sir Edgar Whitehead during the period of the Central African Federation.

23. In my review of court records for the period from 1902 until the 1960s, I could find no case in which a white man was executed for rape. The last execution of a black man for Black Peril took place in 1935.

24. Leonore Davidoff, *The Best Circles: Society, Etiquette and the Season* (London: The Cresset Library, 1986), p. 80.

25. See Nancy F. Cott, "Passionlessness: An Interpretation of Victorian Sexual Ideology, 1790–1850," in *A Heritage of Her Own*, ed. Nancy F. Cott and Elizabeth H. Pleck (New York: Simon and Schuster, 1979); and Frank Mort, *Dangerous Sexualities: Medico-Moral Politics in England since 1830* (London: Routledge & Kegan Paul, 1987). See also Judith Walkowitz, *City of Dreadful Delight: Narratives of Sexual Danger in Late-Victorian London* (London: Virago, 1992), especially pp. 132–134.

26. See Henrika Kuklick, *The Savage Within: The Social History of British Anthropology, 1885–1945* (Cambridge: Cambridge University Press, 1991), pp. 94–98. For a history of the concept of the primitive see Adam Kuper, *The Invention of Primitive Society: Transformations of an Illusion* (London: Routledge & Kegan Paul, 1988).

27. See "Character and Anal Eroticism" (1908) in Angela Richards, ed., *Freud on Sexuality*, trans. James Strachey (London: Penguin Books, 1983), pp. 205–215.

28. Ronald Hyam, *Empire and Sexuality: The British Experience* (Manchester: Manchester University Press, 1990). For a critical review of Hyman see Luise White, *The International Journal of African Historical Studies* 25 (1992): 664–665.

29. See Octave Mannoni, *Prospero and Caliban: The Psychology of Colonization* (New York: Frederick A. Praeger, 1964).

30. In his history of Salisbury, G. H. Tanser admitted that fears of Black Peril damaged race relations and fostered injustice. And yet in his book-length study of the early colonial period he devoted less than two pages to the subject. See G. H. Tanser, *A Sequence of Time: The Story of Salisbury, Rhodesia, 1900 to 1914* (Salisbury: Pioneer Head, 1974), pp. 200–201.

31. See Philip Mason, *The Birth of a Dilemma: The Conquest and Settlement of Rhodesia* (London: Oxford University Press, 1958).

32. Ibid., p. 93.

33. Ibid., p. 107.

34. Dane Kennedy, *Islands of White: Settler Society and Culture in Kenya and Southern Rhodesia, 1890–1939* (Durham: Duke University Press, 1987).

35. Ibid., p. 145.

36. Ibid., pp. 146, 188.

37. John Kelly's work on Fiji provides a good example. During a period of economic crisis in the early 1930s the Indian community in Fiji initiated a series of debates which shocked white administrators about the sexuality of the gods and forms of marriage. Kelly has shown how those debates were in themselves a commentary upon and a challenge to colonial authority. John D. Kelly, *A Politics of Virtue: Hinduism, Sexuality, and Countercolonial Discourse in Fiji* (Chicago: University of Chicago Press, 1991).

38. Charles Van Onselen, *Studies in the Social and Economic History of the Witwatersrand, 1886–1914,* vol. 2, *New Nineveh* (Johannesburg: Ravan Press, 1982), p. 45. Van Onselen argues that the scares coincided with periods of economic recession.

39. Norman Etherington, "Natal's Black Rape Scare of the 1870s," *Journal of Southern African Studies* 15 (1988): 36–53.

40. Ann Stoler, "Carnal Knowledge and Imperial Power: Gender, Race, and Morality in Colonial Asia," in *Gender at the Crossroads of Knowledge: Feminist Anthropology in the Postmodern Era*, ed. Micaela di Leonardo (Berkeley: University of California Press, 1991), pp. 68ff.

41. See Michael Banton, *Racial Theories* (Cambridge: Cambridge University Press, 1989), pp. 77–78.

42. See Ann Stoler, "Carnal Knowledge and Imperial Power." See also Ann Stoler, "Making Empire Respectable: The Politics of Race and Sexuality in Twentieth-Century Colonial Cultures," in *Racial Supremacy in Social Darwinist Theory and Colonial Practice,* ed. J. Breman (Amsterdam: V. U. University Press, 1990).

43. See, for example, Alastair Bonnett, "How the British Working Class Became White: The Symbolic Reformation of Racialized Capitalism," *Journal of Historical Sociology* 11 (September 1998): 316–340; and Noel Ignatiev, *How the Irish Became White* (New York: Routledge, 1995).

44. For an inventive study of Foucault's silence on the subject of empire see Ann Stoler, *Race and the Education of Desire* (Durham: Duke University Press, 1995).

45. Each of the crises was precipitated by the trial of a white man for the killing of an African. In each case the verdict handed down by an all-white jury was justified by the belief that the victim was a Black Peril assailant. See, for example, the trial transcript of *Rex versus Lewis,* Salisbury, August 14, 1911, T2/24/16. An almost identical account is to be found in the *Bulawayo Chronicle,* May 19, 1911; June 19, 1911; and August 15, 1911.

46. Clearly a number of factors shaped urban segregation. See, for example, Maynard W. Swanson, "The Sanitation Syndrome: Bubonic Plague and Urban Native Policy in the Cape Colony," *Journal of African History* 18 (1977): 387–410. For a contrary view see Tsuneo Yoshikuni, "Black Migrants in a White City: A Social History of African Harare, 1890–1925" (Ph.D. diss., University of Zimbabwe, 1989), pp. 33–34; and Philip D. Curtin, "Medical Knowledge and Urban Planning in Colonial Tropical Africa," in *The Social Basis of Health and Healing in Africa,* ed. Steven Feierman and John M. Janzen (Berkeley: University of California Press, 1992), pp. 235–255.

47. In 1935 a South African–born mission teacher named Ndachana became the last man executed for rape. His is the only Black Peril case that has been written about in detail. Stanlake Samkange used the trial transcript as the basis for his famous novel, *The Mourned One* (London: Heinemann, 1975).

2. BLACK PERIL

1. Philip Mason, *The Birth of a Dilemma: The Conquest and Settlement of Rhodesia* (London: Oxford University Press, 1958), p. 197.

2. Terence O. Ranger, *Revolt in Southern Rhodesia, 1896–97* (London: Heinemann, 1979), p. 323.

3. Ibid., p. 125.

4. *Report of the Director of Census, 3/5/1921* (Salisbury: Government Printer, 1922).

5. According to Anthony Chennells, in the novels of the 1920s and 1930s written by men and women who had not been in Rhodesia at the time there were constant references to the uprisings of 1896–1897 and to the threat of another war of resistance. See Anthony Chennells, "Settler Myths and the Southern Rhodesian Novel" (Ph.D. diss., University of Zimbabwe, 1982), pp. 349–350.

6. For an account of tropical neurasthenia in Kenya and Southern Rhodesia see Dane Kennedy, *Islands of White: Settler Society and Culture in Kenya and Southern Rhodesia, 1890–1939* (Durham: Duke University Press, 1987), pp. 15–24.

7. J. W. Gregory, *The Menace of Colour* (London: Seeley, Service & Co. Ltd., 1925), p. 196.

8. Ibid., pp. 195–196.

9. Ian Phimister, *An Economic and Social History of Zimbabwe, 1890–1948: Capital Accumulation and Class Struggle* (London: Longman, 1988), p. 68.

10. Over 1,700 Rhodesian soldiers died in World War One out of a total white community of only 30,000. In the final months of that conflict, Spanish flu killed a further 514 settlers. Lewis H. Gann and Michael Gelfand, *Huggins of Rhodesia: The Man and His Country* (London: George Allen & Unwin Ltd., 1964), pp. 46, 52.

11. For an account of the complex politics involved in that strategy see Martin Chanock, *Britain, Rhodesia, and South Africa, 1900–1945* (London: Frank Cass, 1977).

12. For a history of early Salisbury see Tsuneo Yoshikuni, "Black Migrants in a White City: A Social History of African Harare, 1890–1925" (Ph.D. diss., University of Zimbabwe, 1989), pp. 12–19; and G. H. Tanser, *A Sequence of Time: The Story of Salisbury, Rhodesia, 1900 to 1914* (Salisbury: Pioneer Head, 1974).

13. Yoshikuni, "Black Migrants in a White City," pp. 35–38, 40–41.

14. See the *Rhodesian Herald,* October 17, 1900; October 18, 1900; December 12, 1900; and July 19, 1901.

15. Yoshikuni, "Black Migrants in a White City," p. 3.

16. By the 1970s that figure had risen to almost 80 percent. See R. S. Roberts, "The Settlers," *Rhodesiana* 39 (September 1978): 56–57.

17. See, for example, Paul Rich, *White Power and the Liberal Conscience* (Johannesburg: Ravan Press, 1984). For an account of the foundations of segregation in science see Saul Dubow, *Scientific Racism in Modern South Africa* (Cambridge: Cambridge University Press, 1995).

18. Yoshikuni, "Black Migrants in a White City," pp. 33–34.

19. Lewis H. Gann and Peter Duignan, "Changing Patterns of a White Elite: Rhodesia and Other Settlers," in *Colonialism in Africa, 1870–1960,* vol. 2, ed. Lewis H. Gann and Peter Duigan (Cambridge: Cambridge University Press, 1970), p. 123.

20. Black and White Peril in Southern Rhodesia, Special CID File, 1915 or 1916, S1227/2.

21. Ibid.

22. Ibid.

23. *Rex versus Charlie (alias Shilling),* Salisbury High Court, November 20, 1902, Series S628, No. 150.

24. Telegram from Acting Attorney General, Bulawayo, to Attorney General, Salisbury, undated (1902), Executive Council Minutes, EC4/4/7.

25. Attempted Lynching at Bulawayo, Executive Council Minutes No. 683 of meeting held on October 27, 1902, EC4/4/7.

26. See "Editorial," *Bulawayo Chronicle,* November 25, 1902 and November 29, 1902.

27. There is some discrepancy between the archival records in Pretoria and the archival records in Harare. The following account is based upon the Zimbabwe material.

28. *Rex versus Ziku,* Salisbury High Court, April 29, 1904, Series S628, No. 222.

29. *Rex versus Mudzingawe,* Salisbury High Court, May 3, 1905, Series S628, No. 252.

30. *Rex versus Mananga (alias Jonas Umtali),* Salisbury High Court, April 10, 1913, Series S628, No. 698.

31. *Rex versus Musima,* Salisbury High Court, July 17, 1924, Series S628, No. 1706.

32. *Rex versus Munemu,* Salisbury High Court, October 10, 1928, Series S628, No. 2203.

33. Ibid.

34. See *Rex versus Akutizwi,* Salisbury High Court, August 15, 1924, Series S628, No. 1690.

35. *Rex versus Joseph,* Salisbury High Court, January 27, 1926, Series S628, No. 1863.

36. The following account of the Umtali case is constructed from the transcripts taken at the preliminary hearing held at Umtali. Umtali District Court: Trial Records and Transcripts of the Alukuleta Case, October 22, 1910, D3/7/22.

37. Ibid., p. 4.

38. Resident Commissioner James G. Fair to High Commissioner, November 10, 1910, Correspondence, RC2/4/13.

39. "Editorial," *South Africa,* January 28, 1911.

40. "Women's Petition to Lord Gladstone: More Native Assaults," *The Globe,* February 7, 1911.

41. *Morning Post,* January 27, 1911.

42. The Earl of Kerry asked the Secretary of State whether in commuting the death sentence Gladstone had acted on his own discretion or on the instructions of the Secretary. He was told that Gladstone had not consulted the government in Britain and that his decision would not be reviewed. See *The House of Commons Debates,* February 8, 1911.

43. See "Mr. Harcourt's Defence of Lord Gladstone," *The Standard,* February 11, 1911.

44. The issue was raised again by the Earl of Kerry on February 21, when he asked if a number of petitions from public meetings in Rhodesia protesting the action of Gladstone had reached the secretary. *The House of Commons Debates,* February 10, 1919.

45. Town Clerk Warden, Salisbury, to the Resident Commissioner, January 12, 1911, RC3/3/25.

46. Mrs. Eva Cleveland to the Resident Commissioner, February 21, 1911, RC3/3/25.

47. See *Southern Rhodesia: Preliminary Returns of a Census, 7 May 1911* (Salisbury: Government Printer, 1911).

48. See *The Cape Times (Weekly Edition),* February 1, 1911.

49. Another prominent citizen, Mr. Gordon Forbes, found Gladstone's explanation to be unacceptable, especially his suggestion that the assault did not take place. See "Interview with Mr. Gordon Forbes," *Bulawayo Chronicle,* February 3, 1911.

50. Resident Commissioner Burns Begg, Salisbury, to Lord Gladstone, May 17, 1911. The Alukuleta Case, RC3/3/25.

51. Ibid., pp. 3–4.

52. Notes made by the High Commissioner's Office, Pretoria, October 10, 1911, The Alukuleta Case, RC3/3/25.

53. Ibid.

54. Letter from Lord Gladstone, Cape Town, to Resident Commissioner Burns Begg, April 13, 1914, The Alukuleta Case, RC3/3/25.

55. Resident Commissioner's Office to Lord Gladstone, June 5, 1914, The Alukuleta Case, RC3/3/25.

56. That, at least, was the opinion of Tredgold. See Report by the Attorney General to the Administrator, May 29, 1911, RC3/3/27.

57. The following account of the Hillside case is taken from the transcripts of the Salisbury High Court Criminal Cases, Series S628, No. 570; and *Rex versus Bonali,* May 17, 1911, RC3/7/21.

58. Transcripts of the Salisbury High Court Criminal Cases, Series S628, No. 570, p. 5.

59. They wrote: "We should think that there is no question that this man will be sentenced to death and we ask you to use your influence, that instruction be sent to Lord Gladstone, to see that the full sentence be carried out." Isabella Smith, K. Hinchley, and E. Dauncey of Balham Hills, Harcourt, to Mr. Lewis, March 18, 1911. *Rex versus Bonali,* RC3/7/21.

60. Attorney General Tredgold to Administrator, May 29, 1911, *Rex versus Bonali,* RC3/7/21.

61. Resident Commissioner Burns Begg to High Commissioner, June 7, 1911, *Rex versus Bonali,* RC3/7/21.

62. As a result of this trial there followed a detailed correspondence between Justice Watermeyer, the resident commissioner, and the high commissioner over his interpretation of the ordinance of 1903. The key issues were the violence of the act, the injury sustained by the victim, and the degree of premeditation. They agreed that only where there was violence should the death penalty be enacted. See Letter from Judge Watermeyer to the Resident Commissioner, September 1, 1911, *Rex versus Bonali,* RC3/7/21.

63. The details of the case are taken from the trial transcripts of *Rex versus Nyamadzi (alias Raponzo),* May 18, 1911, Salisbury High Court, Series S628, No. 579.

64. "The Black Peril: Salisbury Lady Assaulted," *Rhodesian Herald,* April 21, 1911.

65. *Rex versus Nyamadzi (alias Raponzo)*, p. 4.

66. Report by Attorney General Tredgold to the Administrator, May 29, 1911, RC3/3/27, p. 3.

67. Resident Commissioner Burns Begg to the High Commissioner, June 6, 1911, RC3/3/27.

68. See *Rex versus Bonali (alias Jim)* and *Rex versus Nyamadzi (alias Raponzo)*, S1289, Capital Punishment Files No. 17 and No. 18.

69. *Rex versus Kuchi (alias Jim)*, Salisbury High Court, January 28, 1913, Series S628, No. 673.

70. Ibid., p. 19.

71. See Lawrence Vambe, *From Rhodesia to Zimbabwe* (London: Heinemann, 1976), pp. 107–128.

72. The only brutal rape in the period before responsible government which reached court occurred in November 1922. Three African men were charged with having raped a woman named Mrs. South at the Bulawayo Golf Course. The crime was notable in three respects: It was probably premeditated, there was more than one assailant, and it involved rape. The accused, Sandy, Bunywana, and Zuzumba, were found guilty, sentenced to death, and executed. See A. F. Russell, Judge's Report to the Attorney General, March 15, 1923, Appeals: Criminal Cases, S337. See also "A Just Penalty," *Bulawayo Chronicle*, March 3, 1923.

73. "A Foul Murder," *Rhodesian Herald*, March 10, 1916.

74. "The Veld Murder," *Rhodesian Herald*, March 24, 1916.

75. There was little press coverage of the case, although one correspondent to the *Rhodesian Herald* was critical of white mothers who allowed their daughters to walk about unaccompanied. "Scribe" felt that on seeing such women, natives would assume they had an immoral purpose and would be tempted to assault them. "White women may be quite certain of this—no native they meet while out alone ever passes them without the thought of assault, at least entering his head." "Scribe," "Letter to the Editor: The Black Peril," *Rhodesian Herald*, March 24, 1916.

76. Lewis H. Gann, *A History of Southern Rhodesia: Early Days to 1934* (New York: Humanities Press, 1969), p. 222.

77. The following account is taken from a newspaper report. See "Alleged Attempted Rape," *Rhodesian Herald*, November 5, 1909.

78. *Rex versus Kolale (alias Kurari)*, Salisbury High Court, April 18, 1910, Series S628, No. 511.

79. *Rex versus Zuzi*, Salisbury High Court, February 2, 1914, Series S628, No. 740.

80. Ibid.

81. Numerous other cases in the court files, including the following, are representative both in terms of the nature of the crime and the sentence imposed. *Rex versus Chinadza (alias Jonas)*, Salisbury High Court, November 17, 1904, Series S628, No. 242. Chinadze was found guilty of the rape of a minor, Olga Maria Karrani, and sentenced to six years' jail and twenty-five cuts. *Rex versus Lewis*, Salisbury High Court, September 17, 1935, Series S628, No. 3386. The accused was found guilty and sentenced to three years' hard labor and ten cuts with the

cane for a sexual assault on a child under three years of age. The child suffered no major physical injury.

82. See Anna Clark, *Women's Silence, Men's Violence: Sexual Assault in England 1770–1845* (London: Pandora, 1987), pp. 48–49, 98–101.

83. A small number of assaults did involve serious injury to the child and resulted in severe jail sentences. One such case from 1919 was that of M'zanywa, who was employed as a "picannin" and charged with the rape of Elsie Waterworth, aged six years. Elsie was seriously injured and M'zanywa was sentenced to death. Because of his age (which was between fifteen and eighteen years) M'zanywa's sentence was commuted by the high commissioner to life imprisonment. See *Rex versus M'zanywa,* Salisbury High Court, May 7, 1919, Series S628, No. 1180.

84. Under customary law sexual contact was not thought of as a private matter; therefore consent was of secondary importance. Before 1908, terms of four years' jail and twenty cuts with the cane were common. By 1935 that had fallen to an average of two years' hard labor. The length of sentences probably resulted from negotiations between traditional authorities and the state. See Diana Jeater, *Marriage, Perversion, and Power: The Construction of Moral Discourse in Southern Rhodesia, 1894–1930* (Oxford: Clarendon Press, 1993).

85. The same was true even when the accused was a member of the BSAC police. In February 1902, a BSAC trooper named John Harding was charged with the rape of Zeedwa, a married woman residing at a village near Salisbury. Because the case rested upon Zeedwa's testimony and that of other African witnesses, Harding was found not guilty. Arnold Price, who, like Harding, was a policeman, was charged in May 1913 with having raped Tambandini, the wife of Mutema, a chief of the Melsetter district. Again there were several witnesses who verified the victim's testimony. Again the case was dismissed. See *Rex versus John Harding,* Salisbury High Court, February 20, 1902, Series S628, No. 111; and *Rex versus Arnold Thimbleby Price,* Salisbury High Court, May 15, 1913, Series S628, No. 702.

3. VIOLENCE AND JUSTICE

1. See Ian Phimister, *Wangi Kolia: Coal Capital and Labor in Colonial Zimbabwe 1894–1954* (Harare: Baobab Books, 1994).

2. The Native Police were a branch of the BSAC police department that dealt exclusively with blacks.

3. J. J. Taylor, "The Emergence and Development of the Native Department in Southern Rhodesia, 1894–1914" (Ph.D. diss., University of London, 1974), p. 173.

4. Correspondence, Resident Commissioner, Salisbury September 10, 1902, RC3/3/6; *Rex versus Byron,* February 22, 1906, RC3/8/3; the case of L. Robinson, 1914, RC3/4/1; Confidential Report, November 30, 1905, RC3/8/3.

5. See Administrator Milton to the High Commissioner, March 28, 1907, Correspondence: Resident Commissioner, RC3/3/15.

6. In 1910 the mines employed 37,000 Africans, which represented less than 30 percent of the industry's annual needs. See Charles van Onselen, *Chibaro: African Mine Labor in Southern Rhodesia* (Johannesburg: Ravan Press, 1980), p. 96.

7. Ibid., pp. 145–147.

8. See M. C. Steele, "The Foundations of a Native Policy: Southern Rhodesia, 1923 to 1933," Ph.D. diss., Simon Fraser University, 1972.

9. Albert Schweitzer, *On the Edge of the Primeval Forest* (London: Hodder and Stoughton, 1922), pp. 101–102. For further commentary on the use of the *sjambok* see Lawrence Vambe, *An Ill-Fated People: Zimbabwe Before and After Rhodes* (London: Heinemann, 1972), p. 107ff.

10. As a result of malaria the spleen can swell and distend below the rib cage.

11. Most legal systems, including Anglo-American criminal law, distinguish between different degrees and kinds of unjustified killing. Under the law used in Southern Rhodesia, Roman-Dutch law, culpable homicide was a lesser category of criminal homicide. Like manslaughter it carried a lesser penalty than the crime of murder.

12. Shirley Weleba, "Trial by Jury in Southern Rhodesia, 1900–1912" (Ph.D. diss., University of Southern California, 1969), pp. 54–57.

13. Philip Mason, *The Birth of a Dilemma: The Conquest and Settlement of Rhodesia* (London: Oxford University Press, 1958), p. 309.

14. *Rex versus George Binns,* Salisbury High Court, February 19, 1901, Series S628, No. 65.

15. It was seen as a significant case and the *Rhodesian Herald* published a full transcript of both the magistrate's hearing and the first trial.

16. The following account of the trial is taken from the transcript of *Rex versus Laidlaw,* Salisbury High Court, May 4, 1908, Series S628, No. 391.

17. Ibid., p. 7.

18. Mason, *The Birth of a Dilemma,* pp. 298–299.

19. Letter from Lord Selbourne to the Resident Commissioner, July 14, 1908, Office of the Administrator: Special Juries, A3/21/87.

20. The new ordinance made eligible all men of European descent and British subjects between the ages of twenty-one and sixty years who had for the previous six months been in receipt of an annual salary of at least 50 pounds. Women were excluded. Despite the changes the matter of jury service remained a vexed issue. In March 1919 the Salisbury Town Council proposed a number of changes to the system. The *Rhodesian Herald,* which supported the proposal, argued that the problem of too-frequent service lay not in the size of the jury roll but in the method used to take the ballot. With regard to purely native cases some grievance was felt by busy men forced to listen to a case about a kraal brawl. They each lost a day of work and felt that such cases should be heard before a magistrate with assessors. See "The Jury System," *Rhodesian Herald,* March 21, 1919.

21. Transcript of debate, the Juries Ordinance, Legislative Council. Printed in *Rhodesian Herald,* June 26, 1908.

22. Tredgold's position was equivocal and in the following months he supported one side and then the other. For example, in December 1908, following the high commissioner's suggestion that trial by jury should be abolished, Tredgold wrote to the administrator supporting the existing system. See Attorney General Tredgold: Memo to the Administrator, December 11, 1908, Office of the Administrator: Juries, A11/2/18/31.

23. Transcript of *Rex versus Murdo Macauley and others,* Salisbury High Court, November 3, 1908, Battlefields Case, Series S628, No. 416, p. 4.

24. Ibid., p. 7.

25. In his postmortem of Mangesi, Dr. Mackenzie found the cause of death to be cardiac dilation brought about by acute pulmonary congestion. The postmortem of Sixpence noted there were no broken ribs and no injuries to the abdomen or skull and that the cause of death was pneumonia and pleurisy. Both reports implied that the floggings had been slight. See "Exhibit: A Post Mortem Report on Mangesi" and "Exhibit B: A Post Mortem of Sixpence" in *Rex versus Murdo Macauley.*

26. "Justus," Letter to the Editor, *Rhodesian Herald,* November 13, 1908.

27. Editorial, *Rhodesian Herald,* November 27, 1908.

28. G. A. Wilder, Letter to the Editor, *Rhodesian Herald,* December 12, 1908.

29. Letter to the Editor, *Rhodesian Herald,* November 25, 1908.

30. Others have found different excuses for the conduct of Rhodesian juries. Shirley Weleba argues that in many cases of culpable homicide and murder by whites of Africans, the guilt of the accused had not been clearly established. In trials involving native testimony there were serious problems with translation. For that reason such evidence was seldom accepted by white juries. See Weleba, "Trial by Jury," pp. 187–224.

31. Selbourne made clear that he was not raising the matter officially, which he did not do until April 1909.

32. Lord Selbourne to Administrator W. Milton, November 27, 1908, Office of the Administrator: Special Juries, A3/21/87.

33. Administrator W. Milton to Lord Selbourne, December 12, 1908, Office of the Administrator: Special Juries, A3/21/87.

34. Lord Selbourne to Administrator W. Milton, December 17, 1908, Office of the Administrator: Special Juries, A3/21/87.

35. See, for example, Mr. Montagu, Office of the Secretary for Mines, to Administrator W. Milton, March 8, 1909, Office of the Administrator: Special Juries, A3/21/87.

36. Notes on conference between the Administrator, Justices Vincent and Watermeyer, and the Attorney General, January 1909, Office of the Administrator: Special Juries, A3/21/87.

37. Memo from Attorney General Tredgold titled "Jury System," undated (April 1909?), Office of the Administrator: Special Juries, A3/21/87.

38. Ibid.

39. Dispatch from High Commissioner Selbourne, Johannesburg, April 14, 1909, to the Resident Commissioner, Correspondence: Miscellaneous Reports 1909–1916, A.12–1909 p. 2.

40. Debates of the Legislative Council, May 26, 1909. Transcript printed in *Rhodesian Herald,* June 4, 1909.

41. Secretary of State to Selbourne, August 13, 1909, Office of the Administrator: Special Juries, A3/21/87.

42. They included the following cases, in which the most severe penalty handed down was a fine of 15 pounds: a) Carl Herman Lange was charged with assault with intent to cause grievous bodily harm because he fired two shots with a revolver at a man named Maomba. He was found not guilty. Umtali Criminal Sessions, October 4, 1909, Series S628, No. 464; b) Charles Henry Walker was

charged with assault with intent to do grievous bodily harm because he shot and wounded a man named Chirinda at a farm outside of Umtali. Walker, who was undefended, was found guilty of common assault under great provocation and fined 15 pounds or six weeks in jail. Umtali High Court, October 4, 1909, Series S628, No. 463; c) William George Lapham was charged in November 1909 with culpable homicide because he killed a laborer named Kapuya. He was found not guilty. Salisbury High Court, November 3, 1909, Series S628, No. 474; d) George Pendrey, a policeman of Salisbury, was charged with eleven counts of striking and kicking natives. He was found guilty and fined 1 shilling on each count. Salisbury High Court, January 1, 1910, Series S628, No. 474.

43. See, for example, *Rex versus Rimbi & Wanamata,* Salisbury High Court, November 3, 1909, Series S628, No. 485.

44. *Rex versus Jordan Stanley Miller,* Salisbury High Court, November 3, 1909, Series S628, No. 475.

45. *Rex versus Frederick Butcher,* May 2, 1910, Salisbury High Court, Series S628, No. 510.

46. The following account of the Forbes case is taken from "Alleged Murder," *Rhodesian Herald,* May 6, 1910, and transcripts of *Rex versus MacLaren Forbes* at Salisbury High Court, April 19, 1910, Series S628, No. 502.

47. "The Black Peril," *Rhodesian Herald,* February 10, 1911.

48. *Bulawayo Chronicle,* February 13, 1902.

49. Letter to the Editor, *Rhodesian Herald,* November 25, 1908.

50. The following account of those events is taken from *Rex versus Lewis,* Salisbury, August 14, 1911, T2/24/16. An almost identical account is to be found in the *Bulawayo Chronicle,* May 19, 1911; June 19, 1911; and August 15, 1911.

51. *Rex versus Lewis,* p. 1.

52. Ibid., p. 14.

53. Ibid., p. 15.

54. *Bulawayo Chronicle,* May 26, 1911.

55. *Rex versus Lewis,* p. 42.

56. Ibid., pp. 10–13.

57. Editorial, *Rhodesian Herald,* July 21, 1911.

58. *Rhodesian Herald,* December 15, 1911.

59. Editorial, *Rhodesian Herald,* July 21, 1911.

60. Those papers included the *Daily Chronicle,* the *Daily Express,* the *Daily News,* the *Stamford and Rutland Guardian,* the *Morning Leader,* and the *Morning Herald.* Much of the South African press condemned the jury and the system of justice in Rhodesia and yet it was those same papers which over the preceding three years had helped to create a climate of hysteria about Black Peril. Among the South African press neither the *Evening Chronicle* nor the *Cape Times Weekly* made any comment critical of the verdict, although the *Pretoria News* referred to the decision as a miscarriage of justice. The *Rand Daily Mail* (August 16, 1911) was even more critical and suggested that the decision attacked the foundations of the British Empire.

61. *Bulawayo Chronicle,* August 24, 1911.

62. *Rhodesian Herald,* August 17, 1911.

63. "Sipan," Letter to the Editor, *Rhodesian Herald,* August 25, 1911. "Si-

pan's" letter is a reminder of just how traumatic the *chimurenga* had been for white settlers and to what extent they had been permanently scarred.

64. *Rand Daily Mail*, August 16, 1911.

65. See *Morning Herald*, August 17, 1911, and *The Times*, August 17, 1911.

66. See question from Mr. McCallum Scott to the Secretary of State for the Colonies. *The House of Commons Debates*, August 18, 1911.

67. John White, Letter to the Editor, *Rhodesian Herald*, August 25, 1911.

68. Simpson's sermon was reprinted in full in the *Rhodesian Herald*. See "The Lewis Case," *Rhodesian Herald*, August 25, 1911.

69. See "Open Letter to the Administrator, Sir William Milton from Ernest Harker, Dean of Salisbury and the Archdeacons of Matabeleland and Mashonaland," *Rhodesian Herald* November 24, 1911.

70. Attorney General Tredgold to the Acting Administrator, August 29, 1911, *Rex versus Lewis*, T2/24/16.

71. Ibid., p. 2.

72. Resident Commissioner to the High Commissioner, August 31, 1911, *Rex versus Lewis*, RC3/8/6.

73. Ibid., p. 3.

74. In her history of the jury system Shirley Weleba cites a number of factors which produced the verdict in the Sam Lewis case. Whites were greatly outnumbered by Africans, the *chimurenga* was in the near past and whites were fearful, whites felt that only by imposing their morality on blacks could they maintain control, white men greatly outnumbered white women and felt the women had to be protected, whites saw Africans as brutal and regarded Black Peril crimes with repugnance, and Africans were charged with rape of their own women in a large number of cases. While such cases were rare in terms of the total population, their frequency was such that many whites served on juries in such cases. See Weleba, "Trial by Jury," pp. 78–79.

75. "Lord Gladstone's Speech," *Rhodesian Herald*, September 8, 1911.

76. "Sir Charles Coghlan's Views," *Rhodesian Herald*, May 3, 1912.

77. The Special Juries Ordinance, No. 13 of 1912.

78. See Appendix, Table B, "Ordinances Introduced as the Result of a Request by the Imperial Authorities," in Claire Palley, *The Constitutional History and Law of Southern Rhodesia, 1888–1965* (Oxford: Clarendon Press, 1966).

79. "W. P. B.," "Letter to the Editor: Trial by Jury," *Rhodesian Herald*, May 31, 1912.

80. It amended the Special Juries Ordinance of 1912 by deleting the words "or by a native against a European" and allowed the accused to have the charge heard before a judge and assessors. If the accused was an African the trial was held by a judge and two assessors who were or had been native commissioners. In such cases the judge had sole discretion regarding sentencing. If the accused was a European he was usually tried by a judge and an ordinary jury consisting of only nine men who were European male citizens and had certain property qualifications. A jury could return a majority verdict. See the Criminal Trials High Court Act, No. 18 of 1927.

81. Lewis H. Gann and Peter Duignan, "Changing Patterns of a White Elite: Rhodesia and Other Settlers," in *Colonialism in Africa, 1870–1960*, vol. 2, ed.

Lewis H. Gann and Peter Duignan (Cambridge: Cambridge University Press, 1970), p. 108.

82. A fellow officer made the following comment on de Laessoe's behavior:

I have always said you were one of the cleverest and ablest men in the Service. I have heard many condemn your methods but the result of your administration is perfect, but the method in my opinion is wrong, it was obtained at too great a cost. I am not able to suggest any methods other than what you adopted to obtain the result which you obtained in your district.

"Report of the Belingwe Enquiry," Correspondence Resident Commissioner, RC3/4/1, p. 87. The comment echoed the criticism made by Kurtz's colleagues in *The Heart of Darkness*. Joseph Conrad, *Heart of Darkness* (New York: W. W. Norton & Company, 1963).

83. Letter from A. Lyton, Acting Secretary Department of Justice, to Secretary of the Prime Minister, April 12, 1939, Correspondence, Office of the Prime Minister, S482/366/39.

84. For an insight into the kind of problems posed by the system see Correspondence, Office of the Prime Minister, S482/366/39.

85. See, for example, Ian Phimister and Charles Van Onselen, *Studies in the History of African Mine Labour in Colonial Zimbabwe* (Gwelo, Zimbabwe: Mambo Press, 1978).

86. Under the terms of the BSAC Charter, settlers had limited control over the political process and the administration of the colony. They could not manage their own defense force or pursue an independent foreign policy. Britain retained a veto over all important legislation, especially laws affecting native policy. See L. H. Gann, *A History of Southern Rhodesia: Early Days to 1934* (New York: Humanities Press, 1969).

87. For a discussion of sexualized violence see Robert J. Stoller, *Perversion: The Erotic Form of Hatred* (Cambridge: Harvester Press, 1976), pp. 8–9.

4. LEGISLATING VIRTUE

1. See Anna Clark, *Women's Silence, Men's Violence: Sexual Assault in England 1770–1845* (London: Pandora, 1987).

2. See Jill Bavin-Mizzi, "Understandings of Justice: Australian Rape and Carnal Knowledge Cases, 1897–1924," in *Sex, Power and Justice: Historical Perspectives on Law in Australia,* ed. Diane Kirkby (Melbourne: Oxford University Press, 1995), pp. 20–22.

3. For a series of essays on the significance of rape see Sylvana Tomaselli and Roy Porter, eds., *Rape: An Historical and Social Inquiry* (London: Basil Blackwell, 1989).

4. See Roy Porter, "Rape: Does It Have an Historical Meaning?" in *Rape: An Historical and Social Inquiry,* ed. S. Tomaselli and Roy Porter (London: Basil Blackwell, 1989), pp. 216–236.

5. See Claire Palley, "The Southern Rhodesian Legal System," in *The Constitutional History and Law of Southern Rhodesia, 1888–1965* (Oxford: Clarendon Press, 1966), pp. 493–563.

6. For a discussion of customary law and its place within colonial administra-

tion and ideology, see Martin Chanock, *Law, Custom and Social Order: The Colonial Experience in Malawi and Zambia* (Cambridge: Cambridge University Press, 1985).

7. The first judge appointed to the High Court was Justice Joseph Vintcent. He was born in the Cape, where his father was a member of the legislature. Vintcent was educated in South Africa and at Cambridge. He served on the bench until his death in 1914. A second judge, John Watermeyer, was appointed in 1896. Watermeyer was also born in the Cape and educated at Cambridge. He was a close friend of William Milton, the administrator. See Michael Kimberley, "Sir Joseph Vintcent, Rhodesia's First Judge," *Rhodesiana* 38 (March 1978): 1–13; and Michael Kimberley, "John Phillip Fairbairn Watermeyer—Rhodesia's Second Judge," *Rhodesiana* 40 (March 1979): 14–21. That pattern of appointments continued for some time. Judge Hopley, who served on the High Court from 1914 until his death in 1919, was born in the Cape, studied law at Cambridge, and practiced as a barrister in Cape Town. He was a personal friend of Rhodes and Starr Jameson. See "Judge Hopley's Death," *Rhodesian Herald*, March 14, 1919.

8. Palley, *Constitutional History*, p. 161.

9. Shirley Weleba, "Trial by Jury in Southern Rhodesia, 1900–1912" (Ph.D. diss., University of Southern California, 1969), p. 48.

10. See Michel Foucault, "La poussiere et le nuage," in *L'impossible prison,* ed. M. Perot (Paris: Editions du seuil, 1980), pp. 29–39.

11. For an account of the weaknesses of the law as a regulatory system see Sally Falk Moore, *Law as Process: An Anthropological Approach* (London: Routledge & Kegan Paul, 1978). See also Christopher L. Tomlins, *Law, Labor, and Ideology in the Early American Republic* (Cambridge: Cambridge University Press, 1993), pp. 318ff.

12. The Criminal Law Amendment Ordinance, No. 13 of 1900, in *Legislative Council Proceedings and Ordinances for 1900* (Salisbury: Government Printer, 1903).

13. Administrator Milton to the High Commissioner, December 17, 1902, A2/4/2.

14. That clause was amended because imperial authorities would not sanction racially discriminatory legislation. See Legislative Council Debates of Southern Rhodesia, 1899–1907, November 12, 1903. Reprinted from *Rhodesian Herald,* SRG2, p. 113.

15. Mr. P. R. Frames, Legislative Council Debates, November 12, 1902, SRG2, p. 114.

16. The ordinance reads: "Any person convicted of the crime of assault with intent to commit rape may be sentenced by the Judge before whom such a person is tried to be hanged by the neck until he is dead, or such person may in the discretion of the Judge be sentenced to any less punishment which the Judge may in the circumstances of the case consider to be sufficient." The Criminal Law Amendment Ordinance, No. 3 of 1903.

17. In November 1902, Mr. Frames moved for the introduction of such legislation, but the motion was defeated by 6 to 3.

18. The ordinance had three sections and said: a) Any white woman or girl who shall voluntarily have illicit sexual intercourse with any native shall upon conviction be liable to imprisonment with or without hard labor for a period not

exceeding two years; b) Any person who procures a white woman or procures a native for such purposes may receive up to five years' hard labor: where such a person is male a further twenty-five lashes in addition; c) Any native who has illicit sexual intercourse with a white woman or girl with her consent shall upon conviction be liable to imprisonment with hard labor for a period not exceeding 5 years. The Immorality Suppression Ordinance, No. 9 of 1903. *Legislative Council Proceedings and Ordinances for 1903* (Salisbury: Government Printer, 1902).

19. Administrator Milton to High Commissioner Milner, Minute No. 90, July 8, 1903, Office of the Administrator, A2/4/2.

20. See Appendix, Table B, "Ordinances Introduced as the Result of a Request by the Imperial Authorities," in Palley, *Constitutional History.*

21. See Terence O. Ranger, *The African Voice in Southern Rhodesia, 1898–1930* (Evanston, Ill.: Northwestern University Press, 1970), pp. 19ff.

22. The Immorality and Indecency Suppression Ordinance, No. 1 of 1916. Legislative Council Debate, May 2, 1916, SRG2, p. 40.

23. Clause 1 of the Immorality and Indecency Suppression Ordinance.

24. See debates of the Immorality and Indecency Suppression Ordinance, May 2 and 5, 1916, Legislative Council Debates, SRG2, pp. 38–46.

25. During the drafting of the immorality ordinance there was some discussion about whether offending white women should face deportation. The attorney general, however, rejected the idea as being foreign to the subject matter of the ordinance. See Attorney General to the Secretary of the Department of the Administrator, March 24, 1916, Correspondence on the Immorality and Indecency Suppression Ordinance of 1916, A3 21/28-9.

26. *Rex versus Kaimulila (alias Perloom),* Salisbury High Court, May 11, 1923, Series S628, No. 1585.

27. *Rex versus Chilumpa,* Salisbury High Court, July 17, 1924, Series S628, No. 1710.

28. *Chibaro,* or forced labor, was used extensively between 1903 and 1912 to drive black workers into mines. Mine work was dangerous: Between 1900 and 1933 over 30,000 men died in mine compounds, mostly from disease. See Charles van Onselen, *Chibaro: African Mine Labor in Southern Rhodesia* (Johannesburg: Ravan Press, 1980), p. 62.

29. See Frank Mort, *Dangerous Sexualities: Medico-Moral Politics in England since 1830* (London: Routledge & Kegan Paul, 1987).

30. Judith Walkowitz, *Prostitution and Victorian Society: Women, Class and the State* (Cambridge: Cambridge University Press, 1980), p. 246.

31. *The Suppression of Betting Houses, Gaming Houses, and Brothels Act: Act No. 36 of 1902: Acts of Parliament Session of 1902* (Cape Town: Cape Times Ltd., 1902).

32. Section 34: "It shall be unlawful for any white woman to voluntarily have illicit sexual intercourse for the purposes of gain with any aboriginal native; and any white woman contravening the provisions of this section shall be liable on conviction to be imprisoned with hard labor for a period not exceeding two years." The Suppression of Betting Houses, Gaming Houses, and Brothels Act, 1902.

33. Before the second Anglo-Boer War draconian legislation was passed in the Transvaal. Under Law No. 11 of 1899 a white woman faced up to five years in jail and could be banished from the republic if she had illicit sexual relations with a

black man. A black man could be jailed for six years and given fifty lashes. After the war began the legislation lapsed. See Nicholas Charles Smythe, "The Origins of Apartheid: Race Legislation in South Africa, 1836 to 1910" (Ph.D. diss., University of Witwatersrand, 1995).

34. Monday, October 13, 1902, *Debates in the House of Assembly Fourth Session of the 10 Parliament, 20 August to the 14 November 1902* (Cape Town: Cape Times, Ltd., 1903), p. 439.

35. Attorney General to the Lieutenant-Governor, Transvaal, September 25, 1902, in Immorality: Sexual Intercourse between White Women and Black Men, LD160 AGS5446/02 (State Archive, Pretoria).

36. Section 19 (1): "Any white woman who voluntarily permits any native to have unlawful carnal connection with her is liable to imprisonment with hard labor for five years." The Immorality Ordinance, No. 46 of 1903, *Statutes of The Transvaal, 1903* (Pretoria: Govt. Printing Office, Transvaal, 1903).

37. Section 3 (i) reads: "Any white woman who voluntarily permits or who incites, solicits, or importunes any native to have unlawful carnal connection with her in circumstances which do not amount to rape, and any native who entices, solicits, or importunes any white woman, to have unlawful carnal connection with him, or to the commission of immoral or indecent acts, shall be guilty of an offence and liable upon conviction to imprisonment with hard labor for a period not exceeding six years and in addition to such imprisonment, to whipping not exceeding twenty-four strokes." The Criminal Law Amendment Act, No. 16 of 1908, *Statutes of The Transvaal, 1908* (Pretoria: Govt. Printing Office, 1908).

38. Second reading of bill by Prime Minister Sir A. H. Hime, May 27, 1903, *Debates of the Legislative Assembly of the Colony of Natal: First Session of the Fourth Parliament,* vol. 23, 1903 (Pietermaritzburgh: Times Printing and Pub. Co., 1903), pp. 202–203. See also the Criminal Law Amendment Act, No. 31 of 1903, *Acts of the Parliament of the Colony of Natal: 1903* (Pietermaritzburg: Times Printing and Pub. Co., 1903), pp. 96–101.

39. See Suppression of Brothels and Immorality Ordinance, No. 11 of 1903, *Orange River Colony Ordinances, 1903* (Bloemfontein: Argus P. & Co., 1903).

40. Callaway explains the absence of such panics in Nigeria in the following way: "The question of European women's 'sexual fear' appears to arise in special circumstances of unequal power structures at times of particular political pressure, when the dominant group perceives itself threatened and vulnerable." Helen Callaway, *Gender, Culture, and Empire: European Women in Colonial Nigeria* (London: Macmillan Press, 1987), p. 237.

41. For example, between 1906 and 1930 seven cases of black-on-white sexual assault were reported in the *Livingstone Mail*. See Karen Hansen, *Distant Companions: Servants and Employers in Zambia, 1900–1985* (Ithaca: Cornell University Press, 1989), pp. 103–104.

42. Ibid., p. 71.

5. EXPLAINING BLACK PERIL

1. After returning to Paris, Mannoni trained as a psychoanalyst under Jacques Lacan at the Ecole Freudienne de Paris. He subsequently published a full-length study of Freud, entitled simply *Freud* (Paris: Editions du Seuil, 1968).

2. Quoted in Elisabeth Roudinesco, *Jacques Lacan and Company: A History of Psychoanalysis in France, 1925–1985,* trans. Jeffrey Mehlam (Chicago: University of Chicago Press, 1986), p. 234.

3. Octave Mannoni, *Prospero and Caliban: The Psychology of Colonization,* trans. Pamela Powesland (New York: Frederick A. Praeger, 1964), pp. 110–111.

4. Philip Mason, *The Birth of a Dilemma: The Conquest and Settlement of Rhodesia* (London: Oxford University Press, 1958), pp. 241–244, 249.

5. See Frantz Fanon, *Black Skin, White Masks,* trans. C. Markham (London: MacGibbon and Kee, 1967).

6. There are numerous variations of the idea of projection and stereotyping. Sander Gilman has observed of Western art that "[b]y the eighteenth century, the sexuality of the black, both male and female, becomes an icon for deviant sexuality in general and the black figure sexualized the scenes in which he or she appeared." Over the next century the figure of the black woman supposedly merged with the prostitute as a symbol of sexual degeneracy. See Sander Gilman, "Black Bodies, White Bodies: Toward an Iconography of Female Sexuality in Late Nineteenth-Century Art, Medicine, and Literature," in *"Race," Writing, and Difference,* ed. Henry L. Gates (Chicago: University of Chicago Press, 1986), p. 228. See also Chapter 3, "The Hottentot and the Prostitute," in Sander Gilman, *Difference and Pathology: Stereotypes of Sexuality, Race, and Madness* (Ithaca: Cornell University Press, 1985).

7. Many writers have noted that guilt about sexual desire is characteristic of Western culture. Some have also argued that in colonial contexts such guilt precipitated racial conflict. The idea is found in Octave Mannoni's *Prospero and Caliban;* Calvin Hernton's *Sex and Racism* (London: Paladin Books, 1970); and in Joseph Conrad's novella *Heart of Darkness.* In the historiography of Southern Rhodesia it is used in Philip Mason's *The Birth of a Dilemma: The Conquest and Settlement of Rhodesia* (London: Oxford University Press, 1958); Richard Gray's *The Two Nations* (London: Oxford University Press, 1960); and Dane Kennedy's *Islands of White* (Durham, N.C.: Duke University Press, 1995). In postmodernist debates it is found in Henry L. Gates, ed. *"Race," Writing, and Difference* and in Sander Gilman's *Difference and Pathology.*

8. Freud was so preoccupied with desire that some of his followers have claimed that the victims of rape actually enjoy the experience. Within psychoanalytic theory there is no zero state of desire. Consequently some analysts have assumed there must also be desire within rape. That idea has of course often been used in courts to the detriment of victims. For an example of the psychoanalytic theory of rape see John Forrester "Rape, Seduction and Psychoanalysis" in Sylvana Tomaselli and Roy Porter, eds., *Rape: An Historical and Social Inquiry* (London: Basil Blackwell, 1989), pp. 56–83.

9. There is no evidence from the press, from official correspondence, or from public debate that Black Peril fears ever had the same significance or intensity in Kenya. The one notable exception, the case involving Ewan Grogan, was contrived for political advantage. The two most important sexual crimes against white women, crimes far worse than any that occurred in colonial Zimbabwe, the Semini and Stumpf cases, did not lead to public hysteria. See "Correspondence Relating to the Flogging of Natives by Certain Europeans," Nairobi, July 1907. London, HM Stationery, 1907, CO 533/28; "Inquest into the Death of Miss Huldas Jane

Stumpf," Kijabe, January 20, 1930, Public Records Office, Kenya, CO 533/394; and transcript "The Semini Case," Supreme Court Criminal Case No. 123 of 1934, Public Records Office, Kenya, CO533/441/1.

10. See, for example, Eduardo Bonilla-Silva, "Rethinking Racism: Toward a Structural Interpretation," *American Sociology Review* 62 (June 1997): 465–480; and Jack Niemonen, "The Role of the State in the Sociology of Racial and Ethnic Relations: Some Theoretical Considerations," *Free Inquiry in Creative Sociology* 23 (May 1995): 27–38.

11. The terms of reference included assaults upon women by men of the same color and of different color; the cause of the crimes with reference to segregation, alcohol, contact of natives with undesirable whites, the divorce of natives from customary life, the employment of native males as domestic servants and native boys to care for female children; and how such attacks could be prevented. *Report of the Commission Appointed to Enquire into Assaults on Women* (Cape Town: Government Printers, 1913), p. 1.

12. Mr. Graham Cross, Witness No. 196, November 7, 1912, Johannesburg, Transcripts of Hearings: Assaults on Women Commission, Pretoria, South African National Archives, pp. 20–21.

13. The report was in fact self-contradictory on this question. At one point it noted that many cases resulted from criminal carelessness by a white woman. At other points it suggested that such was not the case. Ibid., pp. 10 and 24.

14. *Report of the Commission Appointed to Enquire into Assaults on Women,* p. 6.

15. The incidence of black-on-white rape was highest in the Transvaal and the Cape and penalties were more severe in the Transvaal. In the Transvaal during the period 1901 to 1910 eight Coloured men were executed for rape. "Rape Figures for the Period from January 1900 to December 1910," South African Archives, PM1/1/249 120/4/1911.

16. *Report of the Commission Appointed to Enquire into Assaults on Women,* p. 8.

17. See testimony of Rev. Amos Burnet, Frederick Briscoe, and Edwin Bottrill. Witnesses 197, 198, 199, Johannesburg, December 8, 1912, Transcripts, Assaults on Women Commission, K373 1, pp. 22–25.

18. Rev. Frederick Bridgman, Witness 87, August 23, 1912, Durban, ibid., pp. 8–10.

19. The Carnegie Commission of the early 1930s found that white poverty was a major problem. A survey of schools revealed that 17.5 percent of families in the Union, or more than 300,000 whites, lived in poverty. See *The Poor White Problem in South Africa: Report of the Carnegie Commission,* vol. 1 (Stellenbosch: Proc Ecclesia-Drukkery, 1932), p. vii.

20. The commissioner wrote, "By closer contact with the white race in towns the natives have learnt that very often white people lead immoral lives, and that even finely dressed white women make a traffic of their persons." *Report of the Commission Appointed to Enquire into Assaults on Women,* p. 21.

21. Ibid., p. 25.

22. Mr. Cecil Jackson of Pietermaritzburg was concerned about the intimacy between white woman and black servants, particularly in working-class households, and asked the commission, "Would it be possible for the government to

issue a leaflet of warning and distribute it on board each vessel arriving here (South Africa), especially amongst the third-class passengers, because that is the class of woman who is only able to afford one servant as a rule?" Mr. Cecil Jackson, Witness 127, Pietermaritzburg, October 5, 1912, Transcripts, Assaults on Women Commission, K373 1, pp. 46.

23. See Super. Bertram Betts, Witness 162, October 29, 1912, Pretoria Police, pp. 4–6. Oddly enough, the final report contained the allegation that some whites made false claims of sexual assault to defraud blacks of their wages. *Report of the Commission Appointed to Enquire into Assaults on Women,* p. 26.

24. A typical response was that given by Frank Robey of East London: "I think the death penalty is the safest. It is a bit heathenist [*sic*] to suggest the other (ie castration). Of course the man who was so treated would be held up to ridicule by his fellows to the very last day of his life. His life would be a burden to him evermore, especially amongst the natives. It would be a living death for the man. He would have to hide himself from everybody, and go into a strange land." Mr. Frank Robey, Witness 74, East London, August 16, 1912, Transcripts Assaults on Women Commission, K373 1, p. 9. In the final report de Villiers falsely claimed that emasculation had wide support, which then justified his recommending it not as a punishment but as a means for stopping such men from procreating. *Report of the Commission Appointed to Enquire into Assaults,* p. 32.

25. Ibid., p. 11.

26. Ibid., p. 3.

27. For an account of the Sam Lewis case, see Chapter 3: "Violence and Justice."

28. *Report of the Commission Appointed to Enquire into Assaults on Women,* p. 22.

29. East London, July 17, 1912, Transcripts, Assaults on Women Commission, p. 21.

30. Black and White Peril in Southern Rhodesia, Special CID File, 1915 or 1916, S1227/2.

31. That fact has led at least one historian into some confusion. In her study of Shona women, Elizabeth Schmidt uses the term "yellow peril" to refer to the sexual threat posed by white men to black women. Schmidt writes: "While "black peril" was on everyone's lips, some Europeans were more apprehensive about the less-publicized 'yellow peril'—miscegenation as a result of sexual relations between European men and African women." "Ideology, Economics, and the Role of Shona Women in Southern Rhodesia, 1850–1939" (Ph.D. diss., University of Wisconsin-Madison, 1987), p. 414. The term yellow peril was never used in association with sexual assault; in South Africa it referred to the threat posed to the jobs of white workers by imported Asian labor. Throughout the nineteenth and early twentieth centuries that nomenclature was used in the same way in Australia. See Chapter 5: "Black and Yellow Peril: African Women and European Domestic Service" in Schmidt.

32. It does feature quotations taken from other documents for which no sources are given. The absence of court transcripts suggests that few cases of White Peril resulted in criminal charges.

33. Public feeling on this issue is cited by the CID as being the reason for the passing of Ordinance 1903 which made attempted rape a capital offense. Black and White Peril in Southern Rhodesia, Special CID File, S1227/2, pp. 55–56.

34. The activities of two particular women, Louisa Newman and Maud Cotter, were blamed for the Black Peril scares in Bulawayo. On November 11, 1902, they were tarred and feathered by an angry mob before being driven out of the town. Newman, who was of French nationality, had been convicted several times for selling liquor to natives. According to the CID report, Cotter was eventually convicted under the Immorality Ordinance of 1903 and deported. She is said to have died in the Transvaal of syphilis, but as no details are given this story is probably apocryphal. See Special CID File.

35. A second case reads as follows: "In this year [1898] a white constable reports the following circumstances: while passing a house on his beat he noticed a young Jewess standing naked in her room apparently just come out of her bath for a male native was engaged in the process of drying her with a bath towel." The difference between the two women referred to in these case notes was that one was "respectable," the other was Jewish. It was that kind of distinction between "respectable" and "unrespectable" white women that is described in the section dealing with "Female Temperament." Ibid.

36. Ibid., p. 56.

37. Ibid., p. 40. "Limbo" was a slang term for a formal military-style jacket and trousers.

38. Another incident in 1908 involved this same woman. A native cook who had worked for this woman committed suicide. At the inquest letters were produced written by the deceased in which he claimed to have had sexual relations with a number of white women in the country. Ibid.

39. Ibid., p. 40.

40. In the last decades of the nineteenth century fears of national degeneration became the concern of scientists, physicians, clergy, and politicians. They resulted in a number of well-publicized commissions, most notably the Inter-Department Committee on Physical Deterioration of 1904. See Daniel Pick, *Faces of Degeneration: A European Disorder, c. 1848–c. 1918* (Cambridge: Cambridge University Press, 1989).

41. See Dane Kennedy, *Islands of White: Settler Society and Culture in Kenya and Southern Rhodesia, 1890–1939* (Durham: Duke University Press, 1987), pp. 109–127.

42. See Dr. W. M. Hewetson, *Environmental Influences Affecting Blondes in Rhodesia and their Bearing on the Future: A Survey of the Situation from the Medical and Scientific Standpoints* (Salisbury: The Rhodesian Independent Co., Ltd., 1922).

43. Special CID File, p. 26.

44. In Southern Rhodesia the term concubinage referred to any kind of permanent or semi-permanent sexual relationship between a white man and a black or Coloured woman. Because of social disapproval concubinage rarely involved a live-in arrangement.

45. See Jeremy Krikler, "Social Neurosis and Hysterical Pre-Cognition in South Africa," *South African Historical Journal* 28 (1993): 63–97. See also John Pape, "Black and White: The 'Perils of Sex' in Colonial Zimbabwe," *Journal of Southern African Studies* 4 (1990): 699–720.

46. See Arthur de Gobineau, *The Inequality of Human Races*, trans. Adrian Collins (1853; reprint, New York: Howard Fertig, 1967), p. 205.

47. See, for example, J. C. Carothers, "Frontal Lobe Function in the African," *Journal of Mental Science* 97 (January 1952): 122–148.

48. See Sigmund Freud, *Totem and Taboo,* trans. A. A. Brill (1913; reprint, New York: Vintage Books, 1946), p. 3. For an account of Freud's interest in anthropology see Edwin. R. Wallace, *Freud and Anthropology: A History and Reappraisal* (New York: International Universities Press, 1983).

49. Freud writes: "In consequence of the inverse relation holding between civilisation and the free development of sexuality, of which the consequences can be followed far into the structure of our existences, the course taken by the sexual life of a child is just as unimportant for later life where the cultural of social level is relatively low as it is important where that level is relatively high." Sigmund Freud, *Three Essays on the Theory of Sexuality* (1905; reprint, New York: Avon Books, 1962), p. 148.

50. Ibid., p. 73.

51. Freud, *Totem and Taboo,* p. 116–117.

52. Freud, *Three Essays,* pp. 7–73, 87–88, 128–130, and 148.

53. For a history of ethnopsychiatry see Jock McCulloch, *Colonial Psychiatry and the 'African Mind': 1900 to 1960* (Cambridge: Cambridge University Press, 1995). For a history of the sciences of race in South Africa see Saul Dubow, *Scientific Racism in Modern South Africa* (Cambridge: Cambridge University Press, 1995).

54. It is notable that in a standard colonial text on somatic and psychological illness Michael Gelfand, a Southern Rhodesian, made no mention of sexuality. See Michael Gelfand, *The Sick African: A Clinical Study,* 3rd ed. (Cape Town: Juta & Company Ltd., 1957). See in particular pp. 533–589.

55. B. J. F. Laubscher, *Sex, Custom and Psychopathology: A Study of South African Pagan Natives* (London: George Routledge & Sons, 1937).

56. Laubscher wrote: "The active partners are usually the paranoids and the feeble-minded and the passive partners are the epileptics and dull schizophrenics and imbeciles." Laubscher, *Sex, Custom and Psychopathology,* p. 283.

57. See John F. Ritchie, *The African as Suckling and as Adult: A Psychological Study* (1943; reprint, Manchester: Rhodes-Livingstone Institute, 1968).

58. At the First Pan-African Psychiatric Conference held at Abeokuta in 1961 psychiatrist T. A. Lambo presented a paper entitled "Growth of African Children: Psychological Aspects." Although writing ostensibly of the Nigerian family, Lambo relied so heavily upon Ritchie that his argument is indistinguishable from Ritchie's argument in *The African as Suckling.* See T. A. Lambo, "Growth in African Children: Psychological Aspects," in *First Pan-African Psychiatric Conference,* ed. T. A. Lambo (Abeokuta: Government Printer, 1962), pp. 60–64. Ritchie's work also appears in the historiography of the colonial period; in his history of white settlement in Southern Rhodesia Philip Mason refers to Ritchie at length. See Philip Mason, *The Birth of a Dilemma: The Conquest and Settlement of Rhodesia* (London: Oxford University Press, 1958), pp. 84–85.

59. Ritchie, *The African as Suckling,* p. 16.

60. Ibid., pp. 18–19.

61. Laubscher, *Sex, Custom and Psychopathology,* pp. 77–81.

62. For a discussion of modernization theory and its antecedents see Catherine Scott, *Gender and Development: Rethinking Modernisation and Dependency Theory* (London: Lynne Rienner, 1995).

63. *Southern Rhodesian Report of the Director of Census 3/5/1921* (Salisbury: Government Printer, 1922).

64. Tsuneo Yoshikuni, "Black Migrants in a White City: A Social History of African Harare, 1890–1925" (Ph.D. diss., University of Zimbabwe, 1989), p. 17.

65. In that year Salisbury's white population consisted of 2,539 males and 1,037 females, while Umtali's white population consisted of 1,096 males and 469 females. See *Census of Europeans, 1907* (Salisbury: Government Printer, 1908).

66. By 1921 almost one in five whites in the colony were Afrikaners. See R. S. Roberts, "The Settlers," *Rhodesiana* 39 (September 1978): 57.

67. Almost half of the blacks living in Salisbury were migrant workers from Nyasaland, Northern Rhodesia, or Portuguese East Africa and so the image of an ethnically homogenous black population was as much an illusion as the image of an ethnically uniform white community. See *Preliminary Returns of a Census, 7 May 1911* (Salisbury: Government Printer, 1911), p. 3.

68. However, because of migrant labor the number of white women far exceeded that of black women, which probably contributed to fears of Black Peril on the Rand. In 1928 there were 196,000 white women on the Rand but only 29,000 black women. See Jonathan Hyslop, "White Working-Class Women and the Invention of Apartheid," *Journal of African History* 36 (1995): 62.

69. The Committee of Enquiry to Enquire into the Cost of Living found three causes of the high cost of living: Most basic commodities were imported over a great distance; the small local market discouraged farm production; and rail rates were high because of the smallness of the population. See Final Report, Committee of Enquiry to Enquire into the Cost of Living in Southern Rhodesia, 1913, ZAC 4/2/3.

70. See evidence of Mrs. McKeurten, Mrs. W. Macdonald, and Mrs. William Woods. Oral Evidence, Bulawayo, Committee of Enquiry to Enquire into the Cost of Living in Southern Rhodesia, 1913, ZAC 1/1/1, p. 14.

71. According to the committee's final report the average wages and salaries per month for whites were as follows;

Clerks	7 to 15 pounds
Salesmen	20 to 32 pounds
Saleswomen	15 to 25 pounds
Teachers	15 to 17 pounds
Domestic servants	3 to 4 pounds (with board)
Painters	1 pound per day
Carpenters	1 to 5 pounds per day

Final Report, Committee of Enquiry to Enquire into the Cost of Living, 1913, ZAC 4/2/3, p. 59.

72. Witness David McCullough, Oral Evidence, Bulawayo, Committee of Enquiry to Enquire into the Cost of Living, ZCA, 1/1/1, p. 44.

73. Yoshikuni, "Black Migrants in a White City," pp. 19–23.

74. Final Report, Committee of Enquiry to Enquire into the Cost of Living, 1913, ZAC 4/2/3, p. 68.

75. See Pavla Miller, *Transformations of Patriarchy in the West, 1500–1900* (Bloomington: Indiana University Press, 1998), pp. 259–266.

76. For an overview of recent debates on wage labor and family forms, see

Sonya O. Rose, *Limited Livelihoods: Gender and Class in Nineteenth-Century England* (Berkeley: University of California Press, 1992).

77. Mary Douglas writes: "To understand body pollution we should try to argue back from the known dangers of society to the known selection of bodily themes and try to recognise what appositeness is there." Mary Douglas, *Purity and Danger: An Analysis of the Concepts of Pollution and Taboo* (London: Routledge & Kegan Paul, 1966), p. 121.

78. Ibid., p. 4.

79. Maynard W. Swanson, "The Sanitation Syndrome: Bubonic Plague and Urban Native Policy in the Cape Colony," *Journal of African History* 18 (1977): 396.

80. However, this claim by Swanson is not supported by Yoshikuni in his history of Salisbury. Swanson, "The Sanitation Syndrome," p. 388.

81. A contrary view is presented by Yoshikuni in his history of African Harare, in which he claims there was no great fear of infection and that urban segregation came about in an ad hoc manner. Similarly, in an overview of disease, sanitation, and the creation of colonial cities, Curtin argues that the medical model was but one of a number of factors and was by no means the dominant one in promoting segregation. See Yoshikuni, "Black Migrants in a White City," pp. 33–34; and Philip D. Curtin "Medical Knowledge and Urban Planning in Colonial Tropical Africa," in *The Social Basis of Health and Healing in Africa,* ed. Steven Feierman and John M. Janzen (Berkeley: University of California Press, 1992), pp. 235–255.

6. WHITE WOMEN

1. Gertrude Page, *Love in the Wilderness: The Story of Another African Farm* (London: Hurst and Blackett, Ltd., 1907), p. 82.

2. See Helen Callaway, *Gender, Culture, and Empire: European Women in Colonial Nigeria* (London: Macmillan Press, 1987).

3. Doris Lessing, *The Grass Is Singing* (London: Michael Joseph, 1950).

4. In 1920 the Sex Disqualification Removal Ordinance extended to women the same rights enjoyed by men to practice a profession or be admitted to any incorporated society. The only exception was jury service. See the Sex Disqualification Removal Ordinance of 1920, A3/21/83.

5. Deborah Kirkwood, "Settler Wives in Southern Rhodesia: A Case Study," in *The Incorporated Wife,* ed. Hilary Callan and Shirley Ardener (London: Croom Helm, 1984), p. 162.

6. The Sex Disqualification Removal Ordinance of 1920, A3/21/83.

7. In 1900 Jollie married Archibald Colquhoun, the first administrator of Mashonaland. She traveled extensively with him and cooperated with him in the writing of a number of books on travel and politics. She was a member of the executive of the Women's Unionist Association, the Imperial Maritime League, and the National Service League, for whom she was a principal organizer and speaker. After Colquhoun's death she married a farmer, J. Tawse Jollie of Melsetter. Between 1917 and 1919 she was honorary secretary and organizer of the Responsible Government Association and in 1920 she successfully ran for the Eastern Division and entered the Legislative Council as its first female member. See Biographical Note: Ethel Tawse Jollie, RH 8/1/6.

8. Ethel Tawse Jollie, *The Real Rhodesia* (London: Hutchinson & Co., 1924), p. 246.

9. Ibid., pp. 271–272.

10. Ibid., pp. 160–164.

11. For a study of the settler novel see A. J. Chennells, "Settler Myths and the Southern Rhodesian Novel," Ph.D. diss., University of Zimbabwe, 1982.

12. See A. R. Taylor "The Development of Scientific Societies in Rhodesia and Nyasaland" in *Proceedings: The First Federal Science Congress, Salisbury May 18–22, 1960* (Salisbury: Mardon Rhodesian Printers, 1960), pp. 23–34.

13. *Report Director of Census 1936* (Salisbury: Government Printer, 1944), p. 71.

14. During the first decades of colonization teachers in government schools were recruited in London. But the pay was lower than in South Africa and as a consequence many posts were filled by women. N. D. Atkinson, "A History of Educational Policy in Southern Rhodesia" (Ph.D. diss., University of London, 1974), p. 106.

15. See Lewis Gann and Peter Duigan, *White Settlers in Tropical Africa* (Westport: Greenwood Press, 1977); Colin Leys, *European Politics in Southern Rhodesia* (London: Oxford University Press, 1959); Philip Mason, *The Birth of a Dilemma: The Conquest and Settlement of Rhodesia* (London: Oxford University Press, 1958); and G. H. Tanser, *A Sequence of Time: The Story of Salisbury, Rhodesia, 1900 to 1914* (Salisbury: Pioneer Head, 1974).

16. For a review of some of the problems in theorizing a notion of female agency see Margaret Jolly, "Colonizing Women: The Maternal Body and Empire" in *Feminism and the Politics of Difference,* ed. Sneja Gunew and Anna Yeatman (Sydney: Allen & Unwin, 1993), pp. 103–127.

17. Ann Stoler claims that to reduce administrative costs, restrictions on marriage were imposed on males serving colonial administrations and that at some sites demographic imbalances between white men and women were a function of policy. Such an argument supposes that colonial regimes worked with a degree of efficiency which was never achieved in Southern Rhodesia. Rather than seeking to exclude women, the BSAC tried to attract them. See Ann Stoler, "Carnal Knowledge and Imperial Power: Gender, Race, and Morality in Colonial Asia," in *Gender at the Crossroads: Feminist Anthropology in the Postmodern Era,* ed. Micaela di Leonardo (Berkeley: University of California Press, 1991), pp. 58–60, 78–79.

18. *Census of Europeans, 1904* (Salisbury: Government Printer, 1904).

19. The imbalance between white males and females is shown by the following table:

	1904	1911	1926	1936
males	9,000	15,500	19,000	29,800
females	3,600	8,000	17,300	25,700

Report Director of Census, 1936 (Salisbury: Government Printer, 1944), p. 17. Note that the publication of the census was delayed by the war.

The following table, which appears in Ibbo Mandaza's study of Coloured communities in southern Africa, further illustrates that imbalance:

	Males/Females
1901	278/100
1904	246/100
1911	194/100
1921	130/100
1926	126/100
1931	120/100
1936	116/100

Ibbo Mandaza, "White Settler Ideology, African Nationalism and the 'Coloured' Question in Southern Africa: Southern Rhodesia/Zimbabwe, Northern Rhodesia/Zambia, and Nyasaland/Malawi, 1900–1976" (Ph.D. diss., University of York, 1979), p. 274. See also Kirkwood, "Settler Wives in Southern Rhodesia," pp. 143–164.

20. The scheme, which was intended to provide domestic servants, was funded by the secretary of state and by the Rhodesian government and allowed for free passage and rail fares. During the 1930s it was expanded somewhat and in 1937 twenty-three women were granted free passage. See *Report of the Official Secretary: Office of the High Commissioner for Southern Rhodesia for the Year 1928* (Salisbury: Government Printer, 1929), p. 10.

21. See George Orwell, *Burmese Days* (London: Penguin Books, 1934).

22. In his study of nineteenth-century India, Ballhatchet claims that the appearance of significant numbers of British women in the middle of that century widened the perceived gulf between the British and Indians, which hastened the disappearance of the Indian mistress and thereby damaged race relations. It is a tired argument which has never been supported by historical evidence and tells us much more about the author than it does about his subject. See Kenneth Ballhatchet, *Race, Sex, and Class under the Raj: Imperial Attitudes and Policies and their Critics, 1793–1905* (New Delhi: Vikas Publishing Company, 1979).

23. Octave Mannoni, *Prospero and Caliban: The Psychology of Colonization* (New York: Frederick A. Praeger, 1964), p. 115.

24. Ibid., pp. 116–117.

25. Claudia Knapman, *White Women in Fiji 1835–1930: The Ruin of Empire?* (Sydney: Allen & Unwin, 1986), p. 14.

26. Philip Mason, *The Birth of a Dilemma: The Conquest and Settlement of Rhodesia* (London: Oxford University Press, 1958), p. 240.

27. Margaret Strobel, *European Women and the Second British Empire* (Bloomington: Indiana University Press, 1991), p. 7.

28. In addition to Knapman's study of Fiji, see Helen Callaway, *Gender, Culture, and Empire*. For a study of colonial wives in Uganda see Beverley Gartrell, "Colonial Wives: Villains or Victims?" in *The Incorporated Wife*, ed. Hilary Callan and Shirley Ardener (London: Croom Helm, 1984), pp. 165–185. See also the two essays by Deborah Kirkwood on colonial Zimbabwe in the same collection.

29. Ronald Hyam, *Empire and Sexuality: The British Experience* (Manchester: Manchester University Press, 1990), p. 148. See also Ronald Hyam, "Empire and Sexual Opportunity," *Journal of Imperial and Commonwealth History* 14 (January 1986): 34–89.

30. Bristow claims that Jewish militants fighting white slavery initiated the Suppression Act of 1902 in the Cape and the Immorality Act of 1903 in the Transvaal. However, he cites no documentation to support those claims. See Edward J. Bristow, *Prostitution and Prejudice: The Jewish Fights against White Slavery, 1870–1939* (Oxford: Clarendon Press, 1982), p. 243.

31. For an account of life in early Salisbury see Tanser, *A Sequence of Time.*

32. Records show that the brothels were kept under observation to ensure that window blinds were covered at night and that no bedroom was exposed. See Report by Det. Sgt. Delahay, CID, to Office of the Commissioner, December 17, 1911, A/3/28/58-60.

33. H. H. Brown to Mr. Birchenough, BSAC, London, February 4, 1910, A/3/28/58-60.

34. Salisbury Town Council to the Office of the Administrator, March 25, 1910, A/3/28/58-60.

35. See Office of the Administrator to the Salisbury Town Council, March 9, 1909, A/3/28/58-60.

36. Salisbury Town Council to the High Commissioner, April 30, 1909, A/3/28/58-60.

37. Office of the Administrator to Rev. Brown, April 20, 1909, A/3/28/58-60.

38. Southern Rhodesian Constabulary, Salisbury, to Attorney General Tredgold, July 30, 1909, A3/28/60, vol. 2.

39. "The Social Evil," *Rhodesian Herald,* April 21, 1909.

40. "Pioneer Street," *Rhodesian Herald,* April 29, 1909.

41. Those present included the high commissioner, the resident commissioner, town councillors, clergy, and the council's solicitors.

42. Notes of an interview between a deputation and Earl Selbourne, high commissioner at Cecil House, Salisbury, November 10, 1909, A/3/28/58-60, p. 2.

43. Ibid., p. 3.

44. Ibid., pp. 9–12.

45. H. H. Brown to Mr. Birchenough, London, February 4, 1910, A/3/28/58-60.

46. D. Brodie, BSAC, to the Administrator, May 28, 1910, A/3/28/58-60.

47. *Census of Europeans, 1907* (Salisbury: Government Printer, 1908).

48. See Yoshikuni, "Black Migrants in a White City," pp. 26–31.

49. Bristow, *Prostitution and Prejudice,* p. 193.

50. Ibid.

51. Ibid.

52. The Criminal Law Amendment Ordinance, No. 13 of 1900, in *Minutes of the Proceedings of the Legislative Council and Ordinances, Second Session 1900* (Salisbury: Government Printer, 1900).

53. See Attorney General Tredgold, Memo: White Slave Traffic, March 28, 1905, Office of the Administrator, A3/21/15.

54. According to the *Rhodesian Herald* advertisements had appeared in Rhodesian newspapers offering high wages for barmaids to work in the town of Macequece. See "Barmaids Decoyed: White Slave Traffic," *Rhodesian Herald,* August 13, 1912.

55. See Detective Sergeant Rowell, BSAC Police, Umtali, to the Attorney General's Office, September 16, 1912, Office of the Administrator, A3/21/15.

56. Criminal Law Further Amendment Ordinance, No. 4 of 1916.

57. By definition brothels were premises on which a woman worked for a man in selling sexual services. See Legislative Council Debates, May 2, 1916, p. 34. Reprinted from *Rhodesian Herald*.

58. After more than a decade of debate, in 1924 the CID finally carried out an investigation and found that "white slave traffic does not exist in Rhodesia: the immigration laws restrict the entry of prostitutes and without exception every foreign women entering this Colony is the wife, fiance [*sic*] or child of a resident or a *bona fide* entrant for purposes of business." Memo from the Colonial Secretary to the Premier, July 7, 1924, Department of the Administrator, A3/28/84.

59. Mr. Cleveland moved "that it is the opinion of this Council that legislation should be enacted prohibiting the employment of women as barmaids in places licensed to sell intoxicating drink, and that the government be requested to bring in such legislation at an early date." *Legislative Council Debates 1916–1917,* May 12, 1916 (Salisbury: Government Printer, 1917), p. 410.

60. "The Church Synod: The Employment of Barmaids," *Rhodesian Herald,* October 17, 1915.

61. *Legislative Council Debates,* May 12, 1916, p. 414.

62. Mr. McChlery, *Legislative Council Debates,* May 12, 1916, p. 416.

63. The term concubinage covered an assortment of domestic arrangements which served colonial interests in a number of ways. For a discussion of concubinage in terms of race, class, and gender, see Ann Stoler, "Carnal Knowledge and Imperial Power," pp. 58–60, 78–79. See also Ann Stoler, "Making Empire Respectable: The Politics of Race and Sexuality in Twentieth-Century Colonial Cultures," in *Racial Supremacy in Social Darwinist Theory and Colonial Practice,* ed. J. Breman (Amsterdam: V. U. University Press, 1990).

64. Mannoni, *Prospero and Caliban,* p. 113.

65. The Colonial Office was established in 1842. Its primary role was to exercise administrative responsibly for Britain's "white colonies," such as Australia and Canada. The Office later took responsibility for the large African empire which Britain acquired after 1884.

66. The circular was distributed throughout the British Empire but was not sent directly to South Africa or Rhodesia. The memorandum is reproduced in Ronald Hyam's "Concubinage and the Colonial Service: The Crewe Circular (1909)," *Journal of Imperial and Commonwealth History* 14 (1986): 170–186.

67. Gladstone to the Resident Commissioner, June 14, 1910, Cohabitation with Native Girls, RC 3/7/18.

68. A change to the law was hardly necessary, as the first recorded Christian or civil marriage between a white man and an African woman took place in 1920, an event which was viewed with disquiet by the native affairs department. See "The Marriage of Arthur Robinson," Correspondence: Native Department, N3/27/5. See also Chapter 10, note 13.

69. See *Report of the Native Affairs Committee of Inquiry, 1910–1911* (Salisbury: Government Printer, 1911). In *Miscellaneous Reports, 1909–1916* (Salisbury, Government Printer, 1916), p. 7.

70. Attorney General Tredgold, Memo: Native Affairs Committee Report, October 25, 1912, Correspondence, Office of the Administrator, A3/3/18.

71. Letter from the Women's Christian Temperance Union and the Women's Franchise Society of Southern Rhodesia to the Administrator and the Members of the Legislative Council, April 27, 1916, Division of the Attorney General: Immorality Policy Reports 1916–1944, SSS1227/3.

72. See J. C. Blundell, Superintendent of the CID, BSA Police, to the Staff Officer, BSA Police, July 29, 1925, ibid.

73. See *Legislative Council Debates,* May 16, 1921.

74. See transcript from *Legislative Council Debates,* May 9, 1921. Subject of debate: "Intercourse between White Men and Native Women." Office of the Native Department, A/18/34–35, pp. 66ff.

75. Intercourse between White Men and Native Women, *Legislative Council Debates,* May 10, 1921, p. 90.

76. Ibid., pp. 91–92.

77. She moved "that the government be asked to appoint a Commission to inquire into the question of illicit intercourse between black and white, and to suggest the best methods by which to meet the dangers which arise out of that intercourse." Ibid., p. 94.

78. Ibid., p. 102.

79. The term dual mandate is associated with Lord Lugard, the greatest of Britain's colonial administrators. Lugard believed that Britain's imperial role was to benefit Britain herself and also to benefit the colonial people over whom she exercised dominion.

80. Administrator to the London Office, Memo: White Men and Native Women, June 6, 1921, A3/18/35.

81. Chief Native Commissioner of Salisbury, Memo: Miscegenation, June 23, 1921, A3/18/35.

82. Native Commissioner of M'toko, Memo: Miscegenation, June 24, 1921, A3/18/35.

83. "Miscegenation," Minute from Secretary to the Department of the Administrator Drummond Chaplin to the Secretaries for Mines and Works, Treasury, and the Attorney General, August 11, 1921, A3/18/35.

84. See Chapter 10, "Coloureds."

85. Secretary of the Rhodesian Women's League to "The Public of Rhodesia," August 1, 1924, Division of the Attorney General: Immorality Policy Reports 1916–1944, SSS1227/3.

86. J. C. Blundell, Superintendent of the CID, BSA Police to the Staff Officer, BSA Police, July 29, 1925, ibid.

87. "The Menace of Miscegenation," circular distributed by the Gwelo branch of the Rhodesian Women's League (1925), undated and unsigned, ibid.

88. Greta Bloomhill for the Rhodesian Women's League to the Attorney General, Major Hudson, July 9, 1925, ibid.

89. "A Rhodesian Woman" [Mrs. Greta Bloomhill], "Shall We Fail Our Women?" *The Rhodesian,* April 12, 1925.

90. Despite the resolutions passed on this issue some white women were opposed to amendments to the legislation. For example, Mrs. Fripp of the Matabele Women's Institute suggested that imposing penalties on white men would only make it less likely that they would provide for the offspring of such unions. For

most women, however, that question was secondary to the need to combat a cause of Black Peril. See "Miscegenation Condemned," *Bulawayo Chronicle,* April 18, 1931.

91. Mr. A. R. Thompson, Manager Wankie Colliery Limited, to the Honorary Secretary, Rhodesian Women's League, August 5, 1924, Immorality Policy Reports 1916–1944, SSS1227/3.

92. Ibid.

93. The Immorality Act of 1927 outlawed sex between whites and blacks; the Prohibition of Mixed Marriages Act of 1949 outlawed marriage between whites and blacks; and in 1950 and 1957 additional immorality acts prohibited sex between whites and all non-white groups. The laws persisted until 1985. See "To Prohibit Illicit Carnal Intercourse between Europeans and Natives and Other Acts in Relation Thereto." The Immorality Act, No. 5 of 1927, Union of South Africa.

94. See General Smuts to Mr. Huggins, January 30, 1934, Department of the Prime Minister: Miscegenation File. During 1929 there were 319 prosecutions and 212 convictions under the Immorality Act. See also Secretary for Justice, Pretoria, to the Secretary of the Department of Law, Salisbury, May 6, 1930, S482/802/39.

95. Resolution taken at the 1930 Congress, Bulawayo, Historical Manuscripts, Federation of Women's Institutes of Southern Rhodesia, Annual Meetings or Congresses, Minute Book, W05/4/2.

96. See, for example, the Honorary Secretary [Mrs. Fripp] of the Federation of Women's Institutes to the Premier, May 17, 1930, Department of the Prime Minister, S482/802/39. At the 1931 congress held at Gwelo the FWI resolved to petition the government to prohibit marriage between blacks and whites and to introduce legislation rendering relations between European men and African women illegal. The Institutes, however, opposed any legislation which would punish the offender.

97. See Minute from the Secretary to the Premier, April 30, 1930, Department of the Prime Minister, S482/802/39.

98. See "Racial Purity in Southern Rhodesia," *Bulawayo Chronicle,* May 8, 1930.

99. See draft of a bill "To Prohibit Cohabitation Between European Males and Native Females, 1931," Division of the Attorney General: Immorality Policy Reports 1916–1944, SSS1227/3.

100. Chief Native Commissioner to the Secretary of the Premier, May 3, 1930, Department of the Prime Minister, S482/802/39.

101. He wrote to the native commissioner asking him to devise a scheme making white men responsible for the support of mixed-race children. Private Secretary to the Premier to the Chief Native Commissioner, July 1, 1930, Department of the Prime Minister: Miscegenation File, S482/802/39.

102. Address to Delegates, July 10, 1930, Bulawayo, Historical Manuscripts: Federation of Women's Institutes of Southern Rhodesia, Annual Meetings or Congresses, Minute Book, W05/4/2, p. 4.

103. See Minutes: Executive Meeting, November 4, 1930, Federation of Women's Institutes of Southern Rhodesia, Minute Book of Executive Meetings, 1929–1933, WO5/4/4 p. 13, and Mrs. C. E. Fripp, "Miscegenation, or God's Step-Children," read at Gwelo on July 7, 1931 to a private session of the Congress. Federation of Women's Institutes, WO5/1/1/3, p. 8. Her request to have the first

document circulated to all Institute branches was denied; two members objected that it could lead to charges that the Institute was salacious. However, she was allowed to circulate a copy of her personal views on the subject.

104. According to Mrs. Fripp, the South African legislation was introduced following a drought in the Transvaal that had driven many farmers to abandon their wives and children for the gold fields. Consequently many destitute white women sold themselves to wealthy blacks for food. To end the scandal the House passed the legislation in a single secret sitting. Mrs. C. E. Fripp, "Miscegenation," paper read at Gwelo meeting of FWI, November 1930, Confidential, Federation of Women's Institutes, WO5/1/1/3, p. 11.

105. Ibid., p. 10.

106. Ibid., p. 2.

107. Fripp, "Miscegenation, or God's Step-Children," p. 8.

108. Ibid.

109. Ibid., p. 23.

110. Memo: Miscegenation from Moffat, February 12, 1931, Department of the Prime Minister: S482/802/39.

111. Attorney General Hudson to the Premier, November 21, 1930, ibid.

112. Private Secretary to the Prime Minister to the Minister for Internal Affairs, January 29, 1934, ibid.

113. Memo on Miscegenation by Mrs. W. Benjies presented to the Executive Committee, July 1929, Federation of Women's Institutes, Minute Book, Executive Meetings 1929–1933, WO5/4/4.

114. See Terence Ranger, *Are We Not Also Men? The Samkange Family and African Politics in Zimbabwe, 1920–1964* (London: James Currey, 1995); and Michael West, "African Middle-Class Formation in Colonial Zimbabwe, 1890–1965" (Ph.D. diss., Harvard University, 1990).

115. Stoler, "Carnal Knowledge and Imperial Power," p. 60.

7. DOMESTIC LABOR

1. See especially the pioneering work of Ian R. Phimister and Charles van Onselen, *Studies in the History of African Mine Labor in Colonial Zimbabwe* (Gwelo: Mambo Press, 1978).

2. Eric Hobsbawm, *The Age of Empire, 1875–1914* (New York: Vintage Books, 1989), p. 180.

3. Violet Firth, *The Psychology of the Servant Problem: A Study in Social Relationships* (London: The C. W. Daniel Co., 1925), p. 20.

4. See Terence Ranger, "The Invention of Tradition in Colonial Africa" in *The Invention of Tradition*, ed. E. J. Hobsbawm and T. O. Ranger (London: Cambridge University Press, 1983), p. 223.

5. "Your Servant and You: Advice to Housewives on the Treatment of African Domestic Servants," Pamphlet, Department of Public Relations, Southern Rhodesia, 1950.

6. See, for example, Karen Hansen, *Distant Companions: Servants and Employers in Zambia, 1900–1985* (Ithaca: Cornell University Press, 1988), p. 57.

7. Lawrence Vambe, *From Rhodesia to Zimbabwe* (London: Heinemann, 1976), p. 33.

8. Claudia Knapman attacks this idea in her study of colonial Fiji. See "The Mistress-Servant Relationship," in Claudia Knapman, *White Women in Fiji, 1835–1930: The Ruin of Empire?* (Syndey: Allen and Unwin, 1986), pp. 148–160.

9. See Margaret Strobel, *European Women and the Second British Empire* (Bloomington: Indiana University Press, 1991).

10. Despite its economic and social importance, little has been written about domestic labor in southern Africa. The most notable scholarly contributions are Duncan Clarke, *Domestic Workers in Zimbabwe* (Gwelo: Mambo Press, 1974); Jacklyn Cock, *Maids and Madams: Domestic Workers Under Apartheid* (London: Women's Press, 1989); and Charles Pape, "A Century of Servants: Domestic Workers in Zimbabwe 1890–1990" (Ph.D. diss., Deakin University, 1992). For fictional accounts of the complexities of relationships between masters and servants see Doris Lessing, *The Grass Is Singing* and "A Home for the Highland Cattle" in *Five: Short Novels* (London: M. Joseph, 1953).

11. *Southern Rhodesia: Preliminary Returns of a Census 7 May 1911* (Salisbury: Government Printer, 1911), presented to the Legislative Council, 1911. Those figures are probably unreliable. See Chapter 8 on black women, in particular the discussion of Teresa Barnes's work on the census.

12. In his study of the colonial period Richard Gray observed that the views domestic servants formed of whites had disastrous consequences for race relations. See Richard Gray, *The Two Nations: Aspects of the Development of Race Relations in the Rhodesias and Nyasaland* (London: Oxford University Press, 1960), p. 233.

13. The Masters and Servants Ordinance, No. 5 of 1901.

14. Ibid.

15. Dane Kennedy, *Islands of White: Settler Society and Culture in Kenya and Southern Rhodesia, 1890–1939* (Durham, N.C.: Duke University Press, 1987), p. 177.

16. Pape, "A Century of Servants," p. 61.

17. The following table from the 1936 census gives an indication of the importance of domestic labor.

Occupations: Native Males in Employment

Occupation	1911	1921	% increase
Agriculture	13,500	58,500	333%
Mining	41,800	44,000	5%
Domestic	12,100	14,200	17%

Report of the Director of Census, 1936 (Salisbury: Government Printer, 1944), p. 7.

18. Pape, "A Century of Servants," pp. 48–52.

19. "The Servant Problem," *Rhodesian Herald*, June 20, 1913.

20. "Your Servant and You."

21. Sheila Ndlovu, "A History of Domestic Workers in Bulawayo 1930 to 1950" (B.A. honors thesis, University of Zimbabwe, 1986), p. 10.

22. Gertrude Page, *Love in the Wilderness: The Story of Another African Farm* (London: Hurst and Blackett, Ltd., 1907), p. 107.

23. "The Hillside Tragedy," *Rhodesian Herald*, February 26, 1915.

24. See also "Alleged Assault with Intent," *Rhodesian Herald,* February 10, 1911.

25. Gertrude Page, *Jill's Rhodesian Philosophy or The Dam Farm* (London: Hurst & Blackett, 1910), p. 177.

26. One former Bulawayo servant who had worked for a white household in the 1940s admitted to putting his employer's cat into the oven. Ndlovu, "A History of Domestic Workers," p. 16.

27. By 1937 there were 90,000 miners. See Charles van Onselen, *Chibaro: African Mine Labor in Southern Rhodesia* (Johannesburg: Ravan Press, 1980), p. 38.

28. Ibid., p. 51.

29. Ibid., p. 62.

30. "Curfew," "Letter to the Editor: The Black Peril," *Rhodesian Herald,* January 20, 1911.

31. "Justice," Letter to the Editor, *Rhodesian Herald,* January 27, 1911. See also "Onlooker," "Letter to the Editor: The Houseboy System," *Rhodesian Herald,* July 26, 1912.

32. "A Worker," "Letter to the Editor: Male Domestic Servants," *Rhodesian Herald,* February 10, 1911.

33. "Immorality Ordinance: Women's Meeting," *Rhodesian Herald,* May 12, 1916.

34. Black and White Peril in Southern Rhodesia, Special CID File, 1915 or 1916 S1227/2, p. 64.

35. Ibid., pp. 66–68.

36. Report of the Native Affairs Committee of Enquiry 1910–1911, *Miscellaneous Reports, Southern Rhodesia 1909–1916* (Salisbury: Government Printer, 1916), SRG 4, p. 2.

37. Ibid., p. 17.

38. Ibid., p. 39.

39. Herbert Taylor, Chief Native Commissioner, Matabeleland, "Proposals from the Native Affairs Commissioner as Regards Medical Supervision and Industrial Education in Native Areas," July 11, 1911, Superintendent of Natives Conferences: 1911, A3/3/29, p. 8.

40. The Natives Registration Ordinance, No. 5 of 1918, in *Legislative Council Debates* (Salisbury: Government Printer, 1918).

41. Detective Inspector Gwelo to Superintendent of the CID, March 10, 1925, Division of the Attorney General: Immorality Policy Reports 1916–1944, SSS1227/3.

42. Greta Bloomhill for the Rhodesian Women's League, Bulawayo, to the Attorney General, Major Hudson, July 9, 1925, ibid.

43. Superintendent of the CID, Bulawayo, to Staff Officer of the BSA Police, Salisbury, July 29, 1925, ibid.

44. "A Member of the Rhodesian Women's League," Letter to the Editor, *Rhodesian Herald,* November 14, 1929.

45. Report of the Standing Committee on Domestic Service, FWI, July 1930, Federation of Women's Institutes, WO5/10/1, p. 4.

46. Ibid., p. 16.

47. Ibid., p. 69.

48. Ibid., p. 65.

49. Ibid., p. 64.

50. Ibid., p. 36.

51. Ibid., p. 56.

52. Ibid., pp. 19–20.

53. Ibid., pp. 23–24.

54. Ibid., p. 24.

55. Ibid., p. 19.

56. Anna Clark, *Women's Silence, Men's Violence: Sexual Assault in England, 1770–1845* (London: Pandora, 1987), pp. 40–42.

57. Rev. Sketchley, August 29, 1932, Transcripts, Evidence given at Bulawayo before the Committee of Inquiry into the Employment of Native Female Native Domestic Labour, Commissions of Inquiry and Reports, S94.

58. Rev. Neville Jones, Hope Fountain Mission, August 29, 1932, ibid., p. 56.

59. Sister Lois, St. Monica's Mission, Umtali, August 17, 1932, Transcripts, Evidence Given at Umtali before the Female Native Domestic Labour Committee, S94, p. 41.

60. Rev. Mussell, Epworth Mission, September 16, 1932, Transcripts, Evidence given at Salisbury before the Female Native Domestic Labour Committee, S1561/48, p. 160.

61. Bishop Paget and Archdeacon Christalowe, September 16, 1932, ibid., p. 157.

62. The first was tendered in her capacity as an officeholder with the FWI, the second was given as a private citizen. The distinction between her written and oral testimonies suggests that Mrs. Fripp thoroughly disagreed with the cautious role the FWI chose to play at the inquiry.

63. Mrs. Fripp, Federation of Women's Institutes, oral evidence given at Bulawayo, August 30, 1932, Transcripts, Evidence given at Bulawayo before the Female Native Domestic Labour Committee, S94, p. 92.

64. Mrs. Fripp, written evidence given at Bulawayo, August 30, 1932, ibid., p. 93.

65. Mrs. Stewart, August 17, 1932, Transcripts, Evidence given at Umtali before the Female Native Domestic Labour Committee, S94, p. 44.

66. Mrs. Russell, August 30, 1932, Transcripts, Evidence given at Bulawayo before the Female Native Domestic Labour Committee, S94, p. 80.

67. Mr. Stead, Assistant Native Commissioner, August 30, 1932, ibid., p. 84.

68. Mr. Lanning, the Superintendent of Natives, Bulawayo, August 31, 1932, ibid., p. 98.

69. Mr. C. Bullock, September 15, 1932, Transcripts, Evidence given at Salisbury before the Female Native Domestic Labour Committee, S1561/48, p. 142.

70. For an example from a later era of the unequal nature of such relations, see Peter Godwin, *Mukiwa: A White Boy in Africa* (London: Macmillan, 1996).

71. Final Report of the Committee of Inquiry into the Employment of Native Female Domestic Labour, October 27, 1932, S95.

72. Ibid., p. 12.

73. Ibid., p. 16.

74. Secretary of the Female Domestic Labour Committee to the Staff Officer,

Commissioner of Police, December 22, 1931, Evidence given at Salisbury before the Female Native Domestic Labour Committee, S1561/48.

75. Minute from Prime Minister Moffat on the Final Report of the Committee of Inquiry into the Employment of Native Female Domestic Labour, November 17, 1932, ibid.

76. The number of females in domestic service increased in Bulawayo from 62 in 1930 to 1,200 in 1948. They remained a small minority. See Ndlovu, "A History of Domestic Workers," p. 22. See especially Appendix 1. In 1946 almost one-third of Africans who worked in Bulawayo and Salisbury were domestic servants, of whom 92 percent were male. Gray, *The Two Nations,* p. 230. In his study of domestic service in colonial Zimbabwe, Pape points out that by 1990, when male servants were rare in Britain and South Africa, they still predominated in Zimbabwe. See Pape, "A Century of Servants," p. 13.

77. For a discussion of the complex relationship between urban wage labor and rural subsistence see Teresa Barnes, "'We Women Worked So Hard': Gender, Labor, and Social Reproduction in Colonial Harare, Zimbabwe, 1930–1956 (Ph.D. diss., University of Zimbabwe, 1993); and Elizabeth Schmidt, "Ideology, Economics, and the Role of Shona Women in Southern Rhodesia, 1850–1939" (Ph.D. diss., University of Wisconsin-Madison, 1987). Schmidt's dissertation has been published as *Peasants, Traders, and Wives* (London: James Currey, 1992).

8. BLACK WOMEN

1. See Diana Jeater, *Marriage, Perversion, and Power: The Construction of Moral Discourse in Southern Rhodesia, 1894–1930* (Oxford: Clarendon Press, 1933); Teresa Barnes, "'We Women Worked So Hard': Gender, Labor, and Social Reproduction in Colonial Harare, Zimbabwe, 1930–1956" (Ph.D. diss., University of Zimbabwe, 1993); and Elizabeth Schmidt, "Ideology, Economics, and the Role of Shona Women in Southern Rhodesia, 1850–1939" (Ph.D. diss., University of Wisconsin-Madison, 1987).

2. In her history of Shona women Elizabeth Schmidt examines the various strategies women used in their dealings with missionaries, administrators, and male elders to retain control of their own labor, sexuality, and social mobility. See "European Views of African Women" in Schmidt, "Ideology, Economics, and the Role of Shona Women," pp. 263–270.

3. For a discussion of the law, morality, and African marriage see "Marriage and Morality," in Martin Chanock, *Law, Custom and Social Order: The Colonial Experience in Malawi and Zambia* (Cambridge: Cambridge University Press, 1985).

4. See Teresa Barnes, "The Fight for Control of African Women's Mobility in Colonial Zimbabwe, 1900–1939," *Signs* (Spring 1992): 586–608.

5. For example, the Native Pass Further Amendment Ordinance of 1906 required that males above the age of fourteen who were seeking work or traveling carry a certificate of registration.

6. On that question see Barnes, "'We Women Worked So Hard,'" pp. 72–78.

7. Schmidt, "Ideology, Economics, and the Role of Shona Women," pp. 157–158.

8. Barnes, "'We Women Worked So Hard,'" p. 133.

9. See Chapter 4, "Responses by African Men and the Colonial State to Women's Urban Initiatives" in Barnes, "'We Women Worked So Hard,'" pp. 169–273.

10. Similarly, in Malawi the marriage and divorce ordinances of 1902 and 1905 made female consent necessary for a marriage. See Chanock, *Law, Custom and Social Order,* p. 186.

11. See Elizabeth Schmidt, "Patriarchy, Capitalism and the Colonial State in Zimbabwe," *Signs* 16 (Summer 1991): 732–756.

12. Elizabeth Schmidt provides an excellent account of the complex interaction between urban wage labor and rural subsistence cultivation. See Schmidt, "Ideology, Economics, and the Role of Shona Women." See also Eira Punt, "The Development of African Agriculture in Southern Rhodesia with Particular Reference to the Inter-War Years" (M.A. thesis, University of Natal, 1979).

13. Under the colonial administration customary law was reserved for civil cases involving only Africans. Roman-Dutch law was used in criminal cases where a plaintiff or defendant was a European or where customary law was thought "repugnant to natural justice or morality." See Claire Palley, *The Constitutional History and Law of Southern Rhodesia, 1888–1965* (Oxford: Clarendon Press, 1966), p. 494.

14. See Minutes of Proceedings of Superintendents of Natives, October 1909, Department of the Administrator, A3/18/39/14.

15. Native Commissioner Selukwe to the Superintendent of Natives, Gwelo, March 2, 1910, Department of the Administrator, A3/18/39/14.

16. Barnes, "The Fight for Control," p. 591.

17. The committee conducted a wide-ranging inquiry which included reference to social conditions, land tenure, sexual conduct, native marriage, and labor. See Report of the Native Affairs Committee of Enquiry, 1910–1911, presented to the Legislative Council. The committee was chaired by John Graham. Southern Rhodesia Miscellaneous Reports 1909–1916, SRG 4.

18. Ibid., p. 2.

19. Ibid., p. 3.

20. Both African males and white administrators believed in a past sexual purity in traditional society and viewed rising divorce rates as proof of social and moral decay. See Chanock, *Law, Custom and Social Order,* p. 33.

21. Report of the Native Affairs Committee of Enquiry, p. 2.

22. See Barnes, "'We Women Worked So Hard,'" pp. 169–273. For her critique of the work of Schmidt, see pp. 25–30.

23. According to Jeater, there was much lobbying by patriarchs and elders to criminalize adultery, which they saw as a means to re-assert their authority over women and subordinate men. The Natives Adultery Punishment Ordinance of 1916, for example, was directed against mobile women and was the outcome of agitation by patriarchs. Jeater, *Marriage, Perversion, and Power,* pp. 145, 263.

24. Proposed Legislation Making Adultery among Natives a Criminal Offence. J. Taylor, Chief Native Commissioner's Office, Salisbury, to the Secretary of the Department of the Administrator, December 9, 1914, Division of the Attorney General: Immorality Policy Reports 1916–1944, SSS1227/3.

25. Natives Adultery Punishment Ordinance, No. 3 of 1916.

26. Transcripts, Legislative Council debates, May 3, 1916, Office of the Native Department, A/18/34–35, p. 84.

27. Ibid., p. 88.

28. Ibid., p. 93.

29. Ibid., p. 97.

30. Ibid., p. 102.

31. "Intercourse between White Men and Native Women," Transcripts, Legislative Council debates, May 9, 1921, Office of the Native Department, A/18/34–35, pp. 66ff.

32. Natives Adultery Punishment Ordinance, No. 3 of 1916 made any native who committed adultery with a married native woman or who induced such a woman to leave her husband for the purposes of sexual intercourse liable for a fine not exceeding 100 pounds or prison with hard labor for not more than 1 year. White males were exempt from any penalty. In *Legislative Council Debates* (Salisbury: Government Printer, 1916).

33. Criminal Law Further Amendment Ordinance, No. 4 of 1916, ibid.

34. Jeater, *Marriage, Perversion, and Power*, p. 228.

35. In Northern Rhodesia during the 1920s the state made no attempt to restrict the free movement of women. That changed, however, in 1936, when a bill was enacted for the repatriation of women from towns. The bill was supported by patriarchs, who wished to retain control over women, and colonial authorities, who feared the effects of immorality. See Karen Hansen, *Distant Companions: Servants and Employers in Zambia, 1900–1985* (Ithaca: Cornell University Press, 1989), pp. 115, 117–119.

36. Jeater, *Marriage, Perversion, and Power*, p. 246.

37. For an account of missionaries and African girls see Schmidt, "Ideology, Economics, and the Role of Shona Women," pp. 307–341.

38. Attorney General Tredgold to the Secretary of the Department of the Administrator, January 10, 1912, Department of the Administrator, A3/18/39/14.

39. Attorney General Tredgold to the Clerk of Councils, April 27, 1912, ibid.

40. Chief Native Commissioner to Native Commissioner, Rusapi, October 13, 1930, Office of the Chief Native Commissioner: The Status of Native Women, S235/376.

41. Superintendent of Driefontein Mission, Umvuma, to the Superintendent of Natives, Fort Victoria, March 25, 1931, ibid., 24/32–34.

42. Minutes: Native Affairs Advisory Committee, Salisbury, August 11, 1931, ibid., pp. 3–23.

43. Ibid., pp. 31–33.

44. Ibid., pp. 28–50.

45. Ibid., p. 90.

46. Mrs. W. Anderson, London Mission, Lonely Mine, to the Prime Minister, July 6, 1928, Department of the Prime Minister: Miscegenation File 1928–1941, S482/802/39.

47. Native Commissioner, Inyati, to the Superintendent of Natives, Matabeleland, July 25, 1928, ibid. See also Chief Native Commissioner to the Rev. Anderson, August 10, 1928, in the same file.

48. Native Commissioner, Mtoko, to the Chief Native Commissioner, September 10, 1930, Native Department: Immorality at Native Dances, S235/392.

49. Native Commissioner, Mrewa, to the Chief Native Commissioner, Salisbury, September 8, 1930, ibid.

50. Native Commissioner, Inyanga, to the Superintendent of Natives, September 26, 1930, ibid.

51. Native Commissioner, Belingwe, to the Superintendent of Natives, September 18, 1930, ibid.

52. Native Commissioner, Bindura, to the Superintendent of Natives, September 20, 1930, ibid.

53. Chief Native Commissioner Mr. Hudson to the Premier, December 6, 1930, ibid.

54. See Luise White, *The Comforts of Home: Prostitution in Colonial Nairobi* (Chicago: Chicago University Press, 1990).

55. Barnes, "'We Women Worked So Hard,'" p. 171.

56. Jeater, *Marriage, Perversion, and Power,* pp. 178ff.

57. Mr. S. Cooper to the Medical Director, November 29, 1917, Public Health Department: Syphilis, S1173/214.

58. Dr. Fleming to the Native Commissioner, Salisbury, May 25, 1929, Public Health Department: Venereal Disease 1928–1933, S1173/221.

59. The government was to pay for the erection and upkeep of such units while the councils were to be responsible for the detection and examination of cases. See Dr. Fleming to Secretary, Department of the Administrator, June 17, 1919, Public Health Department: Syphilis, S1173/213.

60. Native Commissioner's Office, Shamva, to Native Commissioner, Mazoe, March 3, 1921, Department of Native Affairs, N/22/6.

61. *Annual Report, Public Health Department, for the Year 1927* (Salisbury: Government Printer, 1928), p. 21.

62. Chief Native Commissioner, Salisbury, to the Superintendent of Natives, March 17, 1821, Native Department, N/22/6.

63. *Annual Report, Public Health Department, for the Year 1929* (Salisbury: Government Printer, 1930), pp. 20–21.

64. Transcript of Meeting held at Municipal Offices, Bulawayo, October 6, 1928, Public Health Department, S1173/220, p. 40.

65. Medical Director R. A. Askins to Dr. M. Kane, Rusapi, December 24, 1930, Public Health Department: Venereal Disease 1928–1933, S1173/222.

66. Dr. Kane, Rusapi, to the Medical Director, December 31, 1930, ibid.

67. Dr. Fleming to the Department of the Colonial Secretary, May 6, 1929, S246/531, p. 2.

68. Miss Waters, Memo: Conditions in Salisbury Native Location, May 14, 1929, Department of Native Education, S246/532.

69. Ibid., p. 1.

70. Ibid., p. 2.

71. Evidence from Dr. Hurworth, Municipal Health Officer Salisbury Location, before the Native Affairs Commission 1930, December 5, 1930, Native Department: Inquiry into the Salisbury Native Location, S85, p. 48.

72. Evidence from Mr. Clemo, Assistant Superintendent CID Salisbury, December 9, 1930, ibid., p. 58.

73. Evidence from Rusiti and Munoma Manshona, residents of the Salisbury location, December 9, 1930, ibid., p. 61.

74. Evidence from Mr. John Muketsi, Southern Rhodesian Natives Association, December 6, 1930, ibid., p. 23.

75. Evidence from Major Blundell, Bulawayo CID, Committee of Inquiry into Conditions at the Bulawayo Native Location, 1930, Commission on Committees of Enquiry, ZAN1/1/1, p. 81.

76. Evidence from Mayor H. Peard, ibid., pp. 47–48.

77. Minutes: Mr. Bazeley, Native Affairs Advisory Committee, Salisbury, August 11, 1931, S235/486, pp. 93–94.

78. Barnes, "'We Women Worked So Hard,'" p. 319.

79. Minutes: Native Affairs Advisory Committee, August 11, 1931, p. 95.

80. Ibid., p. 101.

81. The pieces of legislation cited were the Vagrancy Act 23/1879–27/1889; Ordinance No. 16 of 1901; Ordinance No. 4 of 1906; Act No. 14 of 1927; Immorality Laws No. 13 of 1900 and No. 4 of 1916; and Ordinance No. 13 of 1900. See Circular Letter, "Immorality of Native Girls," Office of the Commissioner of the BSAP, Salisbury, to all Superintendents, August 13, 1931, Division of the Attorney General: Immorality: Native Girls, S1227/1, file 913/1931.

82. Minutes: Native Affairs Advisory Committee, August 11, 1931, p. 91.

83. The authority used was Section 9 of Ordinance No. 16 of 1901.

84. Chief Native Commissioner's Office to the Acting Commissioner BSA Police, December 2, 1931, Division of the Attorney General: Immorality: Native Girls, S1227/1, file 913/1931.

85. Circular No. 14: Native Girls Visiting Towns, November 13, 1931, Chief Commissioner's Office to all Native Department Stations, ibid.

86. Salisbury CID to Superintendent CID, Salisbury, October 1, 1934, ibid.

87. The first quarterly return for 1934 showed that 38 women had been warned and 25 had been prosecuted. A further 250 to 300 females were identified as living by doubtful means. Superintendent CID, Salisbury, Memo, April 30, 1934, ibid., file 913/1931.

88. Chief Superintendent CID, Bulawayo, to the Staff Officer, BSAP Salisbury, May 6, 1935, ibid., file 913/1931. Under the terms of the Natives Adultery Punishment Ordinance of 1916, any native who committed adultery with a married native woman or who induced such a woman to leave her husband for the purposes of sexual intercourse was liable for a fine not exceeding 100 pounds or one year's imprisonment.

89. Mr. H. W. Laing to Premier Huggins, December 3, 1934, Department of the Prime Minister: Miscegenation File, S482/802/39.

90. Ibid. *Indunas* means "traditional authorities."

91. C. Bullock, Secretary of Native Affairs, to the Town Clerks of Salisbury, Bulawayo, Gatooma, Umtali, November 16, 1936, Office of the Prime Minister: Native Women in Locations, S482/535/39.

92. Ibid.

93. Diana Jeater's claim that the Natives Registration Act of 1936 effectively ended women's mobility is incorrect. Jeater confuses the ambit and intentions of the act with its application; until the end of the colonial period women did not have to carry passes and therefore enjoyed far greater mobility than did men. Jeater, *Marriage, Perversion, and Power,* pp. 259–260.

94. Barnes, "'We Women Worked So Hard,'" pp. 179ff, 187. For an account of the politics of women's mobility and its connection with the power of the state and of patriarchs, see Chapter 9, "The Closing Door: African Women and Euro-

pean Morality, 1916–1930," in Jeater, *Marriage, Perversion, and Power,* pp. 227–259.

95. Barnes claims that was so until the 1940s. "'We Women Worked So Hard,'" pp. 33, 187.

96. Schmidt, "Ideology, Economics, and the Role of Shona Women," p. 447.

97. Barnes, "'We Women Worked So Hard,'" p. 33.

98. Evidence by Selwyn Bazeley, Transcripts of Committee of Inquiry into the Employment of Native Female Domestic Labour, Bulawayo, 1932, S94, pp. 23–24.

99. Annual Report of the Assistant Native Commissioner, Goromonzi, for the Year ending 31/12/1936, S235/514.

100. At that time native department officers continued to apprehend young women who entered towns alone. They were fingerprinted and their records were sent to the CID. The native commissioner of Bulawayo, Mr. Huxtable, wanted police cooperation in dealing with loitering females and during a meeting with the department in October 1943 he warned that without mutual action there would be an increase in the number of such women who frequented the European residential areas. On the other hand, Huxtable feared that too drastic action would probably increase the incidence of Black Peril cases. See Memo: "Native Females Loafing in Town: Interview with Native Commissioner for Bulawayo, Mr. Huxtable," CID Bulawayo, October 9, 1943, Division of the Attorney General: Immorality: Native Girls, S1227/1, file 913/1931.

9. SYPHILIS

1. For a medical history of white settlement see Michael Gelfand, *Tropical Victory: An Account of the Influence of Medicine on the History of Southern Rhodesia, 1890–1923* (Cape Town: Juta Press, 1953); and *A Service to the Sick: A History of the Health Services for Africans in Southern Rhodesia, 1890 to 1953* (Salisbury: Mambo Press, 1967).

2. G. H. Tanser, *A Sequence of Time: The Story of Salisbury, Rhodesia, 1900 to 1914* (Salisbury: Pioneer Head, 1974), p. 78.

3. During the first decade of colonization few employers provided latrines for servants. Some latrines were built at street corners by the Sanitary Board, but they were inadequate and in 1895 the administrator passed the Townships Sanitary Regulations, No. 109, which required every employer in Salisbury to provide proper latrines. The ordinance, however, was not enforced and as the town grew so did the threat of disease. In 1902 it was estimated that the cost per household of building "native" latrines was between 7 and 15 pounds. See Tsuneo Yoshikuni, "Black Migrants in a White City: A Social History of African Harare, 1890–1925" (Ph.D. diss., University of Zimbabwe, 1989), pp. 44ff. See also G. H. Tanser, *A Sequence of Time,* p. 96.

4. Maynard W. Swanson, "The Sanitation Syndrome: Bubonic Plague and Urban Native Policy in the Cape Colony," *Journal of African History* 18 (1977): 388.

5. For a sociology of the disease in contemporary Europe see Claude Quetel, *History of Syphilis* (Cambridge: Polity Press, 1987).

6. Ibid., p. 7.

7. See Megan Vaughan, "Syphilis and Sexuality: The Limits of Colonial Medical Power," in *Curing Their Ills: Colonial Power and African Illness* (London: Polity Press, 1991), pp. 129–154.

8. For example, in the first decades of this century there was concern in Uganda that the decline in the population due to civil war, smallpox, trypanosomiasis (sleeping sickness), and sexually transmitted diseases would undermine the labor force. Partly for that reason syphilis was declared a dangerous disease under the Dangerous Diseases Ordinance of 1909. See Carol Summers, "Intimate Colonialism: The Imperial Production of Reproduction in Uganda, 1907–1925," *Signs* 16 (Summer 1991). See also Megan Vaughan, "Syphilis in Colonial East and Central Africa: The Social Construction of an Epidemic" in *Epidemics and Ideas: Essays on the Historical Perception of Pestilence,* ed. T. O. Ranger and Paul Slack (Cambridge: Cambridge University Press, 1995), pp. 269–302.

9. Elizabeth Van Heyningen, "Public Health and Society in Cape Town, 1880–1910" (Ph.D. diss., University of Cape Town, 1989), pp. 356–357.

10. Ibid., p. 363.

11. For a social history of the British contagious diseases acts see Judith Walkowitz, *Prostitution and Victorian Society: Women, Class, and the State* (Cambridge: Cambridge University Press, 1980).

12. See the Contagious Diseases Prevention Act, 1885. *Statutes of the Cape of Good Hope: Seventh Parliament, Session 1884–1888* (Cape Town: W. A. Richards & Sons, 1898).

13. Like the contagious diseases acts used in Britain during the 1860s, the Cape legislation was based upon two fallacies: that syphilis was spread principally by a class of prostitutes, and that physicians could identify and treat infected women.

14. Walkowitz, *Prostitution and Victorian Society,* p. 53.

15. Reports on Public Health: 3. On the Operation of the Contagious Diseases Act, 1885, in Appendix 1 to *The Votes and Proceedings of Parliament,* Vol 11, Session 1892 (Cape Town: W. A. Richards & Sons, 1892), pp. 30–31.

16. Claude Quetel, *History of Syphilis* (Cambridge: Polity Press, 1987), p. 255.

17. See, for example, Llewelyn Powys, "How It Happens," in *Ebony and Ivory* (London: Grant Richards Ltd., 1923).

18. Vaughan, "Syphilis in Colonial Africa," pp. 269–302.

19. Compare, for example, the annual medical reports for Kenya and Southern Rhodesia for the years ending 1922, 1925 and 1926.

20. See the individual files contained in Native Department: Venereal Disease among Natives June/July 1900, N1/2/4.

21. Medical Director Fleming to the Chief Secretary, Salisbury, March 22, 1907, Public Health, H2/3/8/1.

22. Transcript of Meeting held at Municipal Offices, Bulawayo, October 6, 1928, Public Health Department, S1173/220, p. 15.

23. Dr. Fleming, Medical Director, Memo: Spread of Venereal Disease among Natives in the Victoria District, September 7, 1907, Public Health, H2/3/8/1, p. 3.

24. For an account of mission medicine in British east and central Africa and its often uneasy relations with the state, see Megan Vaughan, "The Great Dispensary in the Sky: Missionary Medicine," in *Curing Their Ills,* pp. 55–76.

25. Fleming to the Secretary of the Department of the Administrator, November 30, 1909, Public Health: General 1909–1919, H2/10/1.

26. Fleming to the Secretary of the Department of the Administrator, December 15, 1909, ibid.

27. Medical Director Fleming, Estimates for 1912–1913, January 29, 1912, ibid., p. 3.

28. During the first two years of its operation treatment was provided free of charge to African patients. The average supply provided for district surgeons per month was "5,000 Mercury, Calk, and Dovers powder pills, 1 gram each; 1,000 Mercury and Calk pills 1/2 gram each; 7 lbs. of mercurial ointment; 5 lbs. of vaseline; 1 gall blackwash; 1 lb. Blue stone; 5 lb. Calomel and Starch Dusting Powder; 1 gross chip boxes (nested)." Dr. Eaton, Acting Medical Director, to Dr. J. Mitchell, Assistant Medical Officer, August 17, 1916, Public Health, H2/3/8/1.

29. S. Cooper ("Chambrecy") to the Medical Director, November 29, 1911, Public Health Department: Syphilis, S1173/214.

30. S. Cooper to the Medical Director November 29, 1917, ibid.

31. Legislative Council, May 30, 1923, Legislative Council Debates, Vol. 7 (Salisbury: Government Printer, 1923), p. 56.

32. Failure to comply could result in a fine or jail. See "Mines and Works Regulations: Government Notice No. 447 of 1914," Public Health, H2/3/8/2.

33. Secretary, Rhodesia Chamber of Mines to Secretary, Department of the Administrator, May 4, 1923, Public Health, H2/3/8/1. See also The Rhodesian Small Workers and Tributors Association to the Mining Commission at Gatooma, December 12, 1922, Public Health, H2/3/8/2.

34. Mines and Works Regulations: Government Notice No. 447 of 1914, Public Health, H2/3/8/2.

35. Legislative Council Debates, May 30, 1923 (Salisbury: Government Printer, 1923), p. 64.

36. The Medical Director to the Senior Government Medical Officer, Umtali, December 13, 1924, Public Health Department, S1173/212.

37. For example, in November 1925 Dr. A. M. MacKenzie, Senior Government Medical Officer, Gatooma, wrote to the medical director complaining about the cost of syphilis at the Cam and Motor Mine. A. M. MacKenzie, Senior Government Medical Officer, Gatooma, to the Medical Director, November 14, 1925, Public Health Department: Syphilis, S1173/212.

38. Report from the Inspector of Compounds, Bulawayo, September 1926, ibid.

39. T. J. Williams, Medical Officer Ndanga, to the Medical Director, September 22, 1924, ibid.

40. Memo of meeting between the Medical Director, the Native Commissioner, and Acting Chief Native Commissioner, held at the Office of the Medical Director, Salisbury, June 18, 1926, Public Health Department: Syphilis, S1173/213.

41. Chief Native Commissioner to the Secretary of the Premier, January 23, 1928, Public Health Department: Syphilis, S1173/214.

42. See, for example, Report from Dr. Alexander, Rezende Mines Ltd., December 15, 1927, ibid.

43. Rhodesian Herald, January 14, 1928.

44. G. Barratt, Medical Officer, Sinoia, to the Medical Director, Salisbury, May 30, 1928, S246/534.

45. J. S. Liptz, Government Medical Officer, Enkeldoorn, to Medical Director Salisbury, April 18, 1928, ibid.

46. P. Wallace, Filabusi, to the Medical Director, April 23, 1928, ibid.

47. A Northern Rhodesian physician, Dr. McGregor, claimed that in a mere six months he treated some 400 cases of yaws from the Zambesi Valley. When asked why they came to him many of the patients replied "there is no medicine at Wankie" (i.e., in Southern Rhodesia). See Dr. J. McGregor, Medical Officer, Choma, Northern Rhodesia, to the Principal Medical Officer, Livingstone, October 10, 1928; and Medical Director Fleming to the Secretary of the Department of the Colonial Secretary, July 5, 1929, Public Health Department: Yaws in the Zambesi Valley, S246/535.

48. For an account of labor conditions in mines see Ian Phimister and Charles van Onselen, *Studies in the History of African Mine Labor in Colonial Zimbabwe* (Gwelo: Mambo Press, 1978).

49. Minutes of the Conference of Superintendents of Natives, Salisbury, October 31, 1911 to November 3, 1911, Public Health: General 1909–1919, H2/10/1, p. 18.

50. Town Clerk, Salisbury, to the Department of the Administrator, May 11, 1917, Medical Inspections of Urban Natives 1917–1920, H 2/9/2.

51. Town Clerk, Memo from Salisbury Council Meeting to Secretary, Office of the Administrator, April 19, 1917, Public Health, H2/9/2.

52. Ibid.

53. Secretary, Office of the Administrator to the Medical Director, June 18, 1917, ibid.

54. For example, Ordinance No. 16 of 1902 provided for the registration of African servants and the issue of passes to urban areas. See Chief Native Commissioner's Office to the Secretary of the Administrator's Office, August 7, 1917, ibid.

55. J. Robertson, Secretary, Department of the Administrator to the Town Clerk, Salisbury, August 21, 1917, ibid.

56. Report from F. E. Appelyard, Medical Officer, Salisbury, to W. Jenkins, Town Clerk, September 2, 1917, ibid.

57. For further testimony on the extent of that risk see Town Clerk W. Jenkins to the Office of the Administrator, September 26, 1917, ibid.

58. CID, Bulawayo BSA Police to the Secretary of the Office of Administrator, December 12, 1917, ibid.

59. Memo from the Town Clerk, Salisbury, to the Secretary of the Office of Administrator, undated (1918?), ibid.

60. Draft for the Medical Examination of Native Servants (Urban) Ordinance 1918, ibid.

61. Medical Director Fleming to the Acting Commissioner, BSA Police, Salisbury, October 13, 1922, Public Health, H2/3/8/1. See also Fleming to the Assistant Magistrate, Que Que, April 26, 1923, Public Health, H2/3/8/1, in which he questioned the free treatment provided to Africans and demanded to know if all those so treated were paupers and therefore eligible.

62. Town Clerk, Salisbury, to the Medical Director, March 6, 1919, Public Health, H2/9/2.

63. For an account of the epidemic, see Chief Native Commissioner to the Secretary of the Department of the Administrator, November 11, 1918, Administrator Spanish Influenza, A3/12/30/1. See also Roben Mutwira, "Colonial Health Policy: A Case Study of Epidemic Diseases" (M.A. thesis, University of Zimbabwe, 1987).

64. In Kimberley the disease was so devastating that virtually all mines closed, while in Rhodesia the flu killed over 3,000 mine workers. See Charles van Onselen, *Chibaro: African Mine Labor in Southern Rhodesia* (Johannesburg: Ravan Press, 1980), p. 38.

65. It was department policy that European nurses should not treat patients suffering from venereal disease.

66. See Father Butler, Chimanza Mission, to the Medical Director, September 15, 1921, Public Health, H2/3/8/1. The total outlay of anti–venereal disease measures for 1929 was 4,700 pounds. *Report on the Public Health for 1932* (Salisbury: Government Printer, 1933), p. 12.

67. Ibid., p. 12.

68. Medical Director Fleming to the Acting Commissioner BSA Police, Salisbury, October 13, 1922, Public Health H2/3/8/1. The BSAN Police were the British and South Africa Native Police.

69. That rate was estimated at around 0.5 percent. The number of individuals who were identified as being infected with venereal disease were as follows: 14,369 for Salisbury, 37,482 for mine compounds, and 6,577 at Belingwe. See Annual Report, Public Health Department for the Year 1923, Public Health Department, S2419, p. 23.

70. See Public Health Act File, 1922–1924, S1173/357.

71. "The Health Act," *Bulawayo Chronicle*, May 24, 1924.

72. For example, article 27 states: "Where a cleansing station is provided within the district of a local authority or within a reasonable distance therefrom, any person within that district certified by the medical officer of health, school medical inspector or other medical practitioner or by any certified sanitary inspector to be dirty or verminous may on order of the medical officer of health be removed together with his clothing and bedding to such cleansing station and be cleansed within." The Public Health Act 1924, Public Health Act File, 1922–1924, S1173/357, p. 10.

73. See Public Health Act File, 1922–1924, S1173/357.

74. Public Health Department: Venereal Disease 1928–1933, S1173/221.

75. *Report on the Public Health for the Year 1925* (Salisbury: Government Printer, 1926), p. 19.

76. White residents at Gatooma complained that African patients confined to the temporary isolation camp on the town's outskirts would walk down the main street on their way to collect water. See Rossley, Acting Magistrate Gatooma, to the Medical Director, October 24, 1924, Public Health Department: Syphilis, S1173/213.

77. J. W. Lowill, Assistant Native Commissioner Shamva, to the Native Commissioner, Mazoe, January 10, 1933, Public Health Department: Venereal Disease 1928–1933, S1173/224.

78. Many patients were sent to clinics without the formal procedures being followed. See J. Edwards, Gatooma, to the Medical Director, July 8, 1930; and H.

Rochester, BSA Police, Hartley, to the Staff Officer, BSA Police, Salisbury, August 4, 1930, Public Health Department, S1173/222.

79. Transcript of meeting held at municipal offices, Bulawayo, October 6, 1928, Public Health Department, S1173/220, p. 4.

80. Ibid., p. 6.

81. The 1926 return for the Royal Navy for a population of 90,000 men was almost 7 percent, for the Army just over 4 percent. The Royal Air Force was the lowest at 1.7 percent. During 1926 the figure for the total population of New South Wales was 2.6 percent. Ibid., p. 8.

82. Ibid., p. 12.

83. Association of Chambers of Commerce of Rhodesia to the Colonial Secretary, April 22, 1929, S246/531. This was accompanied by a transcript of the proceedings of the chamber's congress.

84. Rhodesian Women's League, Salisbury, to the Colonial Secretary, April 27, 1929, S246/531. The Colonial Secretary was the parliamentarian in charge of colonial affairs. His was the highest office to which the Women's League could directly appeal.

85. For example, at the government medical officers' conferences held in 1929, there was some comment that existing facilities were inadequate and that the problem was serious. See Proceedings, Government Medical Officers' Conferences 1925–1929, Public Health Department, S1173/27–29.

86. The buildings would have cost over 6,000 pounds and the estimated annual running costs would have been almost 3,000 pounds. See Town Clerk, Salisbury Council to the Colonial Secretary, May 5, 1930, S246/531.

87. Medical Officer Fleming to the Department of the Colonial Secretary, May 13, 1930, S246/531.

88. Department of the Colonial Secretary to the Town Clerk of Salisbury, June 19, 1930, S246/531.

89. Senior Government Medical Officer to the Medical Director, December 23, 1927, S246/531.

90. Medical Director to the Secretary of the Department of the Colonial Secretary, February 20, 1928, S246/531.

91. Vaughan, "Syphilis in Colonial East and Central Africa," pp. 286–288.

92. Native Labor Committee Report and Transcripts, 1906, Commissions on Committees of Enquiry, ZAN1/1.

93. Report of the Native Affairs Committee of Enquiry, 1910–1911, Southern Rhodesia Miscellaneous Reports 1909–1916, SRG4, p. 3.

94. This figure is representative for all but purely anecdotal estimates made in the period between 1910 and 1930. See *Public Health Department Annual Report for 1927* (Salisbury:Government Printer, 1928), p. 21.

95. See Carol Summers, "Intimate Colonialism: The Imperial Production of Reproduction in Uganda, 1907–1925," *Signs* 16 (Summer 1991).

96. See annual medical reports for Kenya for the years ending 1922, 1925, and 1926 (Nairobi: Government Printer). These can be found in the Kenya National Archives or at the Public Records Office, Kew.

97. *Annual Medical Report for the Year Ending 31/12/1921, The Colony and Protectorate of Kenya* (Nairobi: Government Printer, 1922), pp. 22–23.

98. See annual medical reports for years ending 1921, 1922, 1923, and 1924.

99. The most famous Black Peril incident in Kenya was most probably invented for political advantage. In March 1907, Ewart Grogan, a leading figure in Kenya's settler community, publicly flogged three Kikuyu rickshaw drivers for having made sexual advances to his sister, Mrs. Dorothy Hunter, and her friend, Miss McDonnell. The flogging was carried out in front of Nairobi's Court House and in front of a crowd of several hundred witnesses. It took place immediately prior to the arrival of the new governor, Hayes Sadler, during a period when the establishment of a Legislative Council was imminent. The flogging was in calculated defiance of established authority. It is probable that Grogan invented the incident in order to gain political leverage. For the most reliable contemporary account see "Transcript: *Crown versus Grogan, Bowker, Burn, Low, Fichat, Gray,*" Town Magistrate, Nairobi, March 25, 1907, Mag. H. O. Dolbey. In *Correspondence relating to the Flogging of Natives by Certain Europeans at Nairobi, July 1907: Presented to both Houses of Parliament* (London: HM Stationery, 1907). See also Leda Farrant, *The Legendary Grogan* (London: Hamish Hamilton, 1981).

100. See Chapter 6 for a discussion of the work of Schmidt, Barnes, and Jeater.

101. Vaughan, "Syphilis in Colonial East and Central Africa," pp. 275–276.

102. Transcript of Meeting between Dr. Fleming and a Delegation from the Bulawayo Landowners and Farmers Association, Municipal Offices, Bulawayo, October 6, 1928, Public Health Department, S1173/220.

103. Dr. Kane, Rusapi, to the Medical Director, December 12, 1930, S1173/222.

10. COLOUREDS, POOR WHITES, AND BOUNDARIES

1. For a discussion of the problems of racial definitions in colonial settings, see Ann Stoler, *Race and the Education of Desire: Foucault's History of Sexuality and the Colonial Order of Things* (Durham: Duke University Press, 1995), 101–116.

2. Ibbo Mandaza, "White Settler Ideology, African Nationalism, and the 'Coloured' Question in Southern Africa: Southern Rhodesia/Zimbabwe, Northern Rhodesia/Zambia and Nyasaland/Malawi, 1900–1976" (Ph.D. diss., University of York, 1979), p. 37.

3. For a later survey of the life conditions of Coloureds, see Mrs. Jean M. Cobb, "General Survey of the Living and Working Conditions of the Coloured Community in the City of Salisbury Municipal Area." Prepared for the Social Services Commission of the Southern Rhodesian Social Hygiene Council, 1938. Prime Minister's Office: The Coloured Community, S246/534.

4. The definitions of a coloured person included "[a]ny person who is neither white nor an Asiatic nor a native," Liquor Act (Chapter 219) Section 2; "[a]ny person who is neither white nor a member of any of the aboriginal tribes of Africa or a person who has the blood of any such tribes or races and lives among or after the manner thereof," Old Age Pension Act (Chapter 287) Section 2; "[a]ny person other than an Asiatic or native who has the blood of an Asiatic or native," Firearm Restriction Act, No. 16 of 1944, Section 2; "[a]ll persons of mixed origin including Hottentot, Cape Malay and Cape Coloured," [Southern Rhodesian Census]. Quoted in *Commission of Inquiry Regarding the Social Welfare of the Coloured Community of Southern Rhodesia.* Report One, Volume Two: *Annexures 1946.*

In *Miscellaneous Reports 1946* (Salisbury:Government Printer, 1946). The report noted that although most definitions included Eurasians as Coloured such a lack of precision was inevitable and of no great significance. See ibid., pp. 9–10.

5. *Southern Rhodesia: Preliminary Returns of a Census, 7 May 1911* (Salisbury: Government Printer, 1911), p. 5.

6. *Report Director of Census 1936 Southern Rhodesia* (Salisbury: Government Printer, 1943), p. 9. Note that because of staff shortages and delays due to the war the report was not published until 1943.

7. See Private Secretary to the Premier to the Chief Native Commissioner, February 5, 1932, Prime Minister's Office 1926–1945, S482/188/39.

8. In surveys conducted after 1904 many Coloureds were either not counted or were classified as European. Mandaza, "White Settler Ideology," 256ff.

9. Ibid., 237–238.

10. For example, in 1924 a dispute broke out at Umtali Hospital over the admission of Coloured patients. Civil Commissioner to the Senior Government Medical Officer, Umtali, August 21, 1924, Ministry of Health, S1173/21.

11. Mr. Fairbridge, Umtali, to Native Commissioner Mr. Bazeley, February 18, 1928, Prime Minister's Office 1926–1945, S482/188/39.

12. One such case was that of Mr. W. Ash of Klein Letaba, who made an application to the minister of native affairs. See Chief Native Commissioner, Salisbury, to the Secretary, Department of Justice, December 1, 1934, Chief Native Commissioner, Annual and Bi-Annual Reports of Half-Caste Births, 1933–1937, S1542/M7.

13. The husband was Arthur Robinson, who at one time served as a private in the army and later joined the BSA Police. He then took up trading in the Ndanga district, where he met his future wife. In October 1920, Robinson married Mary Naberai at the Jichidza Mission; he was forty-two and she was twenty-five. The marriage was viewed with disquiet by the native affairs department, who took it as further proof that Robinson was an unsavory character. See "The Marriage of Arthur Robinson," Correspondence: Native Department N3/27/5.

14. Assistant District Superintendent to the District Superintendent BSA Police, Salisbury, July 5, 1913, Division of the Attorney General: Immorality Policy Reports, 1916–1944, SSS1227/3.

15. One unusual case was that of Heyman Lobel, who was arrested in March 1916 and charged with the rape of two Indian girls with whom he had been cohabiting for some time. He was tried at Bulawayo, found guilty, and sentenced to two years' hard labor. While in Bulawayo prison Lobel attempted to commit suicide by cutting his throat with a razor. "Illicit Intercourse: European Males, Native and Coloured Females," Circular, September 12, 1916, ibid.

16. Ibid.

17. CID, Umtali, to the Assistant Superintendent, Salisbury CID, "Intercourse Europeans and Natives," April 19, 1925, ibid.

18. For example, over a period of four days in June 1920 the department identified twelve cases of white males having sex with black prostitutes. See Superintendent Brundell, CID Bulawayo, to Head Office, Salisbury, July 19, 1920, ibid.

19. Returns of European Males Practising Miscegenation, Gwanda District Office to the Chief Superintendent, Bulawayo CID, May 1930, ibid.

20. An example is the case of George Nickles, a trader and general dealer who lived near the Chilimanzi Reserve, and the Rev. William Withnell, who was in charge of the Holy Cross Mission, located in the reserve. See Rev. William Withnell, Driefontein Mission, Umvuma, to the Administrator, June 26, 1918; and Statement Made before the Superintendent of Natives, Victoria by George Nickles, Trader Living near the Chilimanz Native Reserve, 26 July 1918, Native Department, N3 24/32–34.

21. See, for example, Native Commissioner, Charter District, to Mr. F. Foster, Rhodesdale, Umvuma, August 21, 1914, Native Department, N3 27/1–5.

22. A representative case from 1916 involved John Davies, a magistrate's clerk of Bulawayo. One evening in June of that year Davies visited Bofana, a court messenger with whom he worked, at the native location. Davies demanded to have sex with Bofana's wife; when he protested, Davies dragged Bofana's sister Violet from the hut and brutally raped her. During the subsequent trial Bofana claimed that Davies had visited his hut on a number of occasions and always demanded to "fuck" his wife. Bofana had not reported the matter to the police because he feared he would lose his job. Although the victim's statement was supported by three witnesses, the court found Davies not guilty. Instead he was fined 5 pounds for being in a location without a permit. See Illicit Intercourse: European Males, Native and Coloured Females, 12/9/1916 2/O-G, Division of the Attorney General: Immorality Policy Reports 1916–1944, SSS1227/3.

23. Miscegenation Returns June 1933 to December 1937, Native Commissioner, S1542 M7.

24. Premier to the Secretary, Department of the Colonial Secretary, November 4, 1930, Department of the Prime Minister, S482/802/39.

25. Private Secretary, Prime Minister Moffat to Mr. Hadfield, August 11, 1930, ibid.

26. Secretary to the Premier to the Secretary, Law Department, July 25, 1930, ibid.

27. Mr. Hadfield to the Private Secretary, the Prime Minister, August 26, 1930, ibid.

28. Ibid., p. 2.

29. Premier to the Secretary, Department of the Colonial Secretary, November 4, 1930, ibid.

30. The policy of removing Aboriginal children from the care of their parents continued in Australia until the late 1960s. See also Mandaza, "White Settler Ideology," pp. 364–372.

31. A. G. Yardley, Assistant Native Commissioner, Bindura, to the Native Commissioner, Amandas, November 2, 1934, Annual and Bi-Annual Reports of Half-Caste Births 1933–1937, S1542/M7.

32. Father Burbridge, Campion House, to A. G. Yardley, July 26, 1935, ibid.

33. A. G. Yardley, Assistant Native Commissioner, to Father Burbridge, Campion House, August 9, 1935, ibid.

34. Private Secretary, the Premier to Mr. Hadfield, November 26, 1930, Department of the Prime Minister, S482/802/39.

35. See, for example, the love letters between Frank Green and Martha, aged fifteen years, July 1920, Division of the Attorney General: Immorality Policy Reports 1916–1944, SSS1227/3.

36. He also pointed out that the progeny of such unions were better cared for than were the children of casual relations. Mr. Hadfield to the Private Secretary, the Premier, December 2, 1930, Department of the Prime Minister, S482/802/39.

37. The commission was comprehensive; it took evidence from more than fifty witnesses in thirteen towns. See Report of the Committee into Questions Concerning the Education of Coloured and Half-Caste Children in the Colony 1933, S118. See also Commission of Inquiry into Coloured Employment and Education, S824/154, which contains the submissions, oral evidence, and other documents collected during the inquiry.

38. In 1930 there were estimated to be 1,138 half-caste children in the colony, of whom 379 were acknowledged by their fathers. According to the chief native commissioner, by 1932 the total had fallen to less than 1,000. Report of the Committee into Questions Concerning the Education of Coloured and Half-Caste Children in the Colony, 1933, S118, p. 20.

39. Ibid., p. 27.

40. Ibid., p. 25.

41. Ibid., p. 23.

42. Those children who lived in a semi-European environment and for whom native life was foreign were to be encouraged to enter the Coloured community. The committee recommended the establishment of hostels to give them access to schools. Ibid., p. 23.

43. In 1946 an inquiry was held into the welfare of the Coloured community whose terms of reference included employment, housing, health, and education. Its conclusions mirrored those made by Foggin thirteen years earlier. See *Commission of Inquiry Regarding the Social Welfare of the Coloured Community of Southern Rhodesia*, Report One, Volume Two: *Annexures 1946*. In *Miscellaneous Reports 1946* (Salisbury: Government Printer, 1947).

44. In February 1928 the director of education wrote to the colonial secretary justifying his department's policy. The letter contained the names and histories of thirty Coloured children who for a time had attended white schools. The director's explanation was weak but, as was the case so often with discriminatory practices, the Colonial Office chose not to intervene. See Director of Education to the Secretary, Department of the Colonial Secretary, February 23, 1928, Admission of Coloured Children to European Schools 1924–1939, S824/308.

45. Mandaza "White Settler Ideology," pp. 58–60.

46. See the Education Ordinance of 1903, Department of Education, E2/7/1.

47. Mr. L. Hadfield, Bulawayo, to Mr. Duthie, Director of Education, September 8, 1907, The Coloured School, Bulawayo, E2/10/2/1-3.

48. Director of Education to the Secretary, Advisory School Committee, Bulawayo, April 1, 1912, The Coloured School, Bulawayo, E2/10/2/1-3.

49. Mr. Cowling, Inspector of Schools to the Director of Education, February 1, 1926, The Coloured School, Bulawayo, E2/10/2/1-3.

50. Acting Director of Education to the Secretary Department of the Administrator, March 25, 1911, Admission of Coloured Children into European Schools, E2/3/1.

51. Acting Director of Education to Mr. Gilchrist, August 14, 1916, ibid. In 1934, Foggin acknowledged the principles which had been used by his department for over two decades. Mr. Foggin, Director of Education, to the Secretary, Depart-

ment of Internal Affairs, January 10, 1934, Admission of Coloured Children to European Schools 1924–1939, S824/308.

52. Brownhead was worried that the racial origins of some children would over time become more obvious and that white parents would eventually demand their expulsion. Mr. G. Brownhead, Secretary Bulawayo School's Advisory Committee to the Acting Director Education, Salisbury, February 21, 1911, Admission of Coloured Children into European Schools, E2/3/1.

53. The Gilchrist children were one such case. Their father was European and their mother was born in St. Helena. For a period beginning in 1913 both children attended the Gatooma School, but as the girl became darker her father was asked by the school council to remove her. After an appeal to the director of education the boy, who was of lighter complexion, was allowed to remain enrolled. Mr. Gilchrist, Duchess Hill, to the Director of Education, August 4, 1916, ibid.

54. A typical case from 1911 was that of the Williams children, who were excluded from school at Bulawayo. Mrs. S. Williams to the Administrator, March 28, 1911, ibid.

55. Miss A. Brownlee, Principal Umvuma School to Director of Education, May 8, 1911, ibid.

56. Mandaza, "White Settler Ideology," pp. 154–156.

57. Memo: Grace Maggio, Suspected of Colour, Secretary of the Education Commission to the Minister for Education, May 4, 1942, Half-Caste Children at White Schools 1939–1941, S245/898.

58. Ibid.

59. W. Richards, Assistant Magistrate, Shabani, to the Director of Education, Salisbury, October 18, 1924, Admission of Coloured Children to European Schools 1924–1939, S824/308.

60. Mrs. Lottering to the Director of Education, May 22, 1929, ibid.

61. For a discussion of whiteness see Ruth Frankenberg, *White Women and Race Matters: The Social Construction of Whiteness* (London: Routledge, 1993).

62. That represented more than 300,000 people. *The White Problem in South Africa: Report of the Carnegie Commission*, vol. 1 (Stellenbosch: Proc Ecclesia-Drukkery, 1932), p. vii.

63. N. D. Atkinson, "A History of Educational Policy in Southern Rhodesia" (Ph.D. diss., University of London, 1974), p. 67.

64. For a history of the education system, see Robert John Challis, "The Education Policies of the British South Africa Company in Southern Rhodesia, 1889 to 1914" (B.A. honors thesis, Department of History, University of Cape Town, 1968) and "The Foundation of the Racially Segregated Education System in Southern Rhodesia, 1890 to 1923," (Ph.D. diss., University of Zimbabwe, 1982).

65. Report of the Select Committee of Enquiry into Present Methods and Agencies for Relieving Poverty and Distress, Appointed by the House of Assembly, June 18, 1924, Prime Minister's Office: Correspondence, S482/249/39.

66. The only assistance given to women was by the Loyal Women's Guild, which provided rations and clothing and subsidized rent. In Bulawayo the Guild ran a temporary refugee for destitute women.

67. Report of the Select Committee of Enquiry into Present Methods and Agencies for Relieving Poverty and Distress, p. 8.

68. For an overview of the work of these three figures, see Daniel J. Kevles, *In the Name of Eugenics: Genetics and the Uses of Human Heredity* (New York: Alfred A. Knopf, 1985). For a discussion of the influence of eugenics on Dutch colonial rule, see Ann Stoler, "Carnal Knowledge and Imperial Power: Gender, Race, and Morality in Colonial Asia," in *Gender at the Crossroads of Knowledge: Feminist Anthropology in the Postmodern Era*, ed. Micaela de Leonardo (Berkeley: University of California Press, 1991), pp. 72–76.

69. Dispatch: Premier's Office to the Colonial Secretary, August 8, 1924, Prime Minister's Office: Correspondence, S482/249/39.

70. Ibid.

71. Report on Unemployment and the Relief of Destitution in Southern Rhodesia, 1934, *Miscellaneous Reports, Southern Rhodesia, 1933–1940* (Salisbury: Government Printer, 1940), p. 2.

72. Ibid., pp. 24–25.

73. For a history of the sciences of human inferiority, see Stephen Jay Gould, *The Mismeasure of Man* (New York: W. W. Norton & Company, 1981): and Kevlis, *In the Name of Eugenics*.

74. Following a High Court case in Nyasaland in early 1931, the Colonial Office became concerned about the definitions of race used in east and central Africa. Lord Passfield believed that ordinances such as Southern Rhodesia's Arms and Ammunition Ordinance, No. 2 of 1891, which defined as native a person having any native blood, made it impossible for those of mixed race to improve their social status. Other legislation such as the Interpretation Ordinance, No. 55 of 1929 of Northern Rhodesia that made living among natives a criterion for native status was equally offensive. Passfield wanted to encourage the kind of fluid racial boundaries which Rhodesians found disturbing. To that end the Colonial Office informed all administrations that "[t]he legal status of native half-castes should depend primarily on the standard and mode of their life, and that no obstacle should be placed in the way of native half-castes being classed among members of a higher civilisation where their standard and manner of life justifies such a classification." Following Passfield's memorandum the minister for internal affairs acknowledged that where there was no definite proof of race the "test of general appearance" was to be applied; if necessary that test could be supplemented "by regard being had to the habits of life of the person concerned." Undersecretary of State for the Colonies to the Secretary, Conference of East African Governors, September 21, 1931, ZNA, Sec 1/583.

See also Secretary, Department of Internal Affairs to Winterton and Dazinger, October 17, 1933, Liquor Act 1930: Ruling on the Definition of a Coloured Man, S246/729.

The liquor ordinance of 1897 prohibited the sale of alcohol to Coloureds, which, according to the CID, was necessary to prevent drunken and immoral behavior. Successive attorneys general and administrators were opposed to any change to the law. In supporting the existing legislation in 1924, the administrator argued that any change would lead to increased drunkenness and crime. Their genetic inheritance meant that Coloureds had to be controlled, he argued. The issue of control was always dominant in negotiations about alcohol. See Superintendent, Bulawayo CID to the Staff Officer BSA Police, October 15, 1924, Possession of Liquor and Firearms by Indians and Natives, S246/728; and Memo from the Administrator to the Prime Minister, June 17, 1924, Department of the Prime Minister: The Coloured Community 1926–1945, S482/188/39.

75. Mr. Thornicroft, President of the Coloured Community Service League to the Secretary of the Premier, October 28, 1938, ibid.

76. Mr. E. Taunton, Secretary, Education Commission to the Medical Director, July 3, 1939, Internal Affairs: Coloured and Indian Schools 1937–1948, S245/858.

77. Dr. Baker Jones, Medical Inspector of Schools to the Medical Director, July 28, 1939, Half-Caste Children at White Schools 1939–1941, S245/898.

78. He also made the striking comment that "[c]hildren of mixed European and Bantu descent are not natives and have no long tradition since they are in the transition stage, like the 'middle class' in Gt. Britain," which must have disconcerted his superiors. Ibid.

79. A. P. Martin, Medical Director, to the Secretary, Education Commission, July 31, 1939, ibid.

80. See Saul Dubow's *Scientific Racism in Modern South Africa* (Cambridge: Cambridge University Press, 1995) on the political struggles within the sciences of personality in South Africa.

81. Kevles, *Genetics and the Uses of Human Heredity,* p. 64.

82. See, for example, H. I. Wetherell, "N. H. Wilson: Populism in Rhodesian Politics" *Rhodesian History* No. 6 (1975): 53–76. In his study of scientific racism in South Africa, Saul Dubow found that eugenics played little part in the creation of segregation or the construction of apartheid. See Saul Dubow, *Scientific Racism in Modern South Africa* (Cambridge: Cambridge University Press, 1995).

83. See Stoler, "Carnal Knowledge and Imperial Power."

84. Secretary, Coloured Community Service League to the Secretary, Department of the Prime Minister, July 19, 1939, Department of the Prime Minister: The Coloured Community 1926–1945, S482/188/39.

85. Mr. McLeod of the Eurafrican Association to the Attorney General, December 11, 1931, ibid.

86. Mandaza, "White Settler Ideology," p. 159.

11. CONCLUSION

1. The legislation was influenced by events in southern Africa. During debate Lieutenant Governor Sir Hubert Murray, who drafted the ordinance, consulted the 1913 South African commission's report into Black Peril. According to Amirah Inglis, various factors led to the ordinance, including a struggle for authority between the administration and influential settlers. For a history of the ordinance, see Amirah Inglis, *Not a White Woman Safe: Sexual Anxiety and Politics in Port Moresby, 1920–1934* (Canberra: Australian National University Press, 1974).

2. See Ann Stoler, *Race and the Education of Desire: Foucault's History of Sexuality and the Colonial Order of Things* (Durham: Duke University Press, 1995), pp. 13–16.

3. Even after responsible government came into place in 1923 the BSAC was the major shareholder and controlled railways, mines, and the press. See Ian Phim-

ister, *An Economic and Social History of Zimbabwe, 1890–1948: Capital Accumulation and Class Struggle* (London: Longman, 1988), p. 118.

4. Report from Mr. J. Mylne, Principal Domboshawa School, on Ndachana, March 18, 1935, Ndachana alias Edwin Appeal File Mp-Z 1935, S336.

5. Ndachana's story was used by Stanlake Samkange in his novel *The Mourned One.* The events described by Samkange were taken from the trial transcript and he retained the names of the principal actors. (London: Heinemann, 1975).

6. Three cases heard in the Salisbury High Court, the first in 1929 and the other two in 1935, give a indication of sentences being imposed. In February 1929, Chipeni, an alien native employed at Cranham Farm near Salisbury was charged with assault with intent to rape his employer's daughter, Marjorie Fynn. Miss Fynn was asleep in bed when the attack took place and medical examination found semen stains on her pajamas. Chipeni was found guilty and sentenced to twenty cuts and five years' jail. In July 1935 Kativa, a laborer from Salisbury, was charged with the attempted rape of Violet Mellish, a European woman. Mrs. Mellish, who lived at a Salisbury boarding house, was asleep in her bed when she was awakened by the bedclothes being pulled off and she felt a cold hand on her thigh. She got out of bed, switched on the light, and saw an African man crouching beside the bed with his hands covering his head. Kativa was found guilty of *criminal injuria* rather than attempted rape and sentenced to eighteen months' jail and ten cuts with the cane. In September Kankufa, an unemployed laborer from Salisbury, was charged with housebreaking with intent to commit rape. The assault, committed on a twenty-six-year-old woman named Kathleen Emerick, consisted of lifting the blankets of her bed while she was asleep. Although he did not touch her, Emerick was certain that his intention was rape. In his defense Kankufa claimed that he was hungry and broke into the house in search of food. He was found guilty and sentenced to one year's hard labor for the housebreaking and ten cuts and two years' hard labor for the intent to rape. If any of those cases had been heard in the period before World War One the most likely outcome would have been a death sentence. See *Rex versus Chipeni,* Salisbury High Court, May 17, 1929, Series S628, No. 2294; *Rex versus Kativa (alias Wilson),* Salisbury High Court, July 1935, Series S628, No. 3349; and *Rex versus Kankufa,* Salisbury High Court, October 11, 1935, Series S628, No. 3375.

7. Throughout the transcripts Sister Dobbs is referred to as Miss Dobbs. Report from the Acting Chief Justice R. McIlwaine to the Minister for Justice, July 25, 1925, *Rex versus Ndachana (alias Edwin),* Criminal Sessions, High Court of Southern Rhodesia, 1935, Series S628, No. 3348.

8. Statement by Bessie Nevada Dobbs, S. S., June 13, 1935, in transcripts of Hearing of the Magistrate's Court, Salisbury, June 13, 1935, heard before William Brooks, *Rex versus Ndachana (alias Edwin),* pp. 7, 11.

9. Ibid., pp. 50–51.

10. Evidence from Miss May Bloomfield, *Rex versus Ndachana (alias Edwin).* See also transcript, p. 34.

11. Ibid., p. 19.

12. Exhibit WHB1, Dr. Blackie, Director of Public Health Laboratory Salisbury, Forensic Report, June 5, 1935, *Rex versus Ndachana (alias Edwin).* See also transcript, p. 21.

13. Exhibit ERC1, Dr. Edward Rowlette, May 23, 1935, *Rex versus Ndachana (alias Edwin)*. See also transcript, p. 22.

14. See Report on Ndachana by Sergeant Hansen, Salisbury CID, July 26, 1935, Ndachana (alias Edwin) Appeal File Mp-Z 1935, S336.

15. Judgment of Judge McIlwaine, in *Rex versus Ndachana (alias Edwin)*, pp. 58–59.

16. Statement of Ndachana, ibid., p. 59.

17. Letter by Ndachana, undated (August 1935), Ndachana (alias Edwin) Appeal File Mp-Z 1935, S336.

18. Arthur Shearly Cripps and five others to the Governor asking for clemency, August 28, 1935, ibid., S336.

19. Petitions, ibid., S336.

20. Lawrence Vambe, *From Rhodesia to Zimbabwe* (London: Heinemann, 1976), p. 74.

21. Medical Report on Ndachana by Dr. Rodger, August 24, 1935, Ndachana (alias Edwin) Appeal File Mp-Z 1935, S336.

22. Vambe, *From Rhodesia to Zimbabwe,* pp. 108–109.

23. Prestige was the term used by settlers to define what was most important to them, yet historians have written little about it. For one of the few discussions on the subject see Ann Stoler, "Carnal Knowledge and Imperial Power: Gender, Race, and Morality in Colonial Asia," in *Gender at the Crossroads of Knowledge: Feminist Anthropology in the Postmodern Era,* ed. Micaela de Leonardo (Berkeley: University of California Press, 1991), pp. 63–64. For an analogous but rather different use of the term in a colonial setting see Catherine Hall, "The Economy of Intellectual Prestige: Thomas Carlyle, John Stuart Mill, and the Case of Governor Eyre," *Cultural Critique* (Summer 1989): 167–196.

24. In all Wells identified a group of one hundred and five poor whites, almost 80 percent of whom came from South Africa. See *Report on Unemployment and the Relief of Destitution in Southern Rhodesia, 1934,* in *Miscellaneous Reports, Southern Rhodesia, 1933–1940* (Salisbury: Government Printer, 1940), pp. 24–25.

25. See Bruce Haley, *The Healthy Body and Victorian Culture* (Cambridge: Harvard University Press, 1978), p. 6. See also Norman Vance, *The Sinews of the Spirit: The Ideal of Christian Manliness in Victorian Literature and Religious Thought* (Cambridge: Cambridge University Press, 1985).

26. See Helen Callaway, *Gender, Culture, and Empire: European Women in Colonial Nigeria* (London: Macmillan Press, 1987), pp. 30–54; and Ronald Hyam, *Empire and Sexuality: The British Experience* (Manchester: Manchester University Press, 1990), p. 72.

27. Those characteristics were inscribed in the writings of J. B. F. Laubscher, J. F. Ritchie, and J. C. Carothers. See Jock McCulloch, *Colonial Psychiatry and the "African Mind"* (Cambridge: Cambridge University Press, 1995).

28. For a discussion of these and related debates, see T. Heller, et al., eds., *Reconstructing Individualism: Autonomy, Individuality, and the Self in Western Thought* (Stanford: Stanford University Press, 1986) and V. Beechey and J. Donald, eds., *Subjectivity and Social Relations* (Milton Keynes: Open University Press, 1985).

29. See Pavla Miller, *Transformations of Patriarchy in the West, 1500–1900* (Bloomington: Indiana University Press, 1998).

30. Norbert Elias, *The Civilising Process: State Formation and Civilisation* (Oxford: Basil Blackwell, 1978), p. 235.

31. See, for example, Michel Foucault, *Discipline and Punish: The Birth of the Prison* (London: Penguin Books, 1979).

MONOGRAPHS

Abercrombie, Nicholas, Stephen Hill, and Bryan S. Turner. *Sovereign Individuals of Capitalism.* London: Allen & Unwin, 1986.

Allen, Judith A. *Sex and Secrets: Crimes Involving Australian Women since 1880.* Melbourne: Oxford University Press, 1990.

Anderson, Ben. *Imagined Communities.* London: Verso, 1991.

Appiah, Kwame Anthony. *In My Father's House: Africa in the Philosophy of Culture.* London: Methuen, 1992.

Aries, Philippe, and Andre Bejin, eds. *Western Sexuality: Practice and Precept in Past and Present Times.* Oxford: Basil Blackwell, 1985.

Asad, Talal, ed. *Anthropology and the Colonial Encounter.* Ithaca: Humanities Press, 1975.

Ashcroft, Bill, Gareth Griffins, and Helen Tiffin. *The Post-Colonial Studies Reader.* London: Routledge, 1995.

Ballhatchet, Kenneth. *Race, Sex, and Class under the Raj: Imperial Attitudes and Policies and their Critics, 1793–1905.* New Delhi: Vikas Publishing Company, 1979.

Banton, Michael. *Racial Theories.* Cambridge: Cambridge University Press, 1989.

Barnes, Teresa. "'We Women Worked So Hard': Gender, Labor, and Social Reproduction in Colonial Harare, Zimbabwe, 1930–1956." Ph.D. diss., University of Zimbabwe, 1993.

Barr, Pat. *The Memsahibs: The Women of Victorian India.* London: Secker and Warburg, 1976.

Barry, Kathleen. *Female Sexual Slavery.* New York: New York University Press, 1979.

Brecher, Edward. *The Sex Researchers.* London: Andre Deutsch, 1970.

Bristow, Edward J. *Prostitution and Prejudice: The Jewish Fight against White Slavery, 1870–1939.* Oxford: Clarendon Press, 1982.

———. *Vice and Vigilance: Purity Movements in Britain since 1700.* Dublin: Gill and Macmillan, 1977.

Bulbeck, Chilla. *Australian Women in Papua New Guinea: Colonial Passages, 1920–1960.* Melbourne: Cambridge University Press, 1992.

Burkert, Walter, Rene Girard, and Jonathan Z. Smith. *Ritual Killing and Cultural Formation.* Stanford: Stanford University Press, 1987.

Callan, Hilary, and Shirley Ardener, eds. *The Incorporated Wife.* London: Croom Helm, 1984.

Callaway, Helen. *Gender, Culture, and Empire: European Women in Colonial Nigeria.* London: Macmillan Press, 1987.

Caplan, Pat, ed. *The Cultural Construction of Sexuality.* London: Tavistock Publications, 1987.

Carman, John A. *A Medical History of Kenya: A Personal Memoir.* London: Rex Collings, 1976.

Carothers, J. C. *The African Mind in Health and Disease: A Study in Ethnopsychiatry.* Geneva: World Health Organisation, 1953.

———. *The Psychology of Mau Mau.* Nairobi: Government Printer, 1954.

Cell, John. *The Highest Stage of White Supremacy: The Origins of Segregation in South Africa and the American South.* Cambridge: Cambridge University Press, 1982.

Challis, Robert J. "The Foundation of the Racially Segregated Education System in Southern Rhodesia, 1890 to 1923." Ph.D. diss., University of Zimbabwe, 1982.

Chanock, Martin. *Britain, Rhodesia, and South Africa, 1900–1945.* London: Frank Cass, 1977.

———. *Law, Custom and Social Order: The Colonial Experience in Malawi and Zambia.* Cambridge: Cambridge University Press, 1985.

Chennells, Anthony. "Settler Myths and the Southern Rhodesian Novel." Ph.D. diss., University of Zimbabwe, 1982.

Clark, Anna. *Women's Silence, Men's Violence: Sexual Assault in England, 1770–1845.* London: Pandora, 1987.

Clarke, Duncan. *Domestic Workers in Zimbabwe.* Gwelo: Mambo Press, 1974.

Cock, Jacklyn. *Maids and Madams: Domestic Workers under Apartheid.* London: Women's Press, 1989.

Coward, Rosalind. *Patriarchal Precedents: Sexuality and Social Relations.* London: Routledge & Kegan Paul, 1983.

Davenport-Hines, Richard. *Sex, Death and Punishment: Attitudes to Sex and Sexuality in Britain since the Renaissance.* London: Collins, 1990.

Davidoff, Leonore. *The Best Circles: Society, Etiquette and the Season.* London: The Cresset Library, 1986.

De Gobineau, Arthur. *The Inequality of Human Races.* Trans. Adrian Collins. New York: Howard Fertig, 1967.

Dilman, Ilham. *Freud and Human Nature.* Oxford: Basil Blackwell, 1983.

Dollimore, Jonathan. *Sexual Dissidence: Augustine to Wilde, Freud to Foucault.* Oxford: Clarendon Press, 1991.

Douglas, Mary. *Purity and Danger: An Analysis of the Concepts of Pollution and Taboo.* London: Routledge & Kegan Paul, 1966.

Dubow, Saul. *Scientific Racism in Modern South Africa.* Cambridge: Cambridge University Press, 1995.

Elias, Norbert. *The Civilizing Process: State Formation and Civilization.* Oxford: Basil Blackwell, 1982.

Ellis, Havelock. *Sex in Relation to Society.* London: William Heinemann, 1937.

Fanon, Frantz. *Peau noire, masques blancs.* Paris: Francois Maspero, 1952. Translated by Charles L. Markmann as *Black Skin, White Masks.* London: MacGibbon and Kee, 1967.

———. *Pour la revolution africaine.* Paris: Francois Maspero, 1964. Translated by Haakon Chevalier as *Toward the African Revolution.* London: Pelican Books, 1967.

Farrant, Leda. *The Legendary Grogan*. London: Hamish Hamilton, 1981.

Feierman, Steven, and John M. Janzen, eds. *The Social Basis of Health and Healing in Africa*. Berkeley: University of California Press, 1992.

Firth, Violet. *The Psychology of the Servant Problem: A Study in Social Relationships*. London: C. W. Daniel Co., 1925.

Forster, E. M. *A Passage to India*. 1924. Reprint, London: Penguin Books, 1970.

Foucault, Michel. *Discipline and Punish: The Birth of the Prison*. New York: Random House, 1979.

———. *The History of Sexuality*. Vol. 1. Trans. Robert Hurley. London: Penguin Books, 1978.

Frankenberg, Ruth. *White Women, Race Matters: The Social Construction of Whiteness*. London: Routledge, 1993.

Fredrickson, George. *White Supremacy: A Comparative Study in American and South African History*. New York: Oxford University Press, 1981.

Freud, Sigmund. *Three Essays on the Theory of Sexuality*. Trans. and ed. James Strachey. 1905. Reprint, New York: Avon Books, 1971.

———. *Totem and Taboo: Resemblances between the Psychic Lives of Savages and Neurotics*. Trans. A. A. Brill. 1913. Reprint, New York: Vintage Books, 1946.

Galton, Francis. *Narrative of an Explorer in Tropical South Africa*. London: Ward, Lock & Co., 1889.

Gann, Lewis. H. *A History of Southern Rhodesia: Early Days to 1934*. New York: Humanities Press, 1969.

Gann, Lewis H., and Peter Duigan. *White Settlers in Tropical Africa*. 1962. Reprint, Westport, Conn.: Greenwood Press, 1977.

Gann, Lewis H., and Michael Gelfand. *Huggins of Rhodesia: The Man and His Country*. London: George Allen & Unwin Ltd., 1964.

Gates, Henry. L., ed. *"Race," Writing, and Difference*. Chicago: University of Chicago Press, 1986.

Gelfand, Michael. *A Service to the Sick: A History of the Health Services for Africans in Southern Rhodesia, 1890 to 1953*. Salisbury: Mambo Press, 1967.

——— *The Sick African: A Clinical Study*. 3rd ed. Cape Town: Juta & Company Ltd., 1957.

———. *Tropical Victory: An Account of the Influence of Medicine on the History of Southern Rhodesia, 1890–1923*. Cape Town: Juta Press, 1953.

Gilman, Sander. *Difference and Pathology: Stereotypes of Sexuality, Race, and Madness*. Ithaca, N.Y.: Cornell University Press, 1985.

Gilroy, Paul. *The Black Atlantic: Modernity and Double Consciousness*. Cambridge: Harvard University Press, 1993.

Gray, Richard. *The Two Nations: Aspects of the Development of Race Relations in the Rhodesias and Nyasaland*. London: Oxford University Press, 1960.

Gregory, J. W. *The Menace of Colour*. London: Seeley, Service & Co. Ltd., 1925.

Haley, Bruce. *The Healthy Body and Victorian Culture*. Cambridge: Harvard University Press, 1978.

Hansen, Karen. *Distant Companions: Servants and Employers in Zambia, 1900–1985*. Ithaca: Cornell University Press, 1989.

Hartz, Louis. *The Founding of New Societies*. New York: Harcourt, Brace & World, Inc., 1964.

Heller, Thomas, Morton Sosna, and David E. Wellbery, eds. *Reconstructing Individualism: Autonomy, Individuality, and the Self in Western Thought*. Stanford, Calif.: Stanford University Press, 1986.

Hernton, Calvin C. *Sex and Racism*. London: Paladin Books, 1970.

Hobsbawm, Eric J. *The Age of Empire, 1875–1914*. New York: Vintage Books, 1989.

———. *Nations and Nationalism since 1780: Programme, Myth, Reality*. Cambridge: Cambridge University Press, 1990.

Hobsbawm, Eric J., and T. O. Ranger, eds. *The Invention of Tradition*. London: Cambridge University Press, 1983.

Hodder-Williams, Richard. *White Farmers in Rhodesia, 1890–1965: A History of the Marandellas District*. London: Macmillan, 1983.

Hole, Hugh Marshall. *The Making of Rhodesia*. 1926. Reprint, London: Frank Cass & Co, 1967.

Hyam, Ronald. *Empire and Sexuality: The British Experience*. Manchester: Manchester University Press, 1990.

Ignatiev, Noel. *How the Irish Became White*. New York: Routledge, 1995.

Inglis, Amirah. *Not a White Woman Safe: Sexual Anxiety and Politics in Port Moresby, 1920–1934*. Canberra: Australian National University Press, 1974.

Jeater, Diana. *Marriage, Perversion, and Power: The Construction of Moral Discourse in Southern Rhodesia, 1894–1930*. Oxford: Clarendon Press, 1933.

Jollie, Ethel Tawse. *The Real Rhodesia*. London: Hutchinson & Co., 1924.

Kelly, John D. *A Politics of Virtue: Hinduism, Sexuality, and Countercolonial Discourse in Fiji*. Chicago: University of Chicago Press, 1991.

Kennedy, Dane. *Islands of White: Settler Society and Culture in Kenya and Southern Rhodesia, 1890–1939*. Durham, N.C.: Duke University Press, 1987.

Kevles, Daniel J. *Genetics and the Uses of Human Heredity*. New York: Alfred A. Knopf, 1985.

Kirkby, Diane, ed. *Sex, Power and Justice: Historical Perspectives on Law in Australia*. Melbourne: Oxford University Press, 1995.

Knapman, Claudia. *White Women in Fiji, 1835–1930: The Ruin of Empire?* Sydney: Allen & Unwin, 1986.

Kuklick, Henrika. *The Savage Within: The Social History of British Social Anthropology, 1885–1945*. Cambridge: Cambridge University Press, 1993.

Kuper, Adam. *Anthropologists and Anthropology: The British School, 1922–1972*. London: Penguin Books, 1978.

———. *The Invention of Primitive Society: Transformations of an Illusion*. London: Routledge & Kegan Paul, 1988.

Laubscher, B. J. F. *Sex, Custom and Psychopathology: A Study of South African Pagan Natives*. London: George Routledge & Sons, 1937.

Lee, Marguerite Elaine. "Politics and Pressure Groups in Southern Rhodesia, 1898–1923." Ph.D. diss., University of London, 1974.

Lessing, Doris. *Going Home*. London: Michael Joseph, 1957.

———. *The Grass Is Singing*. London: Michael Joseph, 1950.

———. *Martha Quest*. London: Hart-Davis, MacGibbon, and Kee Ltd., 1964.

Levy-Bruhl, Lucien. *Primitive Mentality*. New York: The Macmillan Company, 1923.

Leys, Colin. *European Politics in Southern Rhodesia*. London: Oxford University Press, 1959.

Lugard, Lord. *The Dual Mandate in British Tropical Africa*. 1922. Reprint, London: Frank Cass & Co., 1965.

Lyons, Maryinez. *The Colonial Disease: A Social History of Sleeping Sickness in Northern Zaire, 1900–1940*. New York: Cambridge University Press, 1992.

Macleod, Roy, and Milton Lewis, eds. *Disease, Medicine, and Empire: Perspectives on Western Medicine and the Experience of European Expansion*. London: Routledge, 1988.

Malinowski, Bronislaw. *Sex and Repression in Savage Society*. New York: New American Library, 1955.

———. *The Sexual Life of Savages in North-Western Melanesia*. London: Routledge & Kegan Paul, 1929.

Mandaza, Ibbo. "White Settler Ideology, African Nationalism, and the 'Coloured' Question in Southern Africa: Southern Rhodesia/Zimbabwe, Northern Rhodesia/Zambia and Nyasaland/Malawi, 1900–1976." Ph.D. diss., University of York, 1979.

Mangan, J. A., and James Walvin, eds. *Manliness and Morality: Middle-Class Masculinity in Britain and America, 1800–1940*. New York: St. Martin's Press, 1987.

Mannoni, Octave. *Prospero and Caliban: The Psychology of Colonization*. New York: Frederick A. Praeger, 1964.

Mason, Philip. *The Birth of a Dilemma: The Conquest and Settlement of Rhodesia*. London: Oxford University Press, 1958.

McClintock, Anne. *Imperial Leather: Race, Gender, and Sexuality in the Colonial Contest*. New York: Routledge, 1995.

McCulloch, Jock. *Black Soul White Artifact: Fanon's Clinical Psychology and Social Theory*. New York: Cambridge University Press, 1983.

———. *Colonial Psychiatry and the "African Mind."* Cambridge: Cambridge University Press, 1995.

Metcalf, Andy, and Martin Humphries, eds. *The Sexuality of Men*. London: Pluto Press, 1985.

Miller, Pavla. *Transformations of Patriarchy in the West, 1500–1900*. Bloomington: Indiana University Press, 1998.

Mintz, Sidney. *Sweetness and Power: The Place of Sugar in Modern History*. New York: Viking Books, 1985.

Mlambo, Eshmael. *Rhodesia: The Struggle for a Birthright*. London: C. Hurst & Co., 1972.

Moore, Sally Falk. *Law as Process: An Anthropological Approach*. London: Routledge & Kegan Paul, 1978.

Mort, Frank. *Dangerous Sexualities: Medico-Moral Politics in England since 1830*. London: Routledge & Kegan Paul, 1987.

Mutambirawa, James A. *The Rise of Settler Power in Southern Rhodesia (Zimbabwe), 1898–1923*. London: Fairleigh Dickinson University Press, 1980.

Mutwira, Roben. "Colonial Health Policy: A Case Study of Epidemic Diseases." MA thesis, University of Zimbabwe, 1987.

Nandy, Ashis. *The Intimate Enemy: Loss and Recovery of Self under Colonialism*. Delhi: Oxford University Press, 1983.

Nietzsche, Friedrich. *Beyond Good and Evil*. Trans. R. J. Hollingdale. London: Penguin Books, 1990.

Nkosi, Lewis. *Mating Birds*. London: Flamingo Books, 1986.

Page, Gertrude. *The Edge of Beyond*. London: Hurst & Blackett, 1908.

———. *Jill's Rhodesian Philosophy or The Dam Farm*. London: Hurst & Blackett, 1910.

———. *Love in the Wilderness: The Story of Another African Farm*. London: Hurst & Blackett, Ltd., 1907.

Palley, Claire. *The Constitutional History and Law of Southern Rhodesia, 1888–1965*. Oxford: Clarendon Press, 1966.

Palmer, Robin. *Land and Racial Domination in Rhodesia*. London: Heinemann, 1977.

Pape, John. "A Century of Servants: Domestic Workers in Zimbabwe, 1890–1990." Ph.D. diss., Deakin University, 1992.

Pearsall, Ronald. *The Worm in the Bud: The World of Victorian Sexuality*. 1969. Reprint, London: Penguin Books, 1983.

Peiss, Kathy, and Christina Simmons, eds. *Passion and Power: Sexuality in History*. Philadelphia: Temple University Press, 1989.

Phimister, Ian. *An Economic and Social History of Zimbabwe, 1890–1948: Capital Accumulation and Class Struggle*. London: Longman, 1988.

———. *Wangi Kolia: Coal, Capital and Labor in Colonial Zimbabwe, 1984–1954*. Harare: Baobab Books, 1994.

Phimister, Ian R., and Charles van Onselen. *Studies in the History of African Mine Labor in Colonial Zimbabwe*. Gwelo: Mambo Press, 1978.

Pick, Daniel. *Faces of Degeneration: A European Disorder, c. 1848–c. 1918*. Cambridge: Cambridge University Press, 1989.

Powys, Llewlyn. *Black Laughter*. London: Grant Richards, 1928.

———. *Ebony and Ivory*. London: Grant Richards, 1923.

Pratt, Mary Louise. *Imperial Eyes: Travel Writing and Transculturation*. London: Routledge, 1992.

Quetel, Claude. *History of Syphilis*. Cambridge: Polity Press, 1987.

Ranger, Terence O. *The African Voice in Southern Rhodesia, 1898–1930*. Evanston, Ill.: Northwestern University Press, 1970.

———. *Are We Not Also Men? The Samkange Family and African Politics in Zimbabwe, 1920–1964*. London: James Currey, 1995.

———. *Revolt in Southern Rhodesia, 1896–97: A Study in African Resistance*. London: Heinemann, 1967.

Ranger, Terence O., and Paul Slack, eds. *Epidemics and Ideas: Essays on the Historical Perception of Pestilence*. Cambridge: Cambridge University Press, 1995.

Ranger, Terence O., and John Weller, eds. *Themes in the Christian History of Central Africa*. London: Heinemann, 1975.

Rich, Paul. *Race and Empire in British Politics*. Cambridge: Cambridge University Press, 1986.

———. *White Power and the Liberal Conscience*. Johannesburg: Ravan Press, 1984.

Richards, Angela, ed. *Freud on Sexuality*. Trans. James Strachey. Ed. Angela Richards. London: Penguin Books, 1983.

Ritchie, J. F. *The African as Suckling and as Adult: A Psychological Study.* 1943. Reprint, Manchester: Manchester University Press, 1968.

Said, Edward. *Orientalism.* London: Routledge and Kegan Paul, 1978.

Samkange, Stanlake. *The Mourned One.* London: Heinemann, 1975.

Schmidt, Elizabeth. "Ideology, Economics, and the Role of Shona Women in Southern Rhodesia, 1850–1939." Ph.D. diss., University of Wisconsin-Madison, 1987.

Schreiner, Olive. *Trooper Peter Halket of Mashonaland.* London: T. Fisher Unwin, 1897.

Scott, James C. *Domination and the Arts of Resistance.* New Haven: Yale University Press, 1990.

Seligman, Adam B. *The Idea of Civil Society.* New York: The Free Press, 1992.

Sharpe, Jenny. *Allegories of Empire: The Figure of Woman in the Colonial Text.* Minneapolis: University of Minnesota Press, 1993.

Smythe, Nicholas Charles. "The Origins of Apartheid: Race Legislation in South Africa, 1836 to 1910." Ph.D. diss., University of Witwatersrand, 1995.

Sontag, Susan. *AIDS and Its Metaphors.* New York: Farrar, Straus, and Giroux, 1989.

Steele, M. C. "The Foundations of a Native Policy: Southern Rhodesia, 1923 to 1933." Ph.D. diss., Simon Fraser University, 1972.

Stoler, Ann. *Race and the Education of Desire: Foucault's History of Sexuality and the Colonial Order of Things.* Durham: Duke University Press, 1995.

Stoller, Robert. J. *Perversion: The Erotic Form of Hatred.* Cambridge: Harvester Press, 1976.

Strobel, Margaret. *European Women and the Second British Empire.* Bloomington: Indiana University Press, 1991.

Tanser, G. H. *A Sequence of Time: The Story of Salisbury, Rhodesia, 1900 to 1914.* Salisbury: Pioneer Head, 1974.

Taylor, J. J. "The Emergence and Development of the Native Department in Southern Rhodesia, 1894–1914." Ph.D. diss., University of London, 1974.

Thompson, Paul. *The Edwardians: The Remaking of British Society.* London: Paladin Books, 1977.

Tomaselli, Sylvana, and Roy Porter, eds. *Rape: An Historical and Social Inquiry.* London: Basil Blackwell, 1989.

Torgovnick, Marianna. *Gone Primitive: Savage Intellects, Modern Lives.* Chicago: University of Chicago Press, 1990.

Tredgold, Robert. *The Rhodesia That Was My Life.* London: Allen & Unwin, 1968.

Vambe, Lawrence. *An Ill-Fated People: Zimbabwe Before and After Rhodes.* London: Heinemann, 1972.

———. *From Rhodesia to Zimbabwe.* London: Heinemann, 1976.

Van Heyningen, Elizabeth. "Public Health and Society in Cape Town, 1880–1910." Ph.D. diss., University of Cape Town, 1989.

Van Onselen, Charles. *Chibaro: African Mine Labor in Southern Rhodesia.* Johannesburg: Ravan Press, 1980.

———. *Studies in the Social and Economic History of the Witwatersrand, 1886–1914.* Vol. 2, *New Nineveh.* Johannesburg: Raven Press, 1982.

Vance, Norman. *The Sinews of the Spirit: The Ideal of Christian Manliness in Vic-

torian Literature and Religious Thought. Cambridge: Cambridge University Press, 1985.

Vaughan, Megan. *Curing Their Ills: Colonial Power and African Illness*. London: Polity Press, 1991.

Walkowitz, Judith. *City of Dreadful Delight: Narratives of Sexual Danger in Late-Victorian London*. London: Virago, 1992.

———. *Prostitution and Victorian Society: Women, Class, and the State*. Cambridge: Cambridge University Press, 1980.

Wallace, Edwin R. *Freud and Anthropology: A History and Reappraisal*. New York: International Universities Press, 1983.

Ware, Vron. *Beyond the Pale: White Women, Racism and History*. London: Verso, 1992.

Weeks, Jeffrey. *Sexuality*. London: Tavistock Publications, 1986.

Weleba, Shirley. "Trial by Jury in Southern Rhodesia, 1900–1912." Ph.D. diss., University of Southern California, 1969.

West, Michael. "African Middle-Class Formation in Colonial Zimbabwe, 1890–1965." Ph.D. diss., Harvard University, 1990.

White, Luise. *The Comforts of Home: Prostitution in Colonial Nairobi*. Chicago: Chicago University Press, 1990.

Wilkinson, Louis, ed. *The Letters of Llewelyn Powys*. London: John Lane, 1943.

Yoshikuni, Tsuneo. "Black Migrants in a White City: A Social History of African Harare, 1890–1925." Ph.D. diss., University of Zimbabwe, 1989.

ARTICLES

Barnes, Teresa. "The Fight for Control of African Women's Mobility in Colonial Zimbabwe, 1900–1939." *Signs* (Spring 1992): 586–608.

Bonilla-Silva, Eduardo. "Rethinking Racism: Toward a Structural Interpretation." *American Sociology Review* 62 (June 1997): 465–480.

Bonnett, Alastair. "How the British Working Class Became White: The Symbolic Reformation of Racialized Capitalism." *Journal of Historical Sociology* 11 (September 1998): 316–340.

Carothers, J. C. "Frontal Lobe Function in the African." *Journal of Mental Science* 97 (1952): 122–148.

———. "Some Speculations on Insanity in Africans and in General." *The East African Medical Journal* 17 (1940): 90–105.

———. "A Study of Mental Derangement in Africans, and an Attempt to Explain Its Peculiarities, More Especially in Relation to the African Attitude toward Life." *Journal of Mental Science* 93 (July 1947): 548–597.

Clarke, D. G. "Settler Ideology and African Underdevelopment." *Rhodesian Journal of Economics* 8 (March 1974): 17–38.

Connell, R. W. "The Big Picture: Masculinities in Recent World History." *Theory and Society* 22 (1993): 597–623.

Cott, Nancy F. "Passionlessness: An Interpretation of Victorian Sexual Ideology, 1790–1850." In *A Heritage of Her Own*, ed. Nancy F. Cott and Elizabeth H. Pleck. New York: Simon and Schuster, 1979.

Crowder, Michael. "White Chiefs of Tropical Africa." In *Colonialism in Africa,*

1870–1960, ed. Lewis H. Gann and Peter Duignan. Cambridge: Cambridge University Press, pp. 320–350.

Curtin, Philip D. "Medical Knowledge and Urban Planning in Colonial Tropical Africa." In *The Social Basis of Health and Healing in Africa,* ed. Steven Feierman and John M. Janzen. Berkeley: University of California Press, 1992.

Etherington, Norman. "Natal's Black Rape Scare of the 1870s." *Journal of Southern African Studies* 15 (1988): 36–53.

Fanon, Frantz. "Reflections sur l'ethnopsychiatrie." *Conscience maghrebine* 3 (1955): 1–2.

Gann, Lewis H., and Peter Duignan. "Changing Patterns of a White Elite: Rhodesia and Other Settlers." In *Colonialism in Africa, 1870–1960,* Vol. 2, ed. L. H. Gann and Peter Duigan. Cambridge: Cambridge University Press, 1970.

Gordon, H. L. "An Enquiry into the Correlation of Civilization and Mental Disorder in the Kenyan Native." *The East African Medical Journal* 12 (February 1936): 327–335.

———. "Sexual Perversions." *Kenya and East African Medical Journal* 6 (1929–1930): 122–130.

Hyam, Ronald. "Concubinage and the Colonial Service: The Crewe Circular (1909)." *The Journal of Imperial and Commonwealth History* 14 (1986): 170–186.

———. "Empire and Sexual Opportunity." *The Journal of Imperial and Commonwealth History* 14 (January 1986): 34–89.

Hyslop, Jonathan. "White Working-Class Women and the Invention of Apartheid." *Journal of African History* 36 (1995): 57–81.

Krikler, Jeremy. "Social Neurosis and Hysterical Pre-Cognition in South Africa: A Case Study and Reflections." *South African Historical Journal* 28 (1993): 63–97.

Lee, M. Elaine "The Origins of the Rhodesian Responsible Government Movement." *Rhodesian History* 6 (1975): 33–52.

McEwan, Peter. "European Assimilation in a Non-European Context." *International Migration* 2 (1964): 107–127.

Moodie, T. D. "Migrancy and Male Sexuality." *Journal of Southern African Studies* 14 (1988): 228–256.

Pape, John. "Black and White: The 'Perils of Sex' in Colonial Zimbabwe." *Journal of Southern African Studies* 4 (1990): 699–720.

Porot, Antoine, and D. C. Arrii. "L'impulsivite criminelle chez l'indigene algerien—ses facteurs." *Annales medico psychologiques* 90 (1932): 588–611.

Porot, Antoine, and C. Sutter. "Les primitives des indigines nord-africans." *Sud Medical et chirurgical* (April 1939): 226–241.

Roberts, R. S. "The Settlers." *Rhodesiana* 39 (September 1978): 55–61.

Sachs, Wulf. "The Insane Native: An Introduction to a Psychological Study." *The South African Journal of Science* 30 (1933): 706–713.

Schmidt, Elizabeth. "Patriarchy, Capitalism, and the Colonial State in Zimbabwe." *Signs* 16 (1991): 732–756.

Sequeria, James H. "The Brain of the East African." *The British Medical Journal* 7 (1932): 581.

Shelley, H., and W. Watson. "An Investigation Concerning Mental Disorders in the

Nyasaland Natives." *Journal of Mental Science* 341 (November 1936): 701–730.

Simons, H. J. "Mental Disease in Africans: Racial Determinism." *Journal of Mental Science* 104 (1958): 377–388.

Stoler, Ann. "Carnal Knowledge and Imperial Power: Gender, Race, and Morality in Colonial Asia." In *Gender at the Crossroads of Knowledge: Feminist Anthropology in the Postmodern Era,* ed. Micaela de Leonardo. Berkeley: University of California Press, 1991.

———. "Making Empire Respectable: The Politics of Race and Sexuality in Twentieth-Century Colonial Cultures." In *Racial Supremacy in Social Darwinist Theory and Colonial Practice,* ed. J. Bremen. Amsterdam: V. U. University Press, 1990.

Summers, Carol. "Intimate Colonialism: The Imperial Production of Reproduction in Uganda, 1907–1925." *Signs* 16 (Summer 1991).

Swanson, Maynard W. "The Sanitation Syndrome: Bubonic Plague and Urban Native Policy in the Cape Colony." *Journal of African History* 18 (1977): 387–410.

This index covers material in the main body of the book but does not refer to
material in the Notes or Bibliography. Therefore, it includes only authors whose
names appear in the text.

JOCK McCULLOCH

has worked as a Legislative Research Specialist in foreign affairs for the
Australian Parliament and at various universities. He is currently employed
at RMIT University, Melbourne, where he is co-founder of the international development studies program. He has worked in Algeria, Zimbabwe, South Africa, and Kenya and is the author of six books, including
Colonial Psychiatry and the "African Mind." Currently he is working on a
history of asbestos mining in southern Africa.